The Golden Age restor'd

For Barbara

The Golden Age restor'd

The culture of the
Stuart Court, 1603–42

GRAHAM PARRY

ST. MARTIN'S PRESS New York

First published by Manchester
University Press 1981

For information, write:
St. Martin's Press Inc.,
175 Fifth Avenue,
New York, N.Y. 10010

Printed in Great Britain
First published in the United States of
America in 1981

ISBN 0-312-33194-0
Library of Congress Catalog Card Number
81-52544

Typeset by August Filmsetting, Reddish, Stockport

Printed in Great Britain by
Butler & Tanner Ltd, Frome and London

Contents

Illustrations

Chronology 1603–49

<table>
<tr><td colspan="2">*Political and social*</td><td>*Cultural*</td></tr>
<tr><td>1603</td><td>(24 March) Accession of James I</td><td></td></tr>
<tr><td>1604</td><td>James's state entry into London
Hampton Court Conference
Union of the Crowns of England and
    Scotland: James takes title of
    King of Great Britain</td><td></td></tr>
<tr><td>1605</td><td>Gunpowder Plot</td><td>*Masque of Blacknesse* performed
Bacon's *Advancement of Learning*
    published</td></tr>
<tr><td>1610</td><td>Prince Henry created Prince of Wales</td><td></td></tr>
<tr><td>1611</td><td></td><td>Authorised Version of Bible published
Chapman's translation of *The Iliad*
    published</td></tr>
<tr><td>1612</td><td>(Nov.) Death of Prince Henry</td><td></td></tr>
<tr><td>1613</td><td>(Feb.) Marriage of Princess Elizabeth
    and the Elector Palatine</td><td></td></tr>
<tr><td>1613–15</td><td></td><td>Inigo Jones and Arundel in Italy</td></tr>
<tr><td>1614</td><td></td><td>Raleigh's *History of the World*
    published</td></tr>
<tr><td>1615</td><td></td><td>Inigo Jones becomes Surveyor of
    Works</td></tr>
<tr><td>1616</td><td>Rise of George Villiers as favourite
The Overbury Trial</td><td>Shakespeare dies
Works of King James published
Folio edition of Jonson's *Works*
    published
Paul van Somer comes to England</td></tr>
<tr><td>1618</td><td></td><td>Daniel Mytens comes to England</td></tr>
<tr><td>1619</td><td>Death of Queen Anne</td><td>Rebuilding of Banqueting House</td></tr>
<tr><td>1620</td><td>Elizabeth and Frederick driven out of
    Bohemia</td><td>Bacon's *Instauratio Magna* published</td></tr>
<tr><td>1620–1</td><td></td><td>(Nov. to Feb.) Van Dyck in England</td></tr>
<tr><td>1623</td><td>Spanish journey of Prince Charles and
    Buckingham</td><td>First Folio of Shakespeare's *Works*
    published</td></tr>
</table>

		Prince Charles acquires the Raphael Cartoons
1625	Death of James I	
	(27 March) Accession of Charles I	
	(13 June) Marriage of Charles to Henrietta Maria, daughter of Henri IV of France	
1626		Bacon dies
1627	Expedition against La Rochelle to help Huguenots	Purchase of Mantua Collection by Charles
1628	Assassination of Buckingham	
1629–30		Rubens in England
1629–40	Period of Absolute Rule by Charles. No Parliaments called	
1631		Donne dies
1632		Van Dyck returns and settles in England
1633	William Laud enthroned as Archbishop of Canterbury	Reconstruction of St Paul's begins Herbert dies. *The Temple* published Donne's *Poems* published
1634	Ship money levied by Charles	
1635		Rubens's ceiling placed in Banqueting House
1636		Wenceslaus Hollar settles in England
1637	Rebellion in Scotland	Jonson dies
1640	Long Parliament assembles	*Salmacida Spolia*, the last Court masque, performed Carew dies. Carew's *Poems* published
1641	Execution of Strafford	Van Dyck dies in London
1642	Outbreak of Civil War	
1649	(30 Jan.) Execution of Charles	

Preface

In this book I have attempted to outline the characteristic iconography that accompanied the reigns of James I and Charles I, and in the light of that iconography to explore a wide range of works of art that were created within the setting of the Stuart Court, either for the express purpose of glorifying the monarch, or with the broader intention of projecting or reflecting the royal interest. The accession of a new dynasty of kings in 1603 saw the deployment of a great variety of images and symbols that declared the distinctive virtues and policies of King James. Some of these images were carried over from Elizabeth's reign, others were invented to emphasise the changes introduced by the new King. A chorus of acclaim greeted James's accession as the beginning of a new golden age, and indeed, after the uncertainty of Elizabeth's last years, the security and peace that the Stuart succession appeared to offer made the future look very bright. Charles also tried to foster the myth of the Stuart golden age, but his emblems of felicity became increasingly unbelievable as the Court isolated itself from the threatening trends in politics and religion that developed during the 1630s.

A major innovation in the Court entertainments of James's reign was the annual masque that crowned the Christmas festivities, and this event, under the management of Ben Jonson and Inigo Jones, rapidly became the principal means of celebrating the sublime powers of the Stuart monarchy. The sequence of masques up to 1640 provides a varied mythology for Stuart rule and forms a repository of images and beliefs enabling us to reconstruct the confident claims made for the benevolent and increasingly absolutist government of James and Charles; this assurance begins to falter only on the very eve of the Civil War. Another fertile source for the imagery of the two reigns lies in the books written under the patronage of the Crown, and especially in their dedications, where the merits of the patron are most fulsomely extolled. Much of the literature discussed in this book is complimentary in tone and extravagantly uncritical in its praise of the myriad virtues of royal and noble patrons. Hyperbole came naturally in an age when flattery was one of the minor arts, yet there was much to be enthusiastic about. Encouragement of the arts at Court met with brilliant results: the active interplay of artist and patron made the Court in both reigns a centre of innovation and achievement, in poetry, painting and architecture. Under James, a great transformation of taste took place, as artists assimilated continental influences that flowed into this country with the relaxation of tension between England and Catholic Europe. In the vanguard of the new taste were Prince Henry and the Earl of Arundel, whose importance I have tried to describe here. Their example helped to form the tastes of Prince Charles, but it also set the pattern for many leading noblemen who were attracted to the cultivated life-style they had pioneered, and during the 1620s and 1630s a whole generation of virtuoso lords arose. Limitations of space restrict me to a presentation of the central figures in this activity, and cause me to concentrate on the main lines of development in literature, architecture and painting. In discussing the more notable acts of patronage, I hope to restore a number of works of art to their original context so that the first intentions of their creators may be more fully understood. I have not attempted to analyse the state of music at the Stuart Court, even though such illustrious figures as Dowland, Tomkins, Gibbons and Ferrabosco were active there, because it seems unrewarding to try to evoke what should be heard and not just described. Moreover, music in this period does not share the same iconography that binds together the other arts and makes them the common expression of a unified court culture.

In recent years, books by Frances Yates, Roy Strong and Stephen Orgel have greatly broadened our understanding of the cultural and intellectual movements of early Stuart England, and I have benefited considerably from their studies of this period.

It is a pleasure to express my gratitude to the President and Fellows of Clare Hall, Cambridge, where I spent a valuable term in stimulating and hospitable surroundings. I have also profited from some extremely helpful conversations with my colleague Professor Bernard Harris, who has been a thesaurus of seventeenth-century knowledge, and with Professor Douglas Jefferson of Leeds University, whose ideas have often opened up a new approach to a subject. My thanks to them both. I am also particularly indebted for advice and opinion to my colleague Dr Timothy Webb, to Dr Michael Hunter of Birkbeck College, and Dr Michael Vickers of the Ashmolean Museum, Oxford. My greatest thanks go to my wife Barbara, who has uncombed the tangles of the text, prepared the typescript, and been a constant source of help and practical suggestion.

[1]

The iconography of James I

King James's triumphal entry into London in March 1604 was one of those moments of composite pageantry that exhibit the complexities of a culture in an intensive and compressed form upon an occasion of particular significance. It was the City's official greeting to the new monarch, a pledging of allegiance, and an elaborate and imaginative statement of the hopes and expectations of the new reign. Combining architecture with emblem, tableau, drama and music, the event demonstrates compactly how the arts served the monarchy by projecting a state mythology, and also offers a view of the iconography prevailing at the beginning of James's reign. The new King, whose character was little known, and who came from remote Scotland, needed an image whose associations would be familiar to his English subjects and courtiers, so an important function of these welcoming ceremonies was to invest James with the symbolism of the old Queen, just as the coronation had invested him with the traditional regalia. They were a form of initiation rite introducing the new King to the roles created for Queen Elizabeth and left vacant by her.

There had not been a royal entry into London since Queen Elizabeth's coronation procession in 1559, and hers had been a modest affair by comparison with James's. She passed under five triumphal arches which carried symbolical figurations of political virtues; the Queen was not only welcomed by her subjects, but she was also given guidance, by means of a series of instructive tableaux, in the art of governing a country which had known years of religious persecution and foreign intervention.[1] One tableau showed her as the descendant of Elizabeth of York, whose marriage to Henry VII had made harmony between the warring Roses and brought peace to the country. Another displayed her enthroned upon 'the seate of worthy governance' sustained by the four virtues trampling down vices; a third showed how the eight beatitudes could be applied to the Queen, while another tableau represented 'Debora the judge and restorer of the House of Israel' in council with her advisers, the nobility, the clergy and the commoners. The central pageant depicted a barren hill juxtaposed against a fertile and flourishing hill, signifying the nation as it had decayed under Mary, and the prosperous commonwealth expected under Elizabeth. Truth, the daughter of Time, was introduced, who presented the Queen with an English Bible. Religious motifs clearly dominated this pageant sequence, which emphasised the need for wise government exercised with the support of and in the spirit of the reformed church. The Queen's entry was a long-remembered success because of her ready participation in the spirit of the day's pageantry: she studied the devices with care, reacted to their implications, and made a number of spontaneous speeches along the route. But as far as one can tell, the architecture of this ceremony was not especially ambitious or remarkable, nor were the tableaux particularly sophisticated or sumptuous: they were in fact fairly commonplace for the time, drawing their intensity from their topicality and from the Queen's response to them.

James's entry was of an altogether different order. It was unprecedentedly grandiose and spectacular, reflecting a knowledge of the tradition of triumphal entries that had developed in northern Europe.[2] The great elaboration of royal symbolism during the last two decades of Elizabeth's reign also ensured that there was an abundance of thematic material to be displayed. Preparations had been lengthy, for James had intended his visit to be part of the coronation festivities on St James's Day, 25 July 1603, but plague had forced the delay of his ceremonial entry, although not of his coronation. The entertainments were entrusted to the playwrights Thomas Dekker and Ben Jonson, while the design of the triumphal arches was given to the architect and joiner Stephen Harrison, in whose illustrated book *Arches of Triumph* we have a full record of the ephemeral architecture of this event.[3] Seven vast arches were erected along the processional route, the largest of which was ninety feet high and fifty feet wide, composed with all the soaring extravagant freedom that wood and plaster permitted. Late Elizabethan architecture, which had always inclined towards the inclusion of symbolic images and patterns in its structures, here reached its ebullient climax in arches crowded with image and emblem, encrusted with Renaissance learning, and exhibiting every variety of ornament from the architectural and iconographic handbooks of the age. Pillars, pyramids, obelisks and domes sprout and swell all over these wonderful hybrid structures. Fantastical decoration is so thickly applied that the basic forms are overwhelmed by the profusion of ornament, mainly of the Netherlandish variety that was so popular at the turn of the century: elaborate strapwork, curlicued cartouches and grotesque caryatids. The unrestrained exoticism of detail and the vigorous and exciting silhouettes gave the arches a theatrical power that was entirely appropriate to this occasion, for the arrival of the new King was a dramatic event of the first order. It was equally appropriate that the reception of the King should be stage-managed by two of London's leading dramatists. The design of the arches was adapted to the notion of public theatre, for several of them incorporated musicians' galleries and elevated stages where brief scenes could be enacted. Living actors mingled with the carved plaster statues in a festive morality show, and the arches themselves, free as they were from the constraints of a functional purpose, became in effect pure examples of the architecture of morality, wherein all the components contributed to the exposition of moral arguments in mythographic form.

The main intention of a triumphal arch is to celebrate, and these frontispieces to the Jacobean era celebrate not the historical achievements of a victor, as did their Roman archetypes, but the imagined virtues and ideals of the ruler. In a sense, too, they are incantatory, conjuring up forces that are expected to influence the King, and in order to realise the full potential of their design, they require the presence of the King to release their message. The arches were so dense with meaning that their interpretation demands 'an Age at least to every part'; their detail was so extravagantly superfluous to the occasion, with a harassed King and uncontrollable crowds, that it is not surprising that Dekker and Jonson and Harrison each published a detailed report of his own devisings so that they could be studied and deciphered at leisure.

Dekker provides an animated prologue to the day in his *Magnificent Entertainment*:

In a moment therefore of Time, are Carpenters, Ioyners, Carvers, and other Artificers sweating at their Chizzells. . . .

Not a finger but had an Office: He was held unworthy ever after to *sucke the Honey-dew of Peace*, that . . . would offer to play the Droane. The Streets are surveyed; heigthes, breadths, and distances taken, as it were to make Fortifications, for the Solemnities. Seven pieces of ground, (like so many fieldes for a battaile) are plotted foorth, uppon which these Arches of Tryumph must shew themselves in their glorie: aloft, in the ende doe they advance their proude foreheads. . . .

The day (for whose sake, these wonders of Wood, clymde thus into the clowdes) is now come; being so earely up by reason of Artificiall Lights, which wakened it, that the Sunne over-slept himselfe, and rose not in many houres after, yet bringing with it into the very bosome of the Cittie, a world of people. The Streets seemde to bee paved with men: Stalles in stead of rich wares were set out with children, open Casements fild up with women.

All Glasse windowes taken downe, but in their places, sparkeled so many eyes, that had it not bene the day, the light which reflected from them, was sufficient to have made one.[4]

Dekker devised a dramatic encounter to surprise the King as he approached the City. St George and St Andrew are to be seen riding together, and the Genius of the City rushes forth from the gate in amazement to enquire about this new-found amity. Genius then sounds two of the day's persistent themes of praise: London, or Troynovant, now receives the descendant of Trojan Brutus, and Peace has spread her blessings over the land:

> soft-handed Peace, so sweetly thrives,
> That Bees in Souldiers Helmets build their Hives:
> When Ioy a tip-toe stands on Fortunes Wheele,
> In silken Robes.

Dekker mentions in passing that this little prelude was not enacted because of confused circumstances, and he and Jonson admit that many of their devices and speeches were not played because of the crowds and noise and James's impatience: so the published descriptions present an idealised account of the royal entry which was in actuality a rather chaotic affair, for the great train of dignitaries, officers of the Court and the nobility en masse proved an unmanageable audience.

The conceit on which the whole pageant was based was that for this special day the City of London had been transformed into the King's Chamber or 'Court Royal', since the King's real presence lay there that day, as well as the greater portion of the aristocracy; thus the Entertainment reflected the qualities of the King's majesty and proclaimed the ideals considered desirable at the new Court. Ben Jonson was responsible for the first arch at Fenchurch, where he exercised his natural aptitude for moralising on public themes by dramatising the relationships that should exist between King and City. On this first arch, in place of the pediment, there was a fifty-foot-wide panorama of the City crested with the spires and pinnacles of its crowded churches. The central figure on the façade represented the British Monarchy, seated beneath the two crowns of England and Scotland, and bearing in her lap a globe inscribed 'Orbis Britannicus. Divisus ab Orbe', 'to shew', as Jonson glosses it, 'that this empire is a world divided from the world', information scarcely novel, but the allusion to the prophetic and imperial poet Virgil reminded the spectator that even in Roman times a special destiny had been seen for Britain which was now in the process of realisation. Prophetic motifs derived from Virgil were to be a prominent feature of the day's ceremonies. Supporting British Monarchy was a figure with whom James professed considerable familiarity: Theosophia,

or *divine Wisedome*, all in white, a blue mantle seeded with starres, a crowne of starres on her head. Her garments figur'd truth, innocence and cleerenesse. Shee was alwayes looking up;

The Londinium Arch from Harrison's *Arches of Triumph* (1604)

in her one hand shee sustayned a dove, in the other a serpent: the last to shew her subtiltie, the first her simplicitie; alluding to that text of Scripture, *Estote ergo prudentes sicut serpentes, et simplices sicut columbae*. Her word, *PER ME REGES REGNANT*. Intimating, how by her, all kings doe governe, and that she is the foundation and strength of kingdomes, to which end, shee was here placed, upon a cube, at the foot of the Monarchie, as her base and stay.[5]

By Jonsonian standards, Divine Wisdom is a fairly simple figure, her attributes being derived from a well-known biblical source, the heraldry of her colours simple, her functions clear. The motto relates the figure to her function, the attributes declare the qualities of the figure. There is an appropriateness, a decorum, in the placing of the figures which the mind readily perceives. As a tableau, the juxtaposition of Monarchy and Divine Wisdom could have been presented at Queen Elizabeth's entry of 1559, but the elaboration which follows in Jonson's scheme shows how much the burdensome book-learning of the English Renaissance had come to dominate courtly art forms. Figure is crowded on figure in emblematic allegories of wise government and the interdependence of City and King. The Genius of the City is seen supported by Sage Counsel and Warlike Force, complex personifications, while the imagined daughters of the Genius—Gladness, Veneration, Promptitude, Vigilance, Affection and Unanimity—act as handmaidens to the Monarchy. Their attributes are of a delightful obscurity. Promptitude, for example, or Prothymia as Jonson styled her,

> was attyr'd in a short tuck't garment of flame-colour, wings at her backe; her haire bright, and bound up with ribands; her brest open, virago-like; her buskins so ribanded: Shee was crowned with a chaplet of trifoly, to expresse readinesse, and opennesse every way; in her right hand she held a squirrell, as being the creature most full of life and quicknesse: in the left a close round censor, with the perfume sodainely to be vented forth at the sides. Her word, *QUA DATA PORTA*. Taken from an other place in VIRGIL, where AEOLUS at the command of IUNO, lets forth the winde. . . . And shew'd that shee was no lesse prepar'd with promptitude, and alacritie, then the windes were, upon the least gate that shall be opened to his high command.[6]

One might guess that this figure was built for speed, though somewhat encumbered by the squirrel. The well-read spectator might have caught the allusion to Virgil and made the right connection. The censer and the squirrel might have suggested the perfume of prompt action, and nimbleness. The trefoil may or may not have been visible at a height. The mottoes of other figures made cryptic allusions to lesser poets such as Claudian and Statius whose context cannot have been widely known, while many of the symbolical attributes were novel introductions that Jonson took from Italian books of iconography. In short, these figures needed an interpreter. The well-educated aristocracy and members of the Court circle were adept at deciphering the allegorical figures, devices and *imprese* that were displayed at feasts and tournaments, where shields bearing emblematic compositions with mottoes were frequently carried or hung, and studied by the spectators who tried to riddle out their meanings and guess their appositeness to the bearer. This love of visual cryptograms with their mottoes as clues was part of the Elizabethan fondness for devices, hidden meanings and verbal games, the courtly Renaissance equivalent of the crossword puzzle. The range of conventional meanings was not extensive, for the vogue for emblem books— which provided the source and explanation of so many devices, as well as increasing their complexity—had not really begun when Jonson introduced his *Entertainment*, only four emblem books in English having been published by 1604. Jonson's difficult inventions then were in advance of current taste and probably in advance of current understanding, for he derived much of his material from Cesare Ripa's *Iconologia*, which was scarcely known in England.[7] The *Iconologia* was a most serviceable and fertile continental emblem book which Jonson used throughout his career to introduce a new gallery of personifications and compound figures into his masques.[8] But on this occasion, who could properly have understood his fictions? Since the characters were living figures who occupied their niches only for a brief time during the royal visit, they could not have been scrutinised by the quick-witted. However, their principal observer was to be King James, and James had long cultivated his reputation for learning. Moreover, his book on the duties of a prince, *Basilikon Doron*, contained numerous verbal illustrations of an emblematic nature. Jonson, therefore, could be seen to be paying a compliment to the royal intelligence, which, like an eagle's vision, penetrated further and more clearly than lesser mortals', though it is doubtful whether James had the patience to linger in thought before the display, undistracted by the noisy multitudes. And although the compliment may have been to James, the prestige of the invention clearly redounded to Jonson, who was using the occasion to announce his own sophisticated command of emblematic display. The minutely detailed account of his contributions that he published soon afterwards was both a permanent record of a transient show, and an advertisement of his own advanced skills in iconography; that his message was well received may be known by the eagerness with which the Court commanded him to write masques in which his symbolic fictions reached their fullest expression.

In order to help his readers, he added an explanation of the complex new forms that he was bringing forward:

The nature and propertie of these Devices being, to present alwaies some one entire bodie, or figure, consisting of distinct members, and each of those expressing it selfe, in [its] owne active spheare, yet all, with that generall harmonie so connexed, and disposed, as no one little part can be missing to the illustration of the whole: where also is to be noted, that the Symboles used, are not, neither ought to be, simply Hieroglyphickes, Emblemes, or Impreses, but a mixed character, partaking somewhat of all, and peculiarly apted to these more magnificent Inventions: wherein, the garments and ensignes deliver the nature of the person, and the word the present office. Neither was it becomming, or could it stand with the dignitie of these shewes (after the most miserable and desperate shift of the Puppits) to require a Truch-man, or (with the ignorant Painter) one to write, *This is a Dog*; or, *This is a Hare*: but so to be presented, as upon the view, they might, without cloud, or obscuritie, declare themselves to the sharpe and learned: And for the multitude, no doubt but their grounded iudgements did gaze, said it was fine, and were satisfied.[9]

It is the complexity of these inventions 'apted to magnificence' that Jonson stresses; they are intellectually demanding and they image the higher truths that lie behind the fabric of society but which are perceived by the philosophical beholder. Indeed, the act of perceiving these truths, with Jonson's tactful help, flatters the beholder into a satisfying estimation of his own powers. One can see, however, that at the opening of this new reign Jonson is introducing an intensified allusive iconography for refined wits. Its initial justification lay in the intellectual and philosophic stature of King James, but once introduced, these symbolic inventions proved very serviceable, and they came to characterise the exclusive Court entertainments of both James and Charles.

As James approached the first triumphal arch, a curtain painted with clouds covering the central area opened to reveal a long Latin inscription in his praise. 'The Allegorie being, that those clouds were gathered upon the face of the Citie, through their long want of his most wished sight: but now, as at the rising of the Sunne, all mists were dispersed and fled.'[10] Then the action began, as the Genius of the City engaged in dialogue with the God of the Thames, a figure modelled on Roman personifications of the Tiber, who up till now had been busy pouring water with live fishes out of his earthen pot. The ancient Genius then recollects the earliest days of Britain, when it was first settled by Trojans, and informs the River that

> When BRUTUS plough first gave thee infant bounds,
> And I, thy GENIUS walk't auspicious rounds
> In every furrow; then did I forelooke,
> And saw this day mark't white in CLOTHO's booke.
> The severall circles, both of change and sway,
> Within this Isle, there also figur'd lay:
> Of which the greatest, perfectest, and last
> Was this, whose present happinesse we tast.

Thames acknowledges that it is difficult to compete with the 'flood of joy that comes with him' and 'drowns the world', but that he flows with a silent rapture. Genius then salutes King James as 'a broade spreading Tree' who will shelter the realm, and praises Queen Anne and Prince Henry as branches of an immortal house:

> So, whilst you mortall are,
> No taste of sowre mortalitie once dare
> Approch your house.

Thus are the Stuarts, the true inheritors of Brutus's line, welcomed in. The old legends of the Trojan foundation of Britain took on new vigour with the accession of James, for he was the first modern king to restore the sovereign unity that the British Isles were fabled to have enjoyed in ancient times. The Tudors had professed descent from the Trojans (who were deemed to have formed the original British population of the islands) in order to emphasise their native British origins as opposed to an alien Norman ancestry, and in order to give historical depth to a recently successful family; since James's right to the English throne derived from Henry VII, he naturally appropriated the myth of the Trojan origin of the Tudors. It was a good deal easier for English poets to celebrate the new King as the descendant of the Trojan Brutus than to represent him as the son of England's Catholic foe, Mary Queen of Scots. As we shall see, the Trojan legend also lay behind the claims of nascent imperialism that would be made several times in the course of the day's entertainment, for the Trojans were the source of empire in the West, as Virgil had incontrovertibly established, and Britain like Rome was settled from Troy.

The royal group next moved to the arch erected by the Italian community in London. This arch, as might have been expected, was architecturally the most chaste and classically correct; it also used paintings to greater effect than any other, although the subject matter was not remarkable for its coherence. The central painting over the archway emphasised the legitimacy of James's inheritance, showing Henry VII giving him the sceptre as the true successor to the Tudor line. There could be no doubt about the relevance of that picture to the day's event, but as for the majority of the allegorical figures which decorated the Italian arch, Dekker was unable to identify them in his description, even though he was the principal pageant master. Two panegyrical incidents stand out, however, one visual, the other verbal. Over the rear archway Apollo was painted 'with all his Ensigns and Properties belonging to him, as a Sphere, Bookes, a Caducaeus, an Octoedron, with other Geometricall Bodies, and a Harpe in his left hand: his right hand with a golden Wand in it, poynting to the battel of *Lepanto*'.[11] The allusion is to the poem that James had written on the Battle of Lepanto, which was a great victory for Christendom and for the Venetians, so it formed a happy point where the Catholic Italians could congratulate James the Christian poet. That Apollo, who had flayed Marsyas for unsuccessful competition, should admire James's work was an ingeniously turned compliment. The Latin speech of the Italians was equally flattering, stating in a phrase from *Basilikon Doron* 'that those people were blest, where a philosopher rules, and where the Ruler playes the Philosopher'. The Italians recognised the vain side of James's character which loved to be praised: his pride at being a poet and philosopher king.

The arch of the Dutch community was next, rising some seventy feet high, its central gable framed by two great fish curled in baroque scrolls, symbols of the fishing trade so important to the Dutch economy. At 'the Heart of the Trophee was a spacious square roome, left open, Silke Curtaines drawn before it, which (upon the approch of his Maiestie) being put by, 17. yong Damsels . . . sate as it were in so many Chaires of State, and figuring in their persons, the 17. Provinces of Belgia, of which every one caried in a Scutchion . . . the Armes and Coate of one'.[12] A simple tableau then. The rest of the arch expounded a more ambitious theme, which was to have an important place in the Jacobean mythology: the role of Divine Providence in James's kingship. A personification of Providence stood on the topmost pedestal of the arch, over a statue of James who was flanked by Justice and Fortitude. The speech reminded James that he enjoyed his throne by Divine Providence: 'God therefore (that guides the Chariot of the world) holds the Raynes of thy Kingdome in his owne hand: It is hee, whose beames, lend a light to thine'.[13]

At the entrance to Cheapside towered an arch of spectacular magnitude, flanked by two great obelisks impaling orbs, with a third obelisk reared high upon the central tower. Symbolising the eternity of fame and the glory of princes, these objects must have cut a remarkable pattern against the London sky. This arch was Dekker's first invention, and he labelled it Nova Arabia Felix. The implications of the title would have been easily understood by his audience, for Arabia Felix, Arabia the Blest, of Ancient Geography was the fertile land of peace and the legendary abode of the Phoenix, the bird of virtue. James's arrival before the arch was the appearance of the new phoenix, the monarch recreated from Elizabeth's funeral pyre, as it were, whose presence made England the New Arabia Felix. Indeed, at his approach, a figure designated as Arabia Britannica gazed gladdened into the skies. The image of the phoenix was commonly applied to James, as Elizabeth's replacement. (The Dutch had just wished him 'the age of a Phoenix' as he stood before their arch.) The idea of the phoenix as the bird of virtue helps to explain the scene that was now enacted by players in the stage above the central archway. Around a fountain sat the five senses, dejected, 'holding Scutchions in their handes: upon which were drawne Herogliphicall bodyes, to expresse their qualities'. The fountain itself trickled weakly; it was inscribed 'The Fount of Virtue'. At its foot, two personages lay sleeping: 'upon their brestes stucke their names, *Detractio, Oblivio*: The one holdes an open Cuppe; about whose brim, a wreath of curled Snakes were winding, intimating that whatsoever his lippes toucht, was poysoned: the other helde a blacke Cuppe coverd, in token of an

The Nova Felix Arabia Arch from Harrison's *Arches of Triumph* (1604)

envious desire to drowne the worth and memorie of Noble persons'.[14] A
figure of Fame stood aloft, in a robe set with eyes and tongues; she laments
that the fountain of virtue is drying up. At this point James approaches the
arch.

Heereupon *Fame* sounding her Trumpet; *Arabia Britannica*, lookes cheerefully up, the
Sences are startled: *Detraction* and *Oblivion* throw off their iron slumber, busily bestowing
all their powers to fill their cups at the Fount with their olde malitious intention to sucke it
drie; But a strange and heavenly musicke suddainly striking through their eares, which
causing a wildnes and quicke motion in their lookes, drew them to light upon the glorious
presence of the *King*, they were suddainly thereby daunted and sunke downe; The Fount
in the same moment of Tyme, flowing fresh and aboundantly through severall pipes, with
Milke, Wine, and Balme, whilst a person (figuring *Circumspection*) that had watcht day and
night, to give note to the world of this blessed Tyme . . . steps forth on a mounted Stage
. . . to deliver to his Maiestie the interpretation of this dumbe Mysterie.[15]

The speech explains to the spectators the sense of this allegorical action.
England is the New Arabia 'in whose spiced nest / A *Phoenix* liv'd and died
in the Sunnes brest'. Elizabeth's death caused the fount of virtue to dwindle,
and the senses to droop, but James is the great restorer, who causes virtue
to spring again and routs the powers of oblivion and detraction:

> Thou being that sacred *Phoenix*, that doest rise,
> From th'ashes of the first: Beames from thine eyes
> So vertually shining, that they bring,
> To Englands new Arabia, a new Spring.

Thereupon music sounded from the galleries in the arch, birdsong filled the
air; two choristers from St Paul's sang in 'sweete and ravishing voyces'
declaring that 'Troynovant is now a Sommer Arbour', a conceit serving as
a transition to the next arch, which was constructed in the form of a raised
arbor with greenery wound round trellis-work, fruit hanging abundantly
among the leaves. Sylvan figures clad in ivy led the King on to this wonderful
bower, known as Hortus Euporiae or the Garden of Plenty, where Peace and
her daughter Plenty have their dwelling. Courtiers would have recognised
the structure as a summer banqueting house of the sort that was erected in
great lords' gardens for the entertainment of Queen Elizabeth or for their
own delight, where they could dine al fresco to the sound of hidden music;
but the arbor was also an image of England, the garden state, a conceit most
familiar to us from the gardeners' scene in *Richard II*. The architecture of
the arch obeys the decorum of the theme: rustic motifs dominate, satyrs
and wood nymphs decorate the structure and the arch is everywhere upheld
by 'terms standing upon pedestals', a term being the sculptured upper
portion of a body shown emerging from a plinth or pedestal, an ornament

considered particularly appropriate for garden statuary in antiquity and in the Renaissance. Within the upper galleries sat the nine Muses and the seven liberal Arts, who formed a consort of musicians. His Majesty was greeted by Vertumnus, the god of gardens, who explained how the King's presence had revivified his garden state and animated the Muses and the Arts who are pleased to live there. He, on behalf of his mistress Peace, offers the garden to King James 'to be disposde after his royal pleasure.'

The Rustic Arch (England's Arbor) from Harrison's *Arches of Triumph* (1604)

The Italian Arch from Harrison's *Arches of Triumph* (1604)

Much music, and a speech at St Paul's School urging the King to have a special care for education, lay between this ideal green image of England and the next spectacular gateway, the New World Arch, which stood ninety feet high and fifty broad. A great rotating globe occupied the centre of the building 'fild with all the degrees, and states that are in the land', from the nobleman to the ploughman; around the globe were the figures of the four elements who

upon the approch of his Maiestie, went round in a proportionable and even circle, touching that cantle of the Globe, (which was open) to the full view of his Maiestie, which being done, they bestowed themselves in such comely order, and stood so, as if the Engine had beene held up on the tops of their fingers.[16]

An interpreter explained how the orb of England had been moving awry as a result of Elizabeth's death, but now, with the arrival of King James, England moves in a right and orderly fashion once again.

> But see, the vertue of a Regall eye,
> Th'attractive wonder of mans Maiestie,
> Our Globe is drawne in a right line agen,
> And now appeare new faces, and new men.

Nature herself had grown disorderly by the old Queen's death, but the new sovereign has restored order and harmony to the elements, which now combine to assist the stability of England:

> See at the peacefull presence of their King,
> How quietly they movde, without their sting:
> . . .
> . . . propping the queint Fabrick that heere stands,
> Without the violence of their wrathfull hands.

Above the globe stood Fortune, as if treading on the moving world, with Virtue enthroned above her 'intimating, that his Maiesties fortune, was above the world, but his vertues above his fortune'. Aloft on the topmost pinnacle was poised Astraea, 'as being newly descended from heaven, gloriously attirde; all her garments beeing thickely strewed with starres: a crowne of starres on her head: a Silver veile covering her eyes'.

Legend recounted that Astraea, the goddess of justice, was the last of the immortals to leave the earth, when the iron age destroyed whatever virtue was left in men; she would only return when a new golden age was at hand. She was a figure powerfully associated with Queen Elizabeth, part of her personal iconography as a virgin goddess restored in a golden age of justice, peace and virtue. Elizabethan poets and polemical writers had enlarged the associations of the Astraea image to include the purity of the reformed religion over which Elizabeth presided, peace throughout her dominions, the expectation of empire and imperial rule for the English monarch, who was of Trojan–British descent and therefore related to the founders of Rome; all were aspects of the golden age renewed. The myth of the return of Astraea had been linked with Virgil's prophetic lines in his Fourth Eclogue, which heralded a new Saturnian age of gold and had been frequently applied to Elizabeth as the inaugurator of a purer world:

> Magnus ab integro saeculorum nascitur ordo.
> Iam redit et virgo, redeunt Saturnia regna.

> [The great line of the centuries begins anew.
> Now the Virgin returns, the reign of Saturn returns.]

These lines now reappear in Dekker's *Entertainment* applied to King James in conjunction with the prominent figure of Astraea, for 'it was now the golden world'.[17] Dekker had already celebrated Elizabeth as Astraea in the opening of his comedy *Old Fortunatus*, played at Court in 1599; now we see him transferring the mythology of Astraea to James.

> And then so rich an Empyre, whose fayre brest,
> Contaynes foure Kingdomes by your entrance blest,
> By Brute divided, but by you alone,
> All are againe united and made One,
> Whose fruitfull glories shine so far and even,
> They touch not onely earth, but they kisse heaven,
> From whence Astraea is descended hither,
> Who with our last Queenes Spirit, fled up thither,
> Fore-knowing on the earth, she could not rest,
> Till you had lockt her in your rightfull brest.[18]

James was here being integrated into the established state mythology. His act of bringing all Britain under one rule could be seen as the prelude to the imperial expansion of the nation which had been a steady theme of later Elizabethan propaganda, fuelled by the myths and legends that foresaw a renewed Roman Empire rising in the West. In accordance with the prophecies in Virgil, the renewed empire would bring in, like that of Augustus, a time of peace, and would usher in a new golden age. It is extraordinary how powerful and widespread was this political fantasy in sixteenth- and seventeenth-century Europe: it was sustained by poets in many nations who considered it as a dream that might at any moment be translated into actuality, and virtually all new rulers in the West were regarded as potential realisers of the new age. The Emperor Charles V had been the first to exploit these themes; as Holy Roman Emperor, there had been some credibility about his ambition to restore the Empire in a reign in which Religion, Justice and Peace were honourably imposed over a great territory by a new Catholic Augustus, and to give imaginative substance to his policies he claimed analogies with Augustus, and exploited the Virgilian prophecies of empire in Book VI of the *Aeneid* and of the return of the golden age in the Fourth Eclogue. Henri IV had picked up the same complex of imagery in his triumphs and pageants to promote his own sense of mission as King of France, so founding the tradition of Augustan imperialism that was to achieve spectacular fulfilment in the reign of Louis XIV. The Tudor propagandists, especially Foxe and Spenser, followed suit in elaborating a similar imperial destiny for Elizabeth, their task being facilitated by the fact that their monarch was the supreme head of a purified religion, a *pontifex maximus*, not a subordinate to a pontiff as were the Catholic monarchs. Elizabeth was a virgin, consonant with the prophecy in Virgil that a virgin shall usher in a new age, and she could also be equated with the myth of the goddess of Justice returned to earth. It was clear that any of the nation states of sixteenth-century Europe that had once formed part of the Roman Empire could lay claim to be the restorer of the *imperium sine fine* that Virgil had prophesied, and in the minds of artists and political theorists such an idea helped clarify the place of a reign or a dynasty in the pattern of history. The imperial dream had become an almost indispensable part of the political ambitions of Western rulers, and was an essential feature of the national consciousness of aspiring European states, for the dream afforded a gratifying glimpse of the special destiny of the nation. For James, as for Elizabeth, imperial pretentions were a way of asserting the emerging power of Britain under the august guidance of a monarch who enjoyed the special favour of providence. Besides, the stirring nature of the times encouraged optimistic speculation: in an age when there were vast transformations in religion, when new worlds were being revealed, when the European stage was crowded with rulers of exceptional powers, it seemed certain that amazing historical events were in the process of formation. The Bible provided one source of divination about the future, classical myth and poetry furnished another. Both could be made to yield the prospect of a glorious vision of the latter days of the world: the return of the golden age was the secular belief, the millenium was the religious conviction, and monarchs were happy to see their reigns viewed as prefatory to or coeval with these events. King James was promptly accommodated into this scheme, just as Elizabeth had been. James's commitment to peace, implicit in his motto *Beati Pacifici* (blessed are the peacemakers) was untiringly repeated by artists of every sort, for it was clearly part of a providential plan. The consequence was that the figure of Peace became the most predictable and over-employed goddess in the Jacobean panthcon. Just as Peace was the consort of both Elizabeth and James, so too the phoenix image was equally transferable, both in its very nature, as the renewal of the uniqueness of royal virtue in one monarch after another, and also in its associations acquired during the Renaissance of *renovatio* or renewal of religion and civilisation, which in England meant Reformation and an anticipated golden age.[19] The phoenix had also acquired strong imperial associations, for it had long been used as a hieroglyph of the renewal of the Roman Empire, as far back as the reign of Constantine. The Astraea image was also reapplied to James, though with less aptness, since Elizabeth's virginity was central to that earlier identification with the goddess. Nevertheless, it is evident that we are witnessing the passing on of the Elizabethan iconography to King James in this triumphal entry into London.

The final arch at Temple Bar brought James face to face with Jonson's work again, a towering mass of classical scholarship to honour the scholar-king. A head of Janus, god of gates, stood uppermost, fourfaced rather than bifrontal, 'as he respecteth all climates, and fills all parts of the world with his maiestie', in the manner of the new King. The principal figures were Peace, Wealth and Quiet, a lady of exceptional emblematic qualities:

a woman of a grave and venerable aspect, attyred in black, upon her head an artificiall nest, out of which appeared storkes heads to manifest a sweet repose. Her feete were placed upon a cube, to shew stabilitie, and in her lap shee held a perpendicular or levell, as the ensigne of evennesse and rest: on the top of it sate a Halcion or kings-fisher.[20]

An assortment of secondary personifications extended from the central figures, such as Safetie trampling on Danger, Felicity on Unhappinesse, signs of Jonson's pedantic insistence on working out allegorical equations to the last term. Jonson believed in the importance of the Latin motto to crystallise the meaning of the visual display, as in the construction of an emblem, and here the word was 'REDEUNT SATURNIA REGNA. Out of Virgil, to shew that now those golden times were returned againe, wherein Peace was with us so advanced, Rest received, Libertie restored, Safetie assured, and all Blessednesse appearing'.[21]

The action involved the Genius of the City, who had welcomed James at the first arch, in an exchange with a Flamen or civic priest, dressed with full respect to the ancient authorities. The Flamen is about to celebrate the Ides of March (i.e. 15 March, the day of the entry) by a sacrifice to Anna Perenna, the day's deity; the Genius rebukes him, and gesturing towards the King and Queen, says, 'Loe, there is hee, / Who brings with him a greater ANNE then shee', who has brought Peace with her, not Mars as Anna Perenna did. The Flamen is dismissed, and Genius swears to tend the flame now sacred to peace, and the interlude closes with the praise of the new and propitious era that James has ushered in.

As the royal party left the City and rode down the Strand, they encountered one final tailpiece thrown up by Jonson at the last moment: a rainbow, the sun, moon and the Pleiades soared between two obelisks seventy feet high. A human comet, Electra, prophesies, like an ancient Sybil, that the new reign shall be free

> No lesse from envie than from flatterie;
> All tumult, faction, and harsh discord cease,
> That might perturbe the musique of thy peace[22]

and at the climactic moment James is hailed as the new Augustus.

How wide they dream! The distance between the King's real and imagined self was immense. His Court was destined to be renowned for its venality, for its intemperance, for favouritism so extreme that it subverted good government, for neglect of affairs of state, and for gross flattery. Yet it was the function of pageantry and symbolic theatre to offer ideal images of kingship and good government, and a mythology for the new reign was essential to public morale and to courtly prestige, as well as being necessary to define the special characteristics of the new monarch. These visual and moral tributes were being offered to a King who had proven his magnanimity and his awareness of royal responsibility in his treatise on kingship *Basilikon Doron* (which had been hurriedly reprinted in London in 1604 for the admiration of his new subjects). Whatever the actualities of James's reign, the mythology invoked by Electra and conferred on James in the parting speech of the *Entertainment* is profoundly important for an understanding of the ways in which poets and artists impose values and historic vision on a contemporary moment. An event as singular as the accession of James provided a proper occasion for prophecy, and it was part of the office of poet to prophesy; Jonson was too completely classical a poet to let the moment slip by unexploited. The speech begins thus: 'The long laments I spent for ruin'd Troy, / Are dried'; and goes on to speak of the renewal of the Augustan world by James:

> (now thou hast closd up IANUS gates,
> And giv'n so generall peace to all estates)
> . . . no offensive mist, or cloudie staine
> May mixe with splendor of thy golden raigne.

A universal harmony shall prevail:

> One pure consent of mind
> Shall flow in every brest, and not the ayre,
> Sunne, moone, or starres shine more serenely faire.[23]

The heavens 'auspicate' a 'lasting glory to AUGUSTUS state'.

The note is insistently Virgilian and imperial, recapitulating themes that had already been stated several times during the progress. It was almost inevitable that James should be saluted as Augustus before the day was out, for so much of the day's imagery had been tending towards such an identification. The revelation of James's new role is the final imaginative climax of the pageant.

Stylistically, the *Entertainment* had demonstrated a sophisticated handling of classical mythology and displayed a notable inclination to cast moral and political wisdom in classical moulds. Biblical material was scarcely employed at all, in contrast with Elizabeth's entry when the purity of Reformed religion was a dominant theme. Folk motifs were notably absent. Instead, classical poetry was used almost throughout to illuminate the action and provide moral depth. The classicising spirit of Jonson in particular ensured that the late Renaissance came to London in a thorough-going way: the city now had its Genius, its priests, its protective spirits, even the costume of antiquity, and in his final desire to see the dawning of a new Augustan age there was doubtless the hinted belief that Jonson would be its Horace, if not its Virgil, and the poetic guardian of its morality. The spectacle mingled delight with instruction, and although given before a vast popular audience, it was essentially courtly in its spirit, elegant, learned and allusive; above all, the prodigious apparatus of the spectacle was directed specifically to one observer, the King, and its meaning functioned in the fullest sense only with his presence. As such, this complex of music, morality and spectacle in its flamboyant architectural setting, aided by mechanical devices and celestial speaking figures, was well on the way to the Court masque.

Apart from the transference of Elizabethan iconography to the new King, the most noticeable feature of the Entertainment is the emphasis on the magical virtue of royalty: many of the scenarios required the presence of the sovereign for their perfect operation: Arabia was *felix* only when the King was there, the world of Britain could be renewed only by his arrival; the fountain of virtue, the reviving arbor, the revolving globe and harmony of the elements, all stressed the unique virtue that lay in the power of royalty, and which had nothing to do with the private person of James Stuart. The suggestions of near-divine power accorded well with James's own view of his status as God's viceroy in Britain. They spoke to his sense of his own infallibility, as a virtuous force beyond the reach of instruction or criticism. In this way, too, the *Entertainment* prefigured the customary presentation of James in the masques of his reign.

Although James received the most splendid welcome accorded to an English sovereign, even in the midst of his glory the seeds of popular disaffection from the Stuarts were being sown. Far from showing a warm pleasure and gratitude at this great display of loyalty and affection mounted by his new subjects, James's haughty self-concern along with his dislike of crowds caused him to hasten tactlessly along the ceremonial way with a minimum of appreciation. He did not attend closely to the scenes or speeches, he did not address the people or show any evident delight. As the historian of his reign records:

He endured this day's brunt with patience, being assured he should never have such another; and his triumphal riding to the Parliament that followed. But afterward in his publick appearances (especially in his sports) the accesses of the people made him impatient, that he often dispersed them with frowns, that we may not say with curses.[24]

Machiavelli wrote that a prince's best fortress will be found in the love of his people; from the very outset of his reign James ignored the good sense of that advice.

James I employed a relatively restricted range of iconographical motifs, in contrast to the forest of symbols with which Elizabeth had surrounded herself. His own primary sense of himself was as the British Solomon, a conceit which called forth the jibe from Henri IV of 'the wisest fool in Christendom' which has stuck to him more surely than his own vain notion. Above all he wished to be known as the Peacemaker, the guarantor of peace in the British Isles, and the bringer of peace to the divided nations of Europe. He mused contentedly on this aspect of his nature in his *Meditation upon the Lord's Prayer*:

I know not by what fortune, the *dicton* of PACIFICUS was added to my title, at my coming into England; that of the Lion, expressing true fortitude, having been my *dicton* before: but I am not ashamed of this addition; for King Salomon was a figure of CHRIST in that he was a king of Peace. The greatest gift that our Saviour gave his Apostles, immediately before his Ascension, was that he left his Peace with them.[25]

Almost all the works of art associated with James sound this theme of Peace with a certain monotony. As we have seen, his triumphal entry into London was variously adorned with figures and emblems expressive of

Peace. Ben Jonson's masques paid homage to this virtue throughout the reign; paintings and engravings of King James usually alluded to the subject; the new Banqueting House was his Temple of Peace. He believed passionately in his role of peacemaker as the providential mission of his reign; he intended to arrange the marriages of his children to knit together the dynasties of Europe in amity, hoping that ties of affection and duty could achieve what religion and war could not, the peace of Europe. His own dread of arms and warfare, and memories of the violence that surrounded him in youth must have helped to mould his disposition, but there can be no doubt about the sincerity of his state policy to avoid war and let the nation enjoy the benefits of prosperity. Peace was one of the greatest gifts that a king could make to his kingdom; James signed a treaty with Spain at the beginning of his reign to end the lingering conflict, and he determined to be distinguished among the rulers of Europe for his wise and peaceful counsels. His motto *Beati Pacifici* asserted divine approval of his policy.

A belief in the divine approval of his kingship permeated James's sense of his own condition. He expounded the theory of the divine right of kings with complete conviction in his political writings, most fully in his *True Law of Free Monarchies* (1598), where he argued that his right to the throne derived directly from God and was hereditary as well as divine. God had created the institution of kingship, and just as he had endowed it with exceptional powers, so he had charged it with exceptional responsibilities. A king was accountable to God alone for his actions. His special attributes could be determined by a study of God's dealings with the kings of the Old Testament.

Kings are called Gods, by the propheticall King David, because they sit upon GOD his Throne in the earth, and have the count of their administration to give unto him. Their office is, to minister Iustice and Iudgement to the people, as the same David saith; . . . to establish good Lawes to his people, and procure obedience to the same. . . . To decide all controversies that can arise among them, as Salomon did.[26]

Because kingship has been ordained by God, a king's condition partakes of divinity in some degree:

Kings are justly called Gods, for that they exercise a manner or resemblance of Divine power upon earth: For if you will consider the Attributes to God, you shall see how they agree in the person of a King. God hath power to create, or destroy, make, or unmake at his pleasure, to give life, or send death, to judge all, to be judged nor accomptable to none: To raise low things, and to make high things low at his pleasure, and to God are both soule and body due. And the like power have Kings.[27]

The sacred nature of his majesty was a living truth for James; he was a spiritual descendant of the Hebrew kings, and he was under the special protection of God, who had endowed him with a divine and luminous wisdom.[28]

Around the twin pillars of Peace and Wisdom twined the imagery of the Jacobean settlement. From the many books which contain praise of the King's distinctive qualities and attributes, we choose two that offer a representative selection of the principal motifs that went into the making of the royal persona. Henry Peacham's book of emblems *Minerva Britanna* (1612) is an invaluable source for conventional attitudes. Peacham was a minor man of letters associated with the household of Prince Henry, and a minor and somewhat fawning courtier. He seems always to have taken an optimistic and uncritical view of his society, offering in his dedications to the more powerful men at Court flattering reflections of their own best selves. Unlike the majority of English emblem writers of this period, who re-used continental designs, Peacham did at least design and draw his own emblems, and thus can be relied on to supply emblems and verse that convey the taste and imagery of the principal figures at Court, where he had a wide acquaintance. Both emblems and verses are somewhat naive in manner, but one suspects that they were tolerated because he was that rather rare creature, a native English artist. Many of the emblems in his book are in fact based on details from James's own *Basilikon Doron*, as a compliment to the King, who, according to Peacham's Epistle to the Reader, was himself a deviser of emblems in his youth: 'Many and very excellent have I seene of his Maiestie's owne Invention, who hath taken herein in his yonger years great delight'. Of the emblems dedicated to King James, the first shows a crown sustained from above by a divine hand, illustrating James's belief that he held the crown by divine right and by divine will.

> Thus since on heaven, thou wholly dost depend
> And from above thy Crowne, and being hast,

so James will be immune to all human malice, a consoling thought for a King who lived in terror of conspiracies. Another represents the lions of Scotland and England upholding the crown of Britain, with the prophecy that

> BELLONA henceforth bounde in Iron Bandes
> Shall kisse the foote of mild triumphant PEACE,
> Nor Trumpets sterne, be heard within their landes
> Envie shall pine and all old grudges cease.

The motto is: *sic pacem habemus*, thus we have peace. One emblem depicts a botanical curiosity, the thistle growing on the same plant as the rose, being watered by the Almighty's hand from heaven. The motto is: *Quae plantavi irrigabo*, what I have planted, I shall water, and the verses once again stress the providence of God that sustains James's rule:

> Magnifique PRINCE, the splendour of whose face,
> Like brightest PHOEBUS vertue doth revive;
> And farre away, light-loathing vice doth chase,
> These be thy Realmes; that under thee do thrive,
> And which unite, GODS providence doth blesse,
> With peace, with plentie, and all happines.

All the motifs of these verses had appeared in some form or other on the triumphal arches of 1604, so one may recognise the constancy of their currency. Of the remaining emblems either dedicated to James or alluding to him, one features a portcullis surmounted by a crown, urging the King to defend his people, another illustrates the motto *Rex medicus patriae*, the King his country's doctor, who must purge and cure the diseases of the body politic; a harp in a bleak landscape proves to be an emblem of Ireland, 'From discord drawne, to sweetest unitie' by James's royal power. Finally, an emblem on the wisdom of Solomon describes his reliance on the book of God's word, and the need of princes to keep their own counsel and judge all for themselves. The little moral truisms that these pages yield convey in some measure the fairly simple views of kingship that James upheld in his own treatise on the subject.

A far more ingenious collection of James's formal attributes may be found in the dedicatory sequence at the beginning of the 1605 edition of Du Bartas's *Devine Weekes and Workes* translated by Joshua Sylvester and dedicated to the King. This epic of the creation by a French Protestant poet enjoyed a considerable vogue in England in the first half of the seventeenth century; it held a particular significance for King James, who had welcomed Du Bartas to Scotland in 1586, and had essayed a translation of part of the 'Second Week' himself as a godly exercise in verse.[29] Sylvester was a pedestrian yet popular translator, and something of a verbal contortionist when left to his own devices. He puts on an extravagant display in the dedicatory preliminaries to the volume, warming up with a few anagrams, such as IACOBVS STVART = Justa Scrutabo; IAMES STVART = A iust master. This latter discovery of his majesty's true nature as shadowed by his name so delights him that he is impelled to compose a sonnet that rings the changes on the phrase, beginning, 'For a iust master have I labour'd long,' and triumphantly concluding, 'My Liege Iames Stuart A Iust Master is'. His unrestrained muse now speaks in tongues and utters sonnets in several languages on the peerless qualities of King James:

> per cantar l'immenza
> Alma Virtù, Valor, Pietà, Prudenza
> Di GIACOMO (gran Salomon Britanno)
> Per di tua Gloria (udita qual è quanta)
> Rapir il mondo in maraviglia santa.

[Singing of the extraordinary virtue of soul, valour, piety and wisdom of James, the great British Solomon, so that the world, recognising your true glory, will be transported by a holy wonder.]

As the world lies spell-bound by James's glory, Sylvester busies himself with erecting a colonnade of twelve emblem poems, each in the shape of a pillar, in honour of the immortal qualities of the King. By means of the repetition of the last line of one poem as the first line of the next, the sequence is given a circular shape, and thus these poetic pillars form a temple consecrated to James. Another architectural poem follows this group, this time in the shape of a pyramid, which perpetuates the memory of Sir Philip Sidney, whose encouragement of Protestant poetry was renowned.

The quality of Sylvester's verse in these poems ranges from the mediocre to the lamentable. The themes that he proposes are too sublime for his powers, and Icarus-like he sinks in trying to fly too high. A vision of the Jacobean phoenix, for example, causes this bathetic plunge:

> From the spicie Ashes of the sacred URNE
> Of our dead Phoenix (dear ELIZABETH)
> A new true PHOENIX lively flourisheth
> Whom greater glories than the first adorne.
> So much (O KING) thy sacred worth presum-I-on
> JAMES, thou just Heire of England's ioyfull UNION.

Sylvester's erratic virtuosity plays on the surface of his subjects: the subjects themselves are the standard motifs of Stuart iconography, already so well established by 1605 as to be conventional. The pillar poems which form a Jacobean shrine carry the main panegyrical themes. The first begins by reminding us of the imperial dimension of James's rule: 'Great Emperor of Europe's greatest Isles', but he is no conqueror but a peaceful man whose fondest dominion is over the arts. Each of the Muses praises the King's accomplishments; Mnemosyne the Mother of the Muses would

> Crowne him (Laureat)
> Whole and sole soveraigne
> Of the Thespian Spring,
> Prince of Parnassus and Pierian State.

Later on even Apollo will cede his laurels to the inspired King, whose pure Protestant strains are incomparable. The royal phoenix rests upon one of the pillars, while the remaining columns commemorate the union of the kingdoms ordained by God, the King's Protestant zeal, his learning and wisdom, and the providential protection extended by God to the Stuarts. The King is addressed as 'Great, Royall Cedar of Mount Libanon', an allusion that introduces us to a fertile line of Jacobean imagery, James as cedar, for this tree was associated with Solomon, James's chosen archetype, and it was also regarded as the king of trees. Cedar imagery abounds in panegyrics upon James. Finally, Sylvester tries to enlarge the range of the King's personae by attempting to transfer the faery imagery of Queen Elizabeth to James:

> But, (my best Guest) welcome great King of *Faerie*,
> Welcome faire *Queene* (his vertues vertuous Love)
> Welcome right *Aeglets* of the royal *Eyrie*.

But this line of flattery will not stick; no amount of imaginative wrapping can transform gross James into the King of Faerie.[30]

James's own *Workes* were published in folio in 1616, gathering together his principal writings on statecraft, biblical interpretation, religious controversy, and social issues such as those confronted in the 'Demonologie', the 'Counterblast against Tobacco', and the reflections on the Gunpowder Plot. The Bishop of Winchester, James Montagu, was charged with the business of editing the book, and his introductions push the art of panegyric dangerously close to deification. 'The King hath set forth divers works in print as the divers works of God are set forth in the Bible', he confidently claims. In matters spiritual, in penetrating the divine mysteries of Revelation, 'God hath given him an understanding Heart in the interpretation of that Booke beyond the measure of other men'. In matters temporal, James has restored the peace of Augustus:

Never hath there been so universall a Peace in Christendome since the time of our Saviour Christ, as in those his Dayes: and, I dare say, as much, if not more, by the procurement of his Maiestie, then by any other earthly meanes in this world . . . With Peace GOD hath given us Plentie . . . never was Justice administered with more libertie from the King, nor more uprightnesse from the Judges. And yet in the free dispensation of Justice, Mercie did never more triumph.[31]

Abstractions such as these suffer a loss of effect when they are not supported by images of masque or pageant, but Bishop Montagu perseveres and mounts the culminating steps of his eulogy: 'GOD hath given us a Solomon, and GOD above all things gave Solomon Wisdome; Wisdome brought him

The titlepage from King James's *Workes* (1616)

Portrait of James I from his *Workes*

Peace; Peace brought him Riches, riches gave him Glory.'³²

Such praise has its visual counterpart in the frontispiece to the book and the facing portrait of the author. Appropriately, this frontispiece is one of the most elaborate confections of the age: an extremely ornate architectural framework encloses the balanced figures of Religion and Peace, the sustaining principles of James's policies. The entablature supports an exciting assortment of spiky ornaments: slender gothic canopies, finials, a central obelisk, and heraldic animals. The obelisk, emblem of the glory of princes, pierces four crowns, those of James's earthly dominions. Above the obelisk hovers a heavenly crown set with stars and suspended by angels: this is the true crown of glory that will be James's hereafter. The crown is set within the sun, the rays of which shine down upon the earthly crowns, a symbol of the divine right by which James rules. This divine right to kingship is complemented by his temporal titles to the crown, exemplified by the royal beasts with their Scottish, Tudor and French blazonry. The gothic canopies, which are guarded by the royal beasts, and each of which has a burning sanctuary lamp hanging beneath it, may well represent the Church of England sheltering the light of the true faith.³³ On one side, a winged figure personifying Religion gazes upwards towards the heavenly crown, leaning on the Cross and holding a sacred text while she tramples on the skeletal form of death. Peace, on the other side, is a splendidly vigorous female, clad in a military tunic to show her preparedness, trampling on the arms of war. A starry crown indicates her heavenly origin, while her gifts to mankind are symbolised by the olive branch and cornucopia that she carries, showing that peace brings abundance.

The portrait of James facing this frontispiece relates the man to the concepts that have been visualised there. He is seated on his throne holding the orb and sceptre; above him, embroidered on the cloth of state is his motto *Beati Pacifici*. The heads of lions adorn the arms of his throne, 'expressing true fortitude'—James's old device when King of Scotland. The sword of Justice lies by him on a Bible. The verses underneath praise James's divine wisdom:

> Crownes have their compasse, length of dayes their date,
> Triumphes their tombes, felicitie her fate:
> Of more than earth, can earth make none partaker,
> But Knowledge makes the KING most like his maker.

Solomon again.

It was as Solomon that Bacon hopefully addressed James when he dedicated to him one of the books of greatest consequence written during his reign, the *Novum Organum*, in 1620. Ever since the first publication of *The Advancement of Learning* in 1605, Bacon had been elaborating and ramifying his immense plan for the systematic investigation of the phenomena of the natural world and the establishing of all the departments of human knowledge concerning the material creation and the nature of the mind on the basis of verified observation. An undertaking of such magnitude requires the patronage of a king if it is to begin, let alone succeed, for experimental philosophy and co-ordinated research involve new methods of working and a new type of institution for their furtherance; the universities with their commitments to the ancient attitudes and disciplines will not serve. 'For why should a few received authors stand up like Hercules' columns, beyond which there should be no sailing or discovery, since we have so bright and benign a star as your Majesty to conduct and prosper us?' he had enquired in the dedication of the *Advancement*.[34] From 1605 onwards Bacon had been striving to gain the King's support for his projects, suggesting that an active encouragement of his scheme would be an act of permanent value to the natural sciences, and a permanent memorial to James's wisdom. For, as Bacon assures him,

there hath not been since Christ's time any king or temporal monarch which hath been so learned in all literature and erudition, divine and human. . . . Your Majesty standeth invested of that triplicity which in great veneration was ascribed to ancient Hermes, the power and fortune of a King, the knowledge and illumination of a Priest, and the learning and universality of a Philosopher. This propriety inherent and individual attribute in your Majesty deserveth to be expressed not only in the fame and admiration of the present time, . . . but also in some solid work, fixed memorial and immortal monument, bearing a character or signature both of the power of a King and the difference and perfection of such a King.[35]

Bacon was right. Royal support of the methodical enquiry into natural causes would have won James lasting renown as the promoter of the new scientific movement. But James was unmoved by the appeal; even though he admired Bacon's political, legal and administrative skills as Lord Chancellor, in which capacity he must have had many occasions to unfold his philosophical ambitions to the King, James was totally unsympathetic to Bacon's vision. With the publication of the *Novum Organum*, which was the major part of Bacon's scheme for the Great Instauration of learning to appear in his lifetime, there came another appeal.

Surely to the times of the wisest and most learned of Kings belongs of right the regeneration and restoration of the sciences. Lastly, I have a request to make . . . that you who resemble Solomon in so many things . . . in the gravity of your judgements, in the peacefulness of your reign, in the largeness of your heart, in the noble variety of the books which you have composed, would further follow his example in taking order for the collecting and perfecting of a natural and experimental history, true and severe . . . such as philosophy may be built upon . . . and . . . rest on the solid foundation of experience of every kind.[36]

Presumably Bacon's naming of the 'College for experimentall Philosophy' in *The New Atlantis* as 'Salomon's House' was a deliberate encouragement to King James to found such a college. He reminds the reader that Solomon was reputed to have been the first to study the natural creation in 'That Natural History which he wrote of all the plants, from the Cedar of Libanus to the moss that groweth out of the wall', and no doubt hopes that Solomon's latter-day reincarnation will advance the study of the natural world with equal zeal.[37] Bacon was warmly thanked for his book, but James's response to its subject-matter was cool, for he observed that like the Peace of God it passed all understanding. Such indifference was representative of the uncomprehending opposition that the scientific movement had to contend with during the first half of the seventeenth century; its content was simply not deemed important in the way that moral philosophy and theology were. Theological controversy and political debate were the subjects that really fired James's interest, and his major act of institutional patronage was to give generous support to the founding of a college of divinity at Chelsea, where Anglican divines should train themselves to engage Catholic controversial-ists. In 1621 he was also disposed 'to found an Academ Roial or College of Honour where lectures and exercises of heroic matter and of the antiquities of Great Britain may be had and holden forever'.[38] Both ventures collapsed for lack of funds, even though the buildings of Chelsea College advanced some way. But to found a college of experimental science was too remote from his interests, and it was his grandson Charles II who would have the honour of patronising the Royal Society.

As he lived by a borrowed name, so James died by it. His funeral sermon preached by John Williams, Bishop of Lincoln, in Westminster Abbey was entitled *Great Britain's Salomon.* Here over the King's mortal body the Bishop rehearsed for the last time all those parallels and coincidences that had given meaning to James's own sense of his reign, discovering them with a freshness that is astonishing when one considers how long they had been current. He opens by showing the inevitability of the comparison when one searches for a biblical archetype for the King.

You know best, that no Booke will serve this turne, but the Booke of Kings: no King, but one of the best Kings: none of the best Kings, but one that reigned over all Israel, which must either be Saul (as yet good) or David or Salomon: no King of all Israel but one of the wisest Kings, which cannot be Saul, but either David or Salomon: none of the wisest Kings, neither, unless he be a King of Peace, which cannot be David, a Man of War, but onely Salomon.[39]

Furthermore, 'Salomon was a type of Christ himself, and by consequence a Patterne for any Christian.' As one might expect with a King so favoured of God, 'Not a particular of his life but was a mysterie of the Divine Providence, to keepe, and praeserve those admirable parts, for the settling and uniting of some great Empire'.⁴⁰ Here the Bishop turns to the idea of imperial destiny that had been a steady theme in the pageantry and propaganda of the reign. He assesses the achievements of James's tenure:

> all kinds of learning highly improved, manufactures at home daily invented, Trading abroad exceedingly multiplied, the Borders of Scotland peaceably settled, the North of Ireland religiously planted, the Navy Royall magnificently furnished, Virginia, New-Found-Land, and New England peopled, the East India well traded, Persia, China and the Mogor [?Mogul] visited, lastly, all the ports of Europe, Afrique, Asia and America to our red crosses freed and opened.⁴¹

When viewed like this, the congregation could recognise that empire of a sort had been achieved under James's reign, the Pillars of Hercules had been frequently passed, new worlds had been ventured upon, peace and religion had been extended to old and new territories. One begins to realise that the hyperboles and figures of praise applied to James bore a genuine relation to certain large truths. In an age of religion, what other nation had so theologically profound a king, one so able to expound and defend the tenets of his religion? In an age disrupted by religious wars, what other nation enjoyed so unbroken a peace as Great Britain? Viewed against Europe, and looking beyond the corruption of the Court and the imperfections of the political scene, Great Britain must have seemed The Fortunate Isles. Given the Protestant tendency to see Britain as the new Israel where the true faith was revealed and maintained, and where God bestowed prosperity and peace, there must indeed have been a divine providence overseeing all, miraculously preserving Elizabeth and bringing her to the throne, and then succeeding her with James. 'Non sine numine Divum, this came not to passe otherwise, then by God's direction.'⁴²

This chapter opened with an account of the emblematic pageantry that heralded the reign of King James; it may appropriately end with the post-humous celebration of the achievements of his reign as set forth in the great commemorative series of paintings by Rubens on the ceiling of the Banqueting House at Whitehall. This sequence was presumably commissioned by Charles I in 1629–30, when Rubens was in London on a diplomatic mission respecting peace between England and Spain; the decoration of the Banqueting House was still unfinished at this time, and Charles did not miss the opportunity to have the principal hall of his palace completed by the

Rubens, 'The Ceiling of the Banqueting House, Whitehall', from an engraving by Gribelin

master painter of the age. Rubens was accustomed to working on the grand scale: during the previous decade he had executed his great baroque fantasies on the ceiling of the Jesuit Church in Antwerp, as well as composing the glorification of the life and reign of Marie de Medici, the demi-goddess who was the mother-in-law of King Charles. Charles must have been largely responsible for the programme of the ceiling, although no instructions survive. However, it is clear that in choosing to glorify the reign of King James in the way he did, Charles was also seeking to justify the divine right of Stuart kings to rule, and the policy of absolute government on which he was then embarking. The choice of subject was eminently well suited to the setting. In this splendid hall, which James had caused to be built, the old King had often seen himself hailed in masques as a god incarnate, whose presence showered blessings on his people, whose power exerted itself in Justice and maintained Peace and Religion in the blessed isles of his kingdom. The action of the masques had expressed the higher truths of his kingship, just as the illusions of the stage had captured the invisible realities of his rule. Now Rubens would cause the ceiling of the hall to open into the illimitable space of a baroque heaven, where James is received into the realm of light, exchanging his earthly crown for the triumphal wreath of everlasting fame. It is a climax in the true spirit of the masque tradition, and the images of Rubens reveal the soul of James's policies and rule as splendidly as did the ephemeral glories of the stage. The impression that the paintings make is spectacular and sublime: there can be no resisting the assertions they so grandly make about the nature of Stuart power; they overwhelm us with their authoritative forms.

The first vision, as we might term these works (for they see into the ideal world where politics have become morality, where the operations of history have been reduced to their intellectual essentials), is of the Birth of Union.[43] The red-robed figure of James leans forward in his throne towards the triangular group of women who support a naked child whom they are about to crown. The two kneeling women represent England and Scotland, and the child represents the fruit of their Union, Great Britain. Aided by the third figure, Minerva, goddess of wisdom, they lower the new crown of the United Kingdom on to his head at James's command. It is the moment when the King's will is being effected, and his will is an instrument of his wisdom, externalised in the figure of Minerva. The King's wisdom is an important theme of the picture, both the active wisdom that Minerva represents, and also his secret wisdom, symbolised by the sphynx behind the throne. As the sphynx image suggests, this secret wisdom is a mysterious power of divine origin, one of the god-like attributes of his kingship. The central composition emphasises the theme of wisdom, for the pose of James on his throne directing his attention to two women carrying a child between them calls to mind the conventional subject of the Judgement of Solomon, where the King is shown in the act of determining the true mother of the disputed child. Rubens has adapted the convention of the scene to the political issue of Union, and in doing so has paid tribute to James's own identification of himself with the Jewish King. The setting, however, is magnificently Roman, within a palatial structure where Tuscan columns uphold a coffered dome; the effect of this setting is to strike an imperial note which echoes the claims to empire that we have seen to be a feature of Jacobean propaganda. Other familiar themes recur: the arms of the new United Kingdom that are borne aloft by putti are wreathed in red and white roses to remind us of the Tudor origins of James's rule, and the royal gift of Peace is demonstrated by the foreground putto who sets fire to a pile of arms, symbolising an end to the strife that has always existed between England and Scotland.

The side panels to this scene carry allegorical motifs which act as marginal glosses to the central action. One shows Hercules subduing a serpent-coiled figure who must represent Envy; the companion panel shows Minerva crushing a vigorous nude. The vanquished figures are generally held to personify rebellion and discontent, Minerva is undoubtedly Wisdom, while Hercules signifies Heroic Virtue, a common identification in Renaissance iconography books.[44] D. J. Gordon has suggested that Minerva and Hercules should be read together 'for Heroic Virtue cannot stand without the helping presence of Wisdom. Mythologically, it was Minerva who advised Hercules and helped him to achieve his labours, that most familiar allegory of heroic virtue. And it is appropriate that these virtues should support the scene of the Union, perfected and maintained by the Wisdom and Heroic Virtue of James.'[45]

The scene of Union is balanced by a painting whose subject is probably best explained as 'The Benefits of the Rule of King James'. Once again the imperial connotations of his rule are emphasised, for Rubens depicts James enthroned like a Roman emperor in a basilican apse beneath a mighty baldachino. Carved on his throne is a lion's head, his old *impresa* of fortitude. A massive commanding figure, with a head like Jove, James offers a protective gesture to Peace and Plenty who embrace at his right hand. Celestial spirits hold a crown of victory signifying the triumph of his policies. Minerva again averts the dangers of war or rebellion, thrusting away from the throne the armed figure of Mars. Minerva is here aided by Mercury, who points with his caduceus at the scene of violence. Mercury was, amongst his other functions, the god of eloquence, and the patron of embassies, and Rubens appears commonly to use his caduceus as a symbol of persuasion by eloquence and by peaceful means.[46] There is also a suggestion of healing power associated with this instrument which was an attribute of the god of medicine. Rubens, who was often employed as an ambassador, must have had considerable sympathy for James's pacific policies, which in these paintings he always depicts working through the agency of the active wisdom of Minerva.

The side panels to 'The Benefits of James's Rule' amplify the central theme, and interact with each other: Reason, or Temperance, holding a bridle, subdues an enemy, and Liberality with her horn of plenty triumphs over Avarice. Liberality or Bounty is a kingly virtue, which flourishes in time of peace, but it must be tempered by Reason, so that its fullness does not swell into corruption.

The commanding centre of the ceiling shows the Apotheosis of King James. The pictorial concept of an apotheosis was part of the armoury of the baroque painters of the Counter-Reformation in the service of the Roman Church. It mingled the conventions of the Assumption of the Virgin with elements of the deification of a Roman emperor. The process was applied most commonly to the greater glory of the saints and martyrs of the Church and was a feature of the rapturous pietism of post-Tridentine Catholicism, but it could be turned to other ends. Rubens had already painted the Apotheosis of Henri IV for Marie de Medici, and had similarly honoured Buckingham, but James's heavenly reception is more magnificent than his predecessors'. He is borne aloft on the back of an eagle, which also bears a great orb, eagle and orb together symbolising his imperial rule and dominion. Justice assists him, as the essential attribute of his kingship, the exercise of which has ensured his lasting glory. Besides her scales, Justice grasps a thunderbolt as a sign of her swiftness: she forms a powerful figure, although perhaps not an entirely plausible reflection of James's judicial behaviour. The personification of Religion, carrying a Bible, and Piety with a flaming urn constitute James's other supporters, representing his public and personal spiritual strengths. The pairing of Religion and Justice expresses the King's duty to God and to his people, twin responsibilities that he had explained in the first two books of *Basilikon Doron*. Cherubs remove the King's earthly crown while other powers prepare to greet him with crowns of higher worth, of oak and laurel. A winged figure of Peace joins with Minerva to bestow the laurel crown. Into this whirling mythological heaven of acclamation and reward James serenely rises, great, good and just, sainted and deified. For a King who ruled by divine right, apotheosis was the perfect consummation. Rubens closes this final vision with two long flanking panels abounding with putti who profusely scatter the fruits of the earth and tumble harmlessly with wild beasts, evoking in classical fashion the earthly paradise of Plenty and Peace which expresses the golden age that James's reign had caused to return.

Thus the familiar elements of Jacobean iconography are gathered in one last splendid scenario. Unity, Peace, Plenty, Religion, Justice, Wisdom (with the Solomonic allusions), Empire, the Golden Age restored, these are the achievements of the Stuart succession. They are also the inheritance of King Charles, who has caused them to be deployed across the ceiling of the hall where so much of the formal business of state was transacted. The political intelligence of Charles and the exuberant grand style of Rubens have combined to render in these scenes images of the absolute authority of the King: the King possesses in himself all the essential wisdom and knowledge of good government; there is no need of human aid or counsel. Seated in his Roman hall beneath his deified father, Charles was surrounded by the rhetoric of absolute power.

Notes to Chapter One

1   See Sidney Anglo, *Spectacle, Pageantry and Early Tudor Policy*, Oxford 1969, pp. 347 ff.
2   The architectural lineage of these arches probably goes back to the splendid entry of Prince Philip (later Philip II of Spain) into Ghent in 1549, which had set new levels of grandeur and allegorical complexity, the details of which had been widely published. In more recent memory, the entry of the Archduke Albert and the Infanta Isabella into Antwerp in 1599 had occasioned arches comparable to the London ones. See Roy Strong, *Splendour at Court*, London 1973, pp. 101–5.
3   We do not know much about Harrison, but it is evident that he had some acquaintance with Renaissance architectural theory, for his arches were constructed on the principle of harmonic proportions, established by the application of mathematical ratios to the component parts, as both Jonson in his commentary and Harrison in his measurements make clear. These structures are therefore very early examples of proportionally conceived architecture in England, even though to the casual eye they appear magnificently irregular.
4   *The Magnificent Entertainment Given to King James*, in *The Dramatic Works of Thomas Dekker*, ed. Fredson Bowers, Cambridge 1964, vol. II, p. 258.
5   Ben Jonson, *The King's Entertainment*, in *Works*, ed. C. H. Herford and P. and E. Simpson, Oxford 1941, vol. VII, pp. 84–5.
6   *Ibid.*, p. 88.
7   First edition 1593. Jonson appears to have been using the 1603 edition for *The King's Entertainment*. See Allan H. Gilbert, *The Symbolic Persons in the Masques of Ben Jonson*, Durham, N.C. 1948, pp. 3–28.

8 See Allardyce Nicoll, *The Stuart Masques and the Renaissance Stage*, London 1937, pp. 155–93.

9 Ben Jonson, *Works*, vol. VII, pp. 90–1.

10 *Ibid.*, p. 90.

11 Dekker, *The Magnificent Entertainment*, p. 265.

12 *Ibid.*, p. 268.

13 *Ibid.*, p. 273. One other feature of the Dutch arch deserves note: its lower sections were adorned with scenes from the everyday life of the Dutch people—weaving, spinning, fishing, buying and selling—an expression of the fundamental Dutch love of genre painting which they included on an architectural form that was everywhere else used to proclaim magnificence.

14 Dekker, p. 276.

15 *Ibid.*, p. 278.

16 *Ibid.*, p. 296.

17 *Ibid.*, p. 297. See also Frances Yates, *Astraea*, London 1975, pp. 29–87, for an extended discussion of this subject.

18 Dekker, p. 298. These verses were delegated by Dekker to Thomas Middleton.

19 See *Astraea*, p. 38. E.g. 'The return of the golden age and the rebirth of the phoenix are symbols with parallel meanings'.

20 Jonson, vol. VII, pp. 97–8.

21 *Ibid.*, p. 100.

22 *Ibid.*, p. 108.

23 *Ibid.*, p. 109.

24 Arthur Wilson, *The Life and Reign of James the First*, 1653, p. 13.

25 *A Meditation upon the Lord's Prayer*, 1619, pp. 93–4.

26 *The True Law of Free Monarchies*, in *The Political Works of James I*, ed. C. H. McIlwain, Cambridge, Mass. 1918, pp. 54–5.

27 *A Speach to . . . the Parliament*, 1609, in McIlwain, *op. cit.*, pp. 307–8.

28 For a full exposition of James's contributions to the theory of divine right, see J. N. Figgis, *The Divine Right of Kings*, 1896, pp. 137–76. Figgis emphasises that James's reliance on the theory was so great because his claim to the English throne rested on descent alone, and had no proper basis in law.

29 Printed in *His Maiesties Poeticall Exercises at Vacant Houres*, 1591.

30 Subsidiary sections of Sylvester's book have their own dedications, and one can sense the desperation of the poet on the fringes of the Court as he tries to attract patronage. The *Second Weeke* has some fifteen dedicatory sonnets, to James, Prince Henry, Egerton, Salisbury, Dorset, Pembroke, Essex and Devonshire among others, slender lines of obligation fulsomely baited, one or more of which might catch the attention of the great lords. A pension, a minor office in the household, or dining rights at one of the lord's tables might result.

31 King James, *Workes*, 1616, sig. e1.

32 *Ibid.*, sig. e2.

33 See M. Corbett and R. W. Lightbown, *The Comely Frontispiece*, London 1979, p. 140.

34 Dedication to the Second Book of *The Advancement of Learning*, 1605, in *The Works of Francis Bacon*, ed. J. Spedding, London 1859, vol. III, pp. 321–2.

35 Dedication to the First Book of *The Advancement of Learning*, *Works*, vol. III, p. 263.

36   Epistle Dedicatory to *The Great Instauration*, translated in *Works*, vol. IV, p. 12.

37   *The New Atlantis*, 1627, p. 16. Although not published until 1627, the work must have been in manuscript by 1620.

38   Quoted in D. H. Willson, *King James VI & I*, London 1956, p. 297.

39   John Williams, *Great Britains Salomon*, 1625, p. 2.

40   *Ibid.*, p. 43.

41   *Ibid.*, p. 52.

42   *Ibid.*, p. 63.

43   The figure of Union had appeared in the marriage masque *Hymenaei* and Union had provided the theme of *The Fortunate Isles, and their Union*, the last of Jonson's masques for James.

44   Heroic Virtue appeared as a figure in *The Masque of Queens*, where he adverted to the occasion when 'my face aversed, in open field / I slew the Gorgon'.

45   D. J. Gordon, 'Rubens and the Whitehall Ceiling', in *The Renaissance Imagination*, ed. S. Orgel, Berkeley and London 1975, p. 43.

46   *Ibid.*, pp. 64–9. Gordon points out that Minerva and Mercury held a special significance for Rubens, who as an ambassador frequently employed in negotiations for peace in the Thirty Years War felt his own mission was well represented by the gods of wisdom and eloquence, so much so that he placed their statues on the portico of his own house in Antwerp.

[2]
The Jacobean masque

Queen Anne was the prime mover behind the great series of masques that were the most distinctive feature of Jacobean Court entertainment. She delighted in extravagant spectacle and costume, and she excelled in dancing. She it was who singled out Ben Jonson to compose the poetry and elaborate the subject of her masques, usually on the basis of a conceit which she furnished him, and she was discerning enough to appoint Inigo Jones as scenic designer, thus releasing his prodigious talents as a theatrical inventor. Her selection of these two artists established them firmly as the foremost image makers at the new Court.

Jonson's standing at Elizabeth's Court had been somewhat precarious, although he was sufficiently prominent to receive a commission from Lord Spencer for a masque to greet Queen Anne at Althorp on her journey to London in 1603, and Sir John Cornwallis had employed him to entertain the King and Queen after they had been a-maying at Highgate in 1604. The King's triumphal entry in the same year had enabled Jonson to advertise the learned splendour of his inventions, and now under Queen Anne's patronage his particular genius as a public poet was fully recognised. Jonson had really been looking for a distinguished Court role for some years; his intentions were in evidence in *The Poetaster* (1601), where he had associated himself with the figure of the poet Horace at the Court of Augustus. His pointed acclamation of King James as the new Augustus in the London entry carried with it some hint of his own position as would-be Horace or Virgil to the new reign. In the event, Jonson exploited the masque commissions he received as the opportunity to create an uncontested position for himself as the official poet of James's Court, while the extensive connections that he made at Court enabled him to cast himself as the poetic arbiter of private morality by means of the verse epistles and satires that he addressed to the eminent personages of his time. When one remembers that Jonson's plays kept their appeal on the popular stage for much of James's reign, one must admire the versatility and energy of a talent which maintained such a variety of poetic roles so skilfully for so long. His presence gave a distinctive moral colouring to the poetic literature of the Jacobean Court, and endowed the Court festivals with a uniformity of style that endured until their cessation in 1640.

Jonson's colleague and eventual rival Inigo Jones had entered the Queen's service from the establishment of her brother Christian IV of Denmark, who doubtless recommended him to the English royal house. Jones already possessed a working knowledge of Italian illusionist theatrical techniques which he appears to have learnt some time between 1597 and 1603 at the Medici Court at Florence, where the spectacular *intermezzi*, combining music, dance, poetry and painting, had reached an extremely sophisticated state.[1] Queen Anne was ambitious to dazzle her Court with masquing splendours comparable to those of the French and Tuscan Courts, and the King was willing to underwrite the immense cost of these rare ventures, because the masques, more than any other form of courtly display, exhibited that quality of magnificence which was felt to be the essential attribute of monarchy in the Renaissance. In the justification that prefaces his account of the Queen's first masque, *Blacknesse* (1605), Jonson hastens to inform the reader that his intention is 'the studie of magnificence', a phrase that links up with the description of Anne on the title page as 'the most magnificent of Queenes'. Magnificence was not simply sumptuousness of display on a scale that only princes could afford; it contained a moral element too, for as Spenser wrote in the Letter prefixed to *The Faerie Queene*, it is the perfection of all the virtues, and hence the Jacobean masque involved the celebration of ideal virtues which were identified dramatically with the King's majesty which was present at the masque. The 'maiestas' or majesty of the King, the spiritual and moral greatness, the glory, dignity and power embodied in the person of the monarch, could be symbolically revealed or made visible in some of its aspects by means of the miraculous discoveries effected by the machinery of the masque, and charged with its full moral grandeur by poetry and fable. Given James's conviction of the divine right of his tenure, and his own sense of himself as a demi-god ('God gave not Kings the stile of Gods in vaine' is the opening line of *Basilikon Doron*, his manual of kingship), the masque provided an eminently appropriate form for demonstrating the numinous powers of majesty in a setting of the utmost splendour. In addition, King James's unrestrained expenditure on masques was significant evidence of his desire to push his Court into the front rank of European monarchies; the parsimonious epoch of Elizabeth was over; the union effected by James had turned England into Great Britain, whose component countries formed a little empire, so the King now sought to assert his new-found greatness in these spectacles presented to the Court.

It was the Queen's pleasure to be the principal performer in these masques, to lead her ladies in dancing on the great festive occasions, after the manner of the French Ballet de Cour; indeed it was the French Court under Marie de Medici that offered a precedent for the Queen to star in a theatrical representation before the Court. This relatively simple ambition was dramatically exalted by the genius of her two artistic executors, for Jonson, as an inveterate moralist and flatterer, with a gift for heightening a scene by mythological allusion, saw the opportunity of turning the Queen's masque into a triumphal celebration of the King's majesty, while Inigo Jones had the technical and artistic mastery that could conjure up an atmosphere of wonder and magic in which Jonson's exalted claims had a brief but intense credibility.

The fact that royalty was involved in the central action of many of the masques and present also in the audience constituted the unique aspect of the genre, which was essentially aristocratic. The dancers in a masque were always of gentle birth, just as the spectators were exclusively drawn from the Court. The King, who did not dance, was the principal spectator, and proximity to the King in the seating reflected the hierarchy of Court circles. Just as the King seated on his throne in the House of Lords represented the centre of political power, authority and honour, so the King seated in his chair of state in the Banqueting House at Whitehall represented the perfection of the moral virtues of kingship: wisdom, justice, temperance and the rest; at least, that was how Ben Jonson cast him, for he made King James the essential point of reference of the Court masques, feigning that the royal presence exerted a defining influence over the fable of the action which thus served to illuminate some quality of his greatness. Jonson had a genius for transforming the flimsy, gay devices of the Queen into fables of monarchical divinity. Above the brilliance of masquing and dancing and music his poetry revealed the mysteries of kingship to a chosen audience of the gently born, who were alone fit to receive such knowledge. In an important sense, the Court masque under Jonson and Jones was a theatre of mysteries. At the culmination of the festal season came the masque, and it is perhaps not entirely coincidental that the most magnificent event of the Court year took place on Epiphany, or Twelfth Night, for a god was indeed revealed amongst men, and a succession of miracles occurred within the Whitehall Banqueting House to witness the presence of divinity in the person of the King. The element of wonder which was the essential accompaniment of these rites was incomparably provided by Inigo Jones through his mastery of light and

motion and the revelation of the transformation scene, when the stage re-
volved or the shutters opened to discover the masquers in a new landscape,
radiant and sublime. Music and the intricacies of formal patterns of dance
provided the harmony which coalesced with the visual magic to induce a
state of consciousness that bordered on the visionary, a state in which truths
concerning the power of majesty could be seen and known to be true, validated on the instant before the Court's believing eyes, and affirmed by the
final dance of concord and assent in which all participated. That the King
had powers that exceeded those of the sun or moon, that he was an essential
cause of Beauty, that his presence could cause a perpetual spring, or an age
of gold, that the King possessed a heroic virtue and secret wisdom that
penetrated, guided and shaped events and was an instrument of divine
providence, all such qualities could be revealed by the action and fable of the
masque.

The business of revealing mysteries to the initiated was particularly
congenial to Ben Jonson. His interest in the private jargon of coteries, sects
and charlatans is a well-known feature of his plays for the popular stage,
reaching a peak in *The Alchemist* where the mysteries of the projectors, the
rituals of transmutation, and the arcane, absurd vocabulary of alchemy
form the principal part of the comedy. But when it came to the serious
matter of the mystery of kingship, in which Jonson himself could act as
hierophant, then his earnestness was complete. The very extensive use that
Jonson made of emblematic figures drawn from sixteenth-century Italian
manuals of mythology indicates how involved he was with the tradition of
secret wisdom conveyed through images to the understanding mind. He
relied especially on Cesare Ripa's *Iconologia*, Natale Conti's *Mythologia*,
Valeriano's *Hieroglyphica*, Cartari's *Imagini degli Dei*, and Giraldi's *De Deis
Gentium*, and these books furnished him with the complex details of the
gods and allegorical figures that fill his masques.[3] The power of these figures
lay in their obscure attributes, details and colouring of costume, all of which
had meaning to those who knew how to interpret them, but which remained
incomprehensible to the uninformed; the figures had a superficial identity
which could fairly easily be known, and a hidden character accessible only
to the learned initiate. So, for example, the dramatic personification of the
elements of Beauty which occurs in *The Masque of Beauty* is superficially
comprehensible as a visual display of the components of Beauty ranged
beneath the figure of Harmony; but to penetrate the symbolism behind the
colours of their dress and the objects that they bear, or to understand why
the throne of Harmony is rotating in a particular manner requires a quite
exceptional degree of learning. In this case the key to the symbolism lay

ultimately in the writings of the Florentine Neo-Platonists. Now Jonson was a learned man, to the point of pedantry, in fact, and had a modest acquaintance with Italian Neo-Platonic theorising and a detailed knowledge of the iconography books, such as those mentioned above, which simplified philosophical theory into visual images, images that Jonson proceeded to introduce on to the Whitehall stage. But very few people at a Court masque possessed such knowledge, and it is doubtful indeed whether they could even make out the finer details of moving figures in the theatre, let alone have the inclination to indulge in philosophic speculation at an extremely sociable occasion when one's mind was probably not at its clearest; hence the need for the published account of the masque, where Jonson could set forth his erudition for the serious reader to digest. Prince Henry, who was one understanding reader, even encouraged him to amplify his notes on certain masques. The important thing for Jonson was that the learning had been present in the masque, and that its statements about the nature of Beauty, Harmony, Love or Heroic Virtue had been made; the philosophic views that had been expounded, the secret operation of powers that had been hinted at, were true and remained true whether or not they were fully understood by the Court. One might draw an analogy with the Mass: the rituals of the ceremony, the formulae, the instruments employed, even the vestments of the celebrants bear witness to certain truths and have a symbolic significance which is only partially understood by those who attend. The central purpose is clear; the rituals are powerful and suggestive, beyond the level of rationality; the meaning of the symbolism can be known in detail by those who desire, but a limited understanding of the theological significance of the words, actions and instruments does not impair the efficacy of the ceremony. The religious analogy is not inappropriate, for both mass and masque solemnly and ceremonially reveal a mystery about the higher powers that operate in the world; where courtiers assumed the roles of deities, demi-urges or ideal qualities, a higher learning was thought the proper accompaniment to these superior selves, as well as being a tribute to the presumed intellectual comprehension of the Court. Jonson explained in the preface to *Hymenaei* (1606) that the higher meaning constituted the 'soul' of the masque, its vital principle:

This it is hath made the most royall Princes, and greatest persons (who are commonly the personaters of these actions) not onely studious of riches, and magnificence in the outward celebration, or shew; (which rightly becomes them) but curious after the most high, and heartie inventions, to furnish the inward parts: (and those grounded upon antiquitie, and solide learnings) which, though their voyce be taught to sound to present occasions, their sense, or doth, or should alwayes lay hold of more remov'd mysteries.

(10–19)

One imagines that the majority of the audience simply enjoyed the super-ficial pleasures of the masque: the sight of the most favoured courtiers appearing as gods or heroes in settings of exceptional beauty, the songs and incidental music, and the brilliantly choreographed dances that were the greatest delight of the evening to spectators and participants alike. We hear of the masquers rehearsing their dances a good two months before the per-formance; indeed, one has the impression that these rehearsals occupied a surprising amount of time for the courtiers and members of the royal family eligible for the masques. Since the music of almost all the masques is lost, and the dances are irretrievable, modern attention concentrates excessively on the documented contributions of Jonson and Jones, with the result that we give too much prominence to the intellectual elements of the genre. This intellectual structure is unquestionably there, but since we tend to read the masques from the standpoint of Ben Jonson, who was only one of a group of collaborators, we exaggerate the importance of his images and learning in the total effect of the revels. There were undoubtedly a few deep 'understand-ers', as he calls them, in the audience, who had some intuition of the 'remov'd mysteries', and we naturally wish to align ourselves with them, but whereas we may remember a particular masque for a novel metaphor of kingship that it introduces, or for a striking architectural design, most of the actual audi-ence of the time probably remembered it for an extraordinary set of capers cut by Prince Henry or Buckingham, or for the colourful costumes of Queen Anne and her ladies.

The first of Queen Anne's masques was *The Masque of Blacknesse*, per-formed at Court on Twelfth Night 1605. Her simple desire was that she and her ladies should appear as blackamoors, a popular form of disguise in festivals in England and Scotland during the preceding decade. Jonson chose to cast the ladies as Aethiopians dwelling by the river Niger, which flows into the Western Ocean. The conceit on which Jonson bases the masque is very simple, a strained fiction which only redeems itself by the graceful opportunities for royal flattery that it permits. The dark ladies have experienced a vision in which they were instructed to seek a land whose name ends in *-tania*, where their complexion shall be refined and their beauty made ideal. Ocean explains that the prophecy refers to Albion or Britannia, a land beyond the reach of the sun that

> leaves that Clymat of the sky
> To comfort of a greater light
> Who formes all beauty with his sight.
> (193–5)

The moon goddess appears and confirms this interpretation; in her praise of

Britain she manages to reiterate briefly a number of the themes that were becoming the familiar accompaniment of James's reign:

> BRITANIA, which the triple world admires,
> This isle hath now recovered for her name;
>   . . . this blest isle
> Hath wonne her ancient dignitie, and stile,
> *A world, divided from the world:*
>
> . . .
>
> Rul'd by a SUNNE, that to this height doth grace it:
> Whose beames shine day, and night, and are of force
> To blanch an AETHIOPE, and revive a Cor's.
> His light scientiall is, and (past mere nature)
> Can salve the rude defects of every creature.
>
> . . .
>
>   This sunne is temperate, and refines
>   All things on which his radiance shines.
>
>   (241–65)

The allusions are easy to grasp: Britannia has recovered her name as a result of the union of the crowns, and is thus restored to her ancient British dignity. 'This blest isle' picks up the old Roman identification of Britain with the Islands of the Blessed, both considered equally remote from the known world; the phrase is suggestive too of the peace that prevails in the land. The translation of the Virgilian *Orbis divisus ab orbe* introduces a phrase that had acquired prophetic status, carrying with it the idea of Britain as a world set apart for a special destiny. The King is the greater sun who exercises an operative virtue over the land and its people; his 'scientall light' is the light of knowledge, analogous to divine wisdom, that plays over his dominion, and like a divine power is recreative, a force above nature, the secret magic of a king. All these themes had been present in the triumphal entry into London the previous year, but now they are incorporated into a full-scale dramatic spectacle as the 'efficient cause' of the masque.

From these large public themes, Jonson moves into esoteric territory as the masquing ladies descend in pairs from their illuminated shell to dance, holding up to the spectators their fans on which were painted their mythological names and symbols. These 'mute hieroglyphics' as Jonson calls them were part of the essential mystery of the masque. In alluding to them, Jonson says that he has chosen this combination of name and image 'as well for strangenesse, as relishing of antiquitie, and more applying to that originall doctrine of sculpture, which the Aegyptians are said, first, to have brought from the Aethiopians'. Mention of the Egyptians virtually guarantees that Jonson intended to put on a display of secret wisdom and ancient knowledge, mysteries in fact. Few if any of the spectators would have been able to decipher them, but it must be assumed that the King's 'scientall light' could penetrate them, for the King was the chief understander of the masque as well as the chief spectator. (One imagines that some means must have been used to enlighten him in advance; certainly Jonson must have explained the devices to the Queen and her ladies.) The presence of a secret wisdom in the images emphasised the ritual element in the masque and suggested that profound and ineffable relationships were being alluded to. All spectators could associate themselves with the veiled but privileged knowledge that was being disclosed to the Court, confident that in their midst there were some several persons wise enough to have full under-standing—principally the King and Queen—but Jonson was by implication making bold claims for the poet as well, for he was the high priest of the mysteries. A golden tree laden with fruit, the geometrical figure Icosahedron in crystal, a pair of naked feet in a river, a salamander, a cloud full of rain, 'an urn sphered with wine', these were the hieroglyphics. They have been interpreted for us by D. J. Gordon, who detects a complex of images suggestive of the waters of life and of paradise, purification and new life. The Queen appears as Aglaia, the leader of the Graces, a name meaning 'splendour or beauty of the spirit', and her association with a fruitful golden tree suggests 'a royal and spiritual beauty fertilising the earth' in a context of paradise restored, all of which concepts must bear on the Britannia of King James.[4]

Such moments of mystery were brief, however, and could not long inter-rupt the audience's pleasure in music, dance and spectacle, although it is clear from a letter of Sir Dudley Carleton that some courtiers had difficulty in comprehending the nature of perspective scenery that Inigo Jones intro-duced into England with this masque.[5] Both Jonson and Jones had to educate their audience into an appreciation of the new hybrid art that they had created, Jonson using the published texts to convey detailed accounts of what the spectators had seen, with clues to the symbolism of costume and setting, Jones relying on the repeated glory of his effects. The ladies who danced in *The Masque of Blacknesse* were probably amongst its chief understanders, for they were a highly sophisticated group of blue-stockings who might have proved a match for the Queen of Navarre and her witty ladies in *Love's Labour's Lost*. They included Lucy, Countess of Bedford, who was the patron of Donne, Chapman, Daniel, Drayton and Jonson, and no stranger to hard meanings or to the aesthetics of the avant-garde. The Countess of Pembroke belonged to the most distinguished literary family in the country; Lady Rich's family background was also notable for literary connections. Lady Mary Wroth was Sir Philip Sidney's niece and a literary intellectual in her own right: she was a competent poet, but her major work was to be a long prose romance *Urania* (1621), containing elaborate descriptions of chivalric encounters in which devices, emblems and *imprese* figured prominently, demonstrating that she was clearly fluent in the language of symbolism. The *Urania* was dedicated to the Lady Susan Vere, the Countess of Montgomery, who also danced in *The Masque of Blacknesse*. In considering the Jacobean Court culture, it would be unwise to underestimate the intelligence of the female participants.

At the end of *Blacknesse*, the masquers promised to return in a year's time to show the transfiguring effects of their visit to 'Britania'. Circumstances intervened, and the sequel, *The Masque of Beauty*, was not presented until 1608, when it was the Queen's pleasure 'again to glorify the Court', in Jonson's words. The phrase has a double meaning, for it suggests both filling the Court with splendour, and also exalting the Court, for all courtiers shared in the royal glory of James that was celebrated in the masque. We learn that the Aethiopian nymphs have been delayed by envious night, but are now approaching on a floating island, where they have erected a Throne of Beauty. One of the introductory figures immediately directs attention to James, whose supernal influence is being revealed by the masque:

> Behold, whose eyes doe dart Promethean fire
> Throughout this all; whose precepts do inspire
> The rest with dutie; yet commanding, cheare;
> And are obeyed, more with love, than fear.
>
> (35–8)

The floating island is discovered, with its Throne of Beauty, a complicated classical structure irradiated with lights in which the masquers sit, each representing some component of Ideal Beauty, under the controlling power of Harmony, 'The World's soule', in the person of the Queen.

This composition has been shown to be well grounded in the Neo-Platonic theory of Beauty with which Jonson was conversant from Florentine sources.[6] The secret analysis of Beauty was an additional dimension, evident to the higher understanders of the Court, but to everyone else the breath-taking spectacle must have seemed self-sufficient. Many of the accessories belonged to the familiar imagery of love poetry: torch-bearing cupids, Venus's rabbits, love arbours bearing golden fruit, the maze of love, the fountains of youth and pleasure. 'In the arbors were placed the musicians, who represented the shades of the old poets, and were attired in a priest-like habit of crimson and purple, with laurel garlands.' This emphasis on the antique, which was a feature of so many of the masques (expressed particularly through the architectural settings and the costumes) was a way of associating the principal figures in the action with the perfected civilisation of classical antiquity and its authoritative knowledge of the world; but it also acted as a form of flattery to the Court at large by implying that its members are all honorary citizens of sage heroic antiquity, an illusion reinforced by the fact that the fabulous beings on stage moved forward at the conclusion of the masque and drew everyone into the dance that took up the rest of the evening.

As the Floating Island advanced towards the front of the stage, the Throne of Beauty turned 'with a circular motion of its own, imitating that which we call *motum mundi*', while the surrounding steps, on which cupids sat, rotated contrariwise 'with analogy *ad motum planetarum*', the whole system moving to the sound of music. Of course the *primum mobile* of this fictive universe was James, the royal One who is the source of Beauty and Love in the world of Great Britain, who has drawn the wandering beauties of the masque to him as souls are drawn to their source, and who has bestowed an ideal beauty on them. As the Queen and her ladies are now shown wearing their proper complexion, their blackness having been dispelled, their Court beauty is identified with ideal beauty, for 'beauty's perfect throne' is now 'peculiar to this place alone'.

The most spectacular of Queen Anne's early masques was *The Masque of Queenes* (1609), for which she specifically requested that Jonson should compose 'some dance or show that might precede hers and have the place of a foil or a false masque'. Royal taste was thus responsible for the 'anti-masque', which now became a convention of the genre, where spirits of disorder were given a brief licence before they were subdued or dispersed by the forces of the principal masque. This device enhanced the virtuous or thaumaturgical powers attributed to majesty by showing them in active and absolute opposition to negative and disruptive agencies; it also considerably enlarged the aesthetic scope of the masque. 'The spectacle of strangeness', as Jonson called the anti-masque, permitted wilder and more mannered dances, as well as an extended range of musical invention to evoke the discord and rude energy of the preliminary antics.[7] The anti-masque also indulged that love of the grotesque which was a persistent trait of Renaissance taste, exemplified by the leering masks that were an accepted part of decoration 'à l'antique'. The grotesqueries of the anti-masque exist as an acknowledgement of the ineradicable strain of 'strangeness' or the irrational in human nature; by being given a place in the masque, the wayward energies of life were fitted into a controlled vision in which their existence was recognised and their relative power defined and limited by higher authorities. The new convention drew out Jones's and Jonson's talent for caricature: Jonson had a well-established theatrical bias in that direction, and Jones, when in Italy, had come into contact with the art of *caricatura*, which he was now able to exploit for costume designs. In addition to these considerations, the rise of the anti-masque also re-established the old tradition of misrule during the Christmas season, now safely integrated into a disciplined work of art.[8]

Jonson decided to open *The Masque of Queenes* with a gathering of witches, twelve of them to match the twelve masquers. The device was calculated to catch the interest of King James, who was the chief authority on witches in the realm, having anatomised their activities in his book of *Demonologie* (1591). The witches' rituals and habits are given large dramatic space, while the notes to the printed text form a sort of *codex maleficarum*, or infernal hagiography. James's book naturally receives first mention, but thereafter we realise that Jonson's interest is more with the witches of antiquity than with the contemporary epidemic; moreover, we deduce that the Greek and Roman writers have made the definitive observations on witchcraft which modern experience can only confirm. The treatment of the subject here is a good example of how Jonson regarded these early masques as a theatre of Graeco-Roman learning, however lightly and entertainingly displayed, for such learning was, in his view, central to the culture of an enlightened Court.[9]

After a vigorous demonstration of the malignant arts, the witches were dispelled in a trice by a chord of music which marked the transition to the House of Fame, on top of which the masquers sat 'upon a throne triumphal in the form of a pyramid and circled with a store of light'. Although the motif of the Hall of Fame had been borrowed from Chaucer, its details were classical, as were the supporting figures of the poets who formed its pillars, and the heroes whom the poets upheld. The masquers were disguised as famous queens of antiquity, and at the summit of the pyramid, symbol of the eternity of fame, sat England's glory, Bel-Anna, Queen of the Ocean. Her headdress bore a celestial sphere, indicative of the infinite power of the royal mind. She was aptly styled Queen of the Ocean, for her consort James was often glossed as Neptune, in recognition of Britain's command of the northern seas. The Queen was presented by Heroic Virtue, the parent of Fame, who came in the guise of Perseus (although Jonson mentions that he could equally well have chosen Hercules) and he proclaimed the paramount Fame-through-Virtue of Bel-Anna, and then saluted that

> most royall, and most happy King,

Of whom *Fames* House, in every part, doth ring
For every vertue; but can give no increase:
Not, though her loudest Trumpet blaze your peace.
                    (432–5)

The queens then descended and, mounted in chariots, led the hags captive about the stage. The witches had earlier been identified with forces hostile to James's policies: their chief had said,

I hate to see these fruicts of a soft peace,
And curse the piety gives it such increase.
Let us disturbe it, then; and blast the light.
                    (144–7)

So the triumphal procession of the queens becomes a characteristic piece of political rhetoric gloriously accomplished through spectacle.

Increasingly, the architecture of the central masque, and in particular the Palladian structures that Jones composed, came to represent the ordered values of the King's rule; the ideal values of the Court were being expressed theatrically by means of the revived antique style upon the Whitehall stage long before Jones could express them in stone for his aristocratic patrons. It evidently took a considerable time for the taste for the new architectural style to be assimilated by the members of the Court and to be employed as a serious framework for their lives, for it was not until 1615–16 that Jones was requested to provide designs for building in the classical manner. Another remarkable feature of the main masque from the very beginning of the series was the lighting. Technical improvements imported by Jones allowed the masquers to be irradiated by an intense light, often variously coloured, which was powerfully suggestive of their near-divine condition. The heroes of the Court were frequently revealed in 'a mine of light' or 'a store of light', transfigured by incandescence. In an age of low candle power, the concentration of light that Jones was able to bring to bear upon the stage was an essential part of the wonder that was the element in which the masque moved.

Wonder actually appeared on stage as one of the leading characters in *The Vision of Delight*, the Christmas masque of 1617.[10] The transformation scene revealed the Bower of Zephyrus, a luxuriant scene of springtime. Wonder is astonished at the miracles wrought by art in the midst of winter, and her amazement increases when Fantasy explains the true cause:

Behold a King
Whose presence maketh this perpetuall *Spring*,

The glories of which Spring grow in that Bower,
And are the marks and beauties of his power.

(201–4)

The poetics and the economics of the masque coincide at this moment, for the magnificence of the King is ultimately responsible for the art of the masque, and the miracle of midwinter spring is a poetic image of the mysterious divine power of kingship that can change the course of nature and create a beneficent pastoral world where Peace is found. The King is explicitly hailed as a god here: 'Whose power is this? what God?' Art is the means of revealing his power, and the proper response is wonder, the emotion natural to those in the presence of the numinous. The masque mounts to a climax in a series of dances of homage and worship of James which effectively constitute a cult of 'Divus Jacobus'. This tendency towards cult worship had strengthened considerably round about 1615–16 and should be related to the shift towards absolutism in his methods of government. Publication of James's *Workes* in 1616 may have been part of this general strategy, for the book disseminated his political and religious wisdom throughout the land, and could be seen as a way of generating confidence in his judgement and reasserting to his subjects his divine right to rule. The pension of one hundred marks awarded to Jonson in the same year may have been a by-product of this policy—a reward from James to the artist who most consistently promoted the divine image of his majesty.

Jonson's own folio of 1616 concluded with *The Golden Age Restor'd*, which had been the Twelfth Night masque of 1615, and which was the first of the intensified presentations of James as a benevolent just spirit presiding over Britain's destinies. The general action of the masque can virtually be deduced from the title: Jove has decreed that the golden age shall be brought back to man. An anti-masque of the Iron Age is routed by Pallas Athena, or Wisdom, who is Jove's instrument; then Astraea, the long-absent goddess of Justice, whose return had anciently been foretold by Virgil as the sign of the renewal of the golden age, is seen descending into a transformed world in company with the personification of the golden age. They choose to dwell in the happy isle of Britain. The arts flourish again, and the race of blessed spirits that once occupied the earth, 'that for their living good now semigods are made', return to serve as the defenders of Justice. The semigods are of course the masquing courtiers, who are discovered in a blaze of light: they pour forth rapturously to dance on the verdant peaceful earth, then unite with the lady masquers to form platonic souls, where male and female principles are perfectly balanced in a prelapsarian harmony. The earth reverts to its pristine bountifulness and peace:

> Then earth unplough'd shall yeeld her crop,
> Pure honey from the oake shall drop,
>   The fountaine shall runne milke:
> The thistle shall the lilly beare,
> And every bramble roses weare,
>   And every worme make silke.

(163–8)

At the end, Astraea senses the presence of the deity: Jove is watching the enactment of his decrees from beneath the cloth of state.

> Of all there seemes a second birth,
> It is become a heav'n on earth,
>   And *Iove* is present here,
> I feele the Godhead: nor will doubt
> But he can fill the place throughout,
>   Whose power is every where.

(228–33)

In 1620 the annual paean was whimsically varied in *News from the New World*, when James was presented with a race of beings created in his own image who live beyond the moon rapt in the contemplation of his greatness:

A race of your owne, form'd, animated, lightned, and heightned by you, who rapt above the Moone far in speculation of your vertues, have remain'd there intranc'd certaine houres, with wonder of the pietie, wisedome, Majesty reflected by you, on them, from the Divine light, to which onely you are lesse. These, by how much higher they have beene carried from earth to contemplate your greatnesse, have now conceiv'd the more haste and hope in this their returne home to approach your goodnesse; and led by that excellent likenesse of your selfe, the truth [danced by Prince Charles], . . . that all their motions be form'd to the musicke of your peace, and have their ends in your favour, which alone is able to resolve and thaw the cold they have presently contracted in comming through the colder Region.

(303–17)

Conceits that verge on sacrilege abound, redeemed by James's settled belief that he was divinely appointed to reign and that his kingship was a temporal extension of divinity. The dancers are asked to study the King as a living Bible:

> Read him as you would doe the booke
> Of all perfection, and but looke
>   What his proportions be;
> No measure that is thence contriv'd,
> Or any motion thence deriv'd,
>   But is pure harmonie.

(340–5)

The King's power is likewise credited with perpetuity and infinity.

A shift into the pastoral key occurs in *Pan's Anniversarie* (1620), an exceptional masque in that it was staged in midsummer to celebrate the King's birthday. James is now Pan, the universal god of nature, in whose honour the inhabitants of Arcadia gather for their annual rites. Pan is here associated with the Fountain of Light, an image used by the Neo-Platonic philosopher Plotinus to express the source of creativity in the universe from which all life flows. The Arcadians, who are the masquers—and by extension all the members of the Court—return to worship at the Fountain, to give thanks for their perfect society, for they have been taught

> By PAN the rites of true societie,
> From his loud Musicke, all your manners wraught,
> And made your Common-wealth a harmonie,
> Commending so to all posteritie
> Your innocence from that faire Fount of light.
>
> (160–4)

The songs of the masquers are no longer songs; they are specifically entitled hymns. Through them Jonson can praise those royal qualities that James was most proud of. James the poet is 'the best of singers, Pan, / That taught us swaines, how best to tune our lays'. In the tangled thickets of the chase, Pan is 'the best of hunters'; he is also 'the best of leaders'. Finally he is hailed as 'best of shepherds, / That keepes our flocks, and us', a conventional pastoral tribute, but one that may have had a specific relevance to James, who occasionally used this persona, as when, for example, he addressed the Star Chamber in 1617 in a speech against duelling, saying that he was a shepherd, because Jacob, from whom his name derived, was a shepherd, and he intended to defend his sheep as a *rex pacificus*.[11] Biblical echoes recalling God the Father can be heard in the hymn that opens:

> PAN is our All, by him we breath, wee live,
> Wee move, we are.
>
> (192–3)

His power banishes disease, 'keepes away all heats and colds', and maintains a perpetual spring in the land: he has restored the earthly paradise, in effect. Recent commentary on the masque has traced the development of the pastoral mode, emphasising its pre-eminence in the Caroline entertainments, for pastoral permits the presentation of absolute power in its most benevolent aspect, as the god of nature.[12] Certainly, one can see this trend strongly at work in *Pan's Anniversarie*, in which the characters place their total faith in the wise, creative and secure direction of the world by the English Pan.

James's own favourite masque was *The Gypsies Metamorphos'd*, which he witnessed three times in 1621, at Buckingham's seat at Burley-on-the-Hill, at Belvoir and at Windsor. This was not, properly speaking, a Court masque, with its ritual exaltation of the King, but one devised by Buckingham to delight his sovereign. The dances in this masque were by all accounts brilliant, and since James had an intense appreciation of dancing, and Buckingham was an outstanding performer, it is not difficult to see why *The Gypsies* was so successful. The action offered a boisterous and verbose account of gypsy life and revels, full of the canting vocabulary that Jonson reeled out so well, and the presentation was exceptional in that the courtiers who were the leading masquers also spoke their parts, instead of leaving the speeches to professional actors as was usual. Given that Buckingham, his brother and friends were the principals, one can see that *The Gypsies Metamorphos'd* was at once a triumphal vehicle for the Buckingham family, and an act of thanksgiving to the King for his favour. This view becomes clear in the scene where the Captain of the Gypsies, played by Buckingham, tells the fortune of the King. After the conventional praise that James will 'make / All Christian differences cease', and be 'the arbiter of war and peace', for which 'of all the world you shall / Be styled James the Just', Buckingham asks:

> But why doe I presume, though true,
> To tell a fortune, Sir, to you,
>   Who are the maker here of all,
> Where none doe stand, or sitt in veiwe,
> But owe theire fortunes unto you,
>   At least what they good fortune call?
>
> My selfe a *Gypsye* here doe shine,
> Yet are you Maker, Sir, of mine.
>
> (334–41)

A critical courtly eye in 1621 might have found the image of the gypsy turned King's favourite an apt reflection on the prodigious rise of Buckingham.

The last two Court masques of James's reign were closely related to each other. *Neptune's Triumph for the Returne of Albion* (1624) was written to celebrate the safe return to England of Prince Charles from his fruitless journey to Spain to woo the Infanta, but owing to a quarrel over precedence between the French and Spanish ambassadors, the masque had to be cancelled, and Jonson reworked the central scene into the following year's production, *The Fortunate Isles*. The failure of the Spanish match was regarded in political circles as a diplomatic fiasco, although it caused much popular rejoicing, for James's policy of an alliance with Spain through a royal marriage was widely disliked, in spite of the fact that James regarded it as the keystone of his policy for a general European peace. In *Neptune's Triumph*, Jonson endeavoured to write a masque that would convert the royal discomfiture into a victory of James's will. He therefore concentrated on the happy return of Prince Charles, under the name of Albion, from the dangerous paths of his adventures. The god responsible for his preservation is Neptune, the familiar persona of King James. To assist Albion, Neptune has sent Hippius, 'his powerful manager of Horse', an allusion to Buckingham, who was Master of the King's Horse, and Proteus, father of disguise, the secret agent Cottington. There is no reference to the failure of the mission; we learn only that the 'great commands' of Neptune have been executed, and that the god has dispatched a floating island to bring home the travellers. All this information is delivered in a preliminary comic exchange between a poet and a Whitehall cook in a scene which mimics the gossip around the Palace about the nature of the evening's entertainment. The cook is convinced that his own art can produce confections as spectacular as those of the designer of a masque, and pours scalding condemnations on the pretentions of artists. In this exchange between poet and cook, the contrivance and artificiality of the masque are freely admitted: it is a spectacle or show that has been painstakingly put together. This deliberate playing down of the elements of surprise and wonder seems intended to berate the Court in humorous fashion for its unwillingness to respond wholeheartedly to the effects of verse and spectacle, for, to judge by surviving letters and observations on the Jacobean masque, there were always some courtiers who failed to understand the significance of the action, or who were critical of the effects, being interested only in the dancing.[13] The central masque, which presents Prince Charles and his companions on the floating island seated beneath the tree of harmony, followed by three transformation scenes—a maritime palace, a seascape, and the British fleet discovered—must have been intended to overwhelm critical coolness by the sheer lavishness of spectacle, and by the position of the Prince at the heart of it. When the diplomatic quarrel caused the performance to be cancelled, the triple-phased main masque was too powerful to be abandoned, so Jones and Jonson re-used it as the centrepiece for what was in fact to be James's last masque.

The title, *The Fortunate Isles and their Union*, reminds us how consistent and sustained the themes of royal praise had been during twenty-one years of Stuart rule, for these topics would have been current at the time of the London entry of 1604. The floating island of *Neptune's Triumph* has now been named Macaria, the 'blessed' isle, and has been conflated with the classical image of the Islands of the Blest, where the heroes and great poets live eternally. The introducer explains that a critical moment in history has arrived when all the fortunate islands shall be joined together. As the islands of Great Britain have already been united by James, Macaria has been instructed to attach herself to the Kingdom. The implied background is The Thirty Years' War, which was spreading all over Europe, but which left Britain untouched, a state of affairs that was attributed to James's policies of peace. The floating island is discovered, with Apollo, god of poetry, hovering in the air above with Harmony and the spirits of music. Below sits Prince Charles with his companions in the guise of ancient heroes, beneath palm trees that were the symbols of James's peace and the victory of his policies. Singing inhabitants of the island leave the stage and move towards James's throne, praising Britain as the true Elysium. The ancient poets flood into the Hall, into Stuart England, as if it were an extension of their classical home. Prince Charles is lifted aloft as all celebrate his coming marriage to the French princess, 'joining the bright lily and the rose'. The long-delayed miracles of Inigo Jones's art are finally performed, and the blessed spirits go about the Court once more, singing of the ladies' beauty and inviting them into the revels.

With Prince Charles's emergence as principal masquer, Jonson's later masques tended to revert to actions centring on heroic figures, after the fashion of the early masques for Queen Anne and Prince Henry, for their function is now to provide a heroic context for the heir as well as praise for the King. But in other respects great changes had occurred. Perhaps the most important was that the anti-masques had developed into miniature comedies, for a variety of reasons: Jonson must have felt that comedy and the central masque were compatible; there was a precedent for comedy in the Italian *intermezzi* that Jonson admired, and his own comic inventions generally pleased the Court taste; moreover, comedy was very much a part of the old tradition of Twelfth Night revels. Also, during the last decade of James's reign, Jonson was no longer writing for the public stage, but his comic genius was by no means exhausted, and it flourished in the hybrid genre of the masque. The themes of these comic preludes were usually related to the display of the masque proper: for example, in *The Fortunate Isles*, the introductory scenes show the gulling of Merefool by a pretended member of the Rosicrucian Brethren, who promises him strange powers, visions of the great philosophers and more:

> tinct the tip,
> The very tip o' your nose, with this *Collyrium*,

And you shall see i'the aire all the *Ideas*,
Spirits, and *Atomes*, Flies, that buz about
This way, and that way, and are rather admirable,
Then any way intelligible.

(187–92)

But this is charlatanism, and the visions delusions. In contrast the main masque offers an efficacious magic, whose illusions are images of a higher reality, where ideas may indeed be seen in the air, and spirits, all platonically related to the figures of majesty and the splendour of the Court circle.

Over the years the main masque grew more extensive and visually self-sufficient. In its earlier phase a large area of the meaning relied on the symbolic attributes and costumes of the figures for its elucidation, requiring an active learned intelligence to riddle out the secrets. The later masques tend to transmit their meaning by visual magic and splendour of spectacle, through a unified sequence of scenes which promote by means of architectural and landscape settings aided by music, a relatively simple yet sublime glorification of the monarch and the chief masquers. The visual powers begin to predominate over the verbal and intellectual, and in this we see the growing ascendancy of Inigo Jones over Ben Jonson in the ordering of the masques, an ascendancy which would give a quite different character to the masques of Charles's reign.

The Jacobean masques projected idealised images of the King, the royal family, and the courtiers, so that all members of the Court were annually involved in a ritual that celebrated the perfection of their world. The normal conditions of morality and decorum that prevailed at James's Court were of a strikingly different order, and the King himself fell embarrassingly short of being the model prince that he had described to his son and his subjects in *Basilikon Doron*. James was a dirty, ill-favoured man whose personal habits verged on the disgusting even in an age accustomed to squalor. He ate and drank in an uncouth way, he slobbered a good deal, he suffered from gout which made his movements ungainly. His thick Scots accent was barely intelligible to the English at first, though it was clear that he swore a lot, and was excessively given to bawdiness in his talk. He paid little attention to his dress, which was frequently soiled, and his whole bearing was graceless and undignified. As his reign wore on, he became increasingly addicted to drink, eventually developing that florid, blotchy countenance that his later portraits record. The ruling passion of his life was hunting, for which he was notoriously willing to neglect the business of state, yet even here his conduct was less than regal: he had a habit of tearing open a freshly slaughtered deer and plunging his hands and feet into the entrails, then splashing his courtiers' faces with blood as a token of the goodly fellowship of the chase. Towards the ladies of the Court he behaved boorishly, taking little pleasure in their company except when bawdiness got the better of him. Since gallant and chivalric behaviour helped to set the noble tone of princely establishments everywhere, James's grossness in this respect was especially damaging to the character of his Court. The departure of Queen Anne to her separate household in 1606, provoked by incompatibility and the dread of bearing more children, encouraged the atmosphere of Whitehall to degenerate even further. The King's homosexual proclivities alienated many leading courtiers, and disaffection was increased when favourites such as Carr or Villiers were promoted into the aristocracy.

The most notorious excesses of the reign took place when James was visited by his brother-in-law the King of Denmark in 1606, when the drinking and revelry got entirely out of hand. Sir John Harington's famous letter describing the riotous festivities at Theobalds, where Robert Cecil entertained the two Kings, deserves quotation because of the uncommon freshness of the picture, and because it was precisely the sort of gossip that spread around the country and did so much to damage the reputation of the Court among the more sober, pious and industrious sections of society.

The sports began each day in such manner as persuaded me of Mahomet's paradise. We had women and indeed wine too of such plenty as would have astonished each sober beholder. Our feasts were magnificent, and the two royal guests did most lovingly embrace each other at table; I think the Dane hath strangely wrought on our good English nobles, for those whom I never could get to taste good liquor now follow the fashion and wallow in beastly delights. The ladies abandon their sobriety and roll about in intoxication. There hath been no lack of good living: shows, sights and banquetings from morn to eve. One day a great feast was held, and after dinner the representation of Solomon his Temple and the coming of the Queen of Sheba was made before their Majesties. The lady who did play the Queen's part did carry most precious gifts to both their Majesties; but forgetting the steps arising to the canopy overset her caskets into his Danish Majesty's lap and fell at his feet, though I rather think it was in his face. Much was the hurry and confusion; cloths and napkins were at hand to make all clean. His Majesty then got up and would dance with the Queen of Sheba; but he fell down and humbled himself before her and was carried to an inner chamber and laid on a bed of state, which was not a little defiled with the presents of the Queen which had been bestowed on his garments, such as wine, cream, jelly, beverage, cakes, spices and other good matters. The entertainment went forward and most of the presenters went backward or fell down, wine did so occupy their upper chambers. Now did appear Hope, Faith and Charity. Hope did assay to speak but wine rendered her endeavours so feeble that she withdrew and hoped the King would excuse her brevity. Faith was then all alone for I am certain she was not joined with good works, but left the court in a staggering condition. Charity came to the King's feet and seemed to cover the multitude of sins her sisters had committed. In some sort she made obeisance and brought gifts, but said she would return home again as there was no gift which heaven had not already given his Majesty. She then returned to Hope and Faith who were both sick and spewing in the lower hall. Next came Victory in bright armour and presented a rich sword to the King who did not accept it but put it by with his hand; but Victory did not triumph long, for after much lamentable utterance she was led away like a silly captive and laid to sleep on the outer steps of the ante-chamber. Now did Peace make entry and strive to get foremost to the King; but I grieve to tell how great wrath she did discover unto her attendants and much contrary to her semblance most rudely made war with her olive branch and laid on the pates of those who did oppose her coming. I did never see such lack of good order, discretion and sobriety as I have now done.[14]

A more honourable setting for nobility was provided during the years 1608–12 by the Court of Prince Henry, which was manly, chivalric, pious in an invigorating way, a place of encouragement and reward for the arts, so it is not surprising that the finer spirits of the age were attracted there. After Henry's death in 1612 there was no alternative centre, yet the tone of James's Court did not improve. On the contrary, it sank to its nadir with the prolonged and unsavoury Overbury affair of 1615–16.

The area of literature that most commonly portrayed Court life was the drama, and here a court was almost synonymous with lust, lechery, treachery and pride. Even though the action of most Jacobean plays takes place abroad, and very often in the legendary depravity of Italy, one has the impression that the persistently critical view of Court life in drama drew much of its conviction from the experience of the English Court. It would be a great exaggeration to suggest that the murderous darkness of Webster's tragedies was an image of Whitehall society, yet the insistent horror of Court life in these plays presumably had its roots in a definite popular prejudice about the luxury and corruption bred by the palace. No one would dissent from Antonio's assertion in *The Duchess of Malfi* that

> a prince's court
> Is like a common fountain, whence should flow
> Pure silver drops in general,

yet these lines seem to carry an implied reproof that princes' courts are very far from being places of honour and virtue, and the statement stands out in the play as a desperate wish unlikely to be fulfilled. The vigorous line of anti-Court moralising and satire that runs through the plays of Middleton, Webster and Tourneur indicates a well-founded prejudice against the whole ethos of the Court, while Shakespeare's representations of Court life from *Hamlet* to *Cymbeline* do not provide much material for the panegyrist. Of course, much of this animus may be explained by convention and dramatic utility, yet there remains none the less an enduring impression of

moral repugnance, a feeling that the Court is an infectious centre of rotten- \
ness in society. This sensation comes across much more strongly in the plays \
written during James's reign than it did in those written under Elizabeth, \
and the difference is not simply a matter of literary intensity but the result \
of social observation and dismayed expectations. Indignation and outrage \
at the degeneracy of the Court reach their height in *The Revenger's Tragedy*,
written about 1606–7, in which the luxurious evil of the palace is spectacularly evoked and energetically condemned. The lustfulness of courtiers, the
vain pride of their costume, the prodigal excess of food and drink, the
treachery, hypocrisy, and intrigue that never cease, all the phosphorescent
decadence of Court society glows before the audience in this play, and
underneath the theatrical exaggeration one can hear a steady puritan note
of censure. This note has an authentic sound, for besides the predictable
denunciations of the vices of high life, there are a number of contemporary
grievances vented, particularly the recurring complaint about the sheer
wastefulness of the Court and its wanton superfluities that cause the nobility
and the fashionable gentry to convert their real wealth from land and
property into an ephemeral display of costume, feasting and general ostenta-
tion which served to maintain status at Court. The reckless expense that the \
Court promoted not merely nourished an immoral society but was also seen \
to be destroying the economic stability of the country. \

Support for this view came, rather surprisingly, from Ben Jonson himself,
for in many of the poems he addressed to friends and patrons, he warns them
against the damaging seductions of Court life, and compliments the wisdom
of those that stay in self-sufficient contentment on their own estates.
Through these poems, where Jonson sets himself up as a moralist of the
Jacobean age, runs a strong sense of the decadence of the times, redeemed
only by the integrity and conduct of those noblemen he admires.[15] Even
here, however, in these private poems, the poet never permits his censure to
approach the sacred precincts of majesty, for Jonson was never disloyal to
his sovereign.

During the early years of his reign, James managed his rich inheritance
unwisely, in the view of many Englishmen who had admired the more
austere and responsible conservatism of Queen Elizabeth, and this mis- \
management tended to distance his Court from public sympathy. James \
spent improvidently on Court entertainments, and encouraged his courtiers \
into excessive expenditure. His too generous and too mercenary granting of \
titles undermined the reputation of the nobility and tarnished his own \
reputation as the source of honour in the land. His curt rejection at the
Hampton Court Conference of the Puritan appeal for a greater say in church

affairs alienated a numerous body of subjects from his policies. The growing use of the monopoly system to raise money for the royal treasury angered the merchants of the City. James's ill-concealed dislike of his subjects *en masse* was highly impolitic, as was his reluctance to go about amongst his people. Against such discontents, the iconography that was elaborated for James had an important function, for it served to remind the Court, which was still the focus of power in the nation, of the enduring benefits that the King had brought with him: union, peace, an apparent prosperity, a succession assured through his children, and divine approval of his kingship. The claims of empire were a flattering premonition of what Stuart rule might achieve, and certainly during the lifetime of Prince Henry there was every hope that the future would be as bright as the artists feigned. Ultimately, however, these reassurances needed to be given to a far broader audience than the Court, but they were not, and the Stuart line was the less secure as a result of the limited proclamation of its virtues.

Notes to Chapter Two

Throughout this chapter, the line references to Jonson's masques refer to the texts in Jonson's *Works*, ed. Herford and Simpson, volume VII.

1   See John Summerson, *Inigo Jones*, Harmondsworth, 1966, p. 17.

2   The moments of magic in Shakespeare's late plays, where miracles are performed to the accompaniment of music, such as the reviving of Hermione, or of Imogen or Thaisa, would appear to take their form from comparable moments in the Jacobean masque, when the inducing of a heightened consciousness through music and poetry and light created a mood of wonder in which intuition and acceptance of a higher order of truth than the causal or rational could occur. A state of mind in which faith can override impossibility was the special creation of the rituals of the masque world, rituals which also have some affinity with the thaumaturgical scenarios evolved by the Jesuits in their churches in Counter-Reformation Italy. Given the currency of miracles in Court masques, Shakespeare may well have been moved to appropriate the mode for his own special purposes in his final phase.

3   For studies of these figures, see Allan Gilbert, *The Symbolical Figures in Jonson's Masques*, and D. J. Gordon, *The Renaissance Imagination*.

4   See D. J. Gordon, pp. 136–41.

5   See Stephen Orgel's observations on the letter in *The Illusion of Power*, Berkeley, 1975, p. 34. Carleton also complained about the indecorum of the Queen and her ladies appearing in blackface. Jonson must have sensed this problem too, for hereafter the masquers were given roles which could be seen as exalted transformations of their eminence at Court.

6   D. J. Gordon, pp. 141–54.

7   Jonson's account of the witches' dance runs as follows: 'With a strange and sodayne

Musique, they fell into a *magicall Daunce*, full of praeposterous change, and gesticulation, but most applying to theyr property: who, at theyr meetings, do all thinges contrary to the custome of Men, dauncing, back to back, hip to hip, theyr handes ioyn'd, and making theyr *circles* backward, to the left hand, with strange phantastique motions of theyr heads, and bodyes' (ll. 344–50).

8   The licence of misrule reaches its height in *The Irish Masque* of 1613 with the liberties taken by the stage Irishmen in addressing the King with excessive familiarity. Misrule appears as a character in *Christmas His Masque*, 1616.

9   One should also bear in mind that Prince Henry had specifically asked Jonson to document his sources for the masque, a request which must have been an irresistible appeal to his pedantry.

10   The true 'vision of delight' that evening was the Virginian princess Pocahontas, who had been received at Court, and was present at the performance of this masque.

11   See D. H. Willson, p. 308.

12   See S. Orgel, *The Illusion of Power*, pp. 50–3.

13   Of the recorded observations on the masque by contemporaries, only the letters of the Venetian ambassador show a consistently favourable appreciation of what was being presented year after year, and he would have had experience of comparable fêtes in Italy. Otherwise, the regular letter-writers, such as Chamberlain and Carleton, and the occasional witnesses, had very mixed reactions, sometimes being unable to submit to the illusions of the theatre, or complaining about verbosity or obscurity. It is apparent that the art of Jonson and Jones was too sophisticated for many of their audience. None the less, both James and Charles recognised that the masque was an invaluable act of state policy, and they were prepared to spend great sums of the order of £3000 to £4000 a time out of an enfeebled exchequer to have the arts annually combine in their honour.

14   See Sir John Harington, *Nugae Antiquae*, ed. Thomas Park, 1804, vol. I, pp. 348–54.

15   See, for example, 'To Sir Robert Wroth', 'To Elizabeth, Countesse of Rutland', 'To Katherine, Lady Aubigny', 'An Epistle to a Friend, to Perswade him to the Warres'.

[3]
The court of Henry, Prince of Wales

King James named his eldest son Henry Frederick, and by that first name asserted his descent from Henry VII, the first of the Tudor kings, thus establishing the authenticity of his claim to the throne of England. Queen Elizabeth consented to stand as his godmother, so the omens were auspicious. The traditional genealogy of the Tudors, making much use of Geoffrey of Monmouth's *History*, traced the line back to Cadwallader, the last king of British blood, then to King Arthur, and ultimately to the Trojan Brutus, the legendary founder of Britain. The Tudors represented themselves as fulfilling the ancient prophecy that kings of Arthur's line, of British race, would return and rule the land; the Stuarts, as side-shoots of the Tudors, were equally strong supporters of this Arthurian theory of descent, especially James VI of Scotland who saw himself as the probable heir to Elizabeth and the reunifier of all Britain. According to the contemporary fashion for anagrams, whereby it was believed that a man's name concealed his destiny, and that destiny could be discovered by ingenious rearrangement of the latters of his name, 'Charles Iames Stuart' was prophetic of 'Claimes Arthur's Seat'. So too Prince Henry's name was ingeniously anagrammatised from 'HENRICVS FRIDERICVS STEVARTVS' into 'ARTHVRI IN SEDE FVTVRVS CRESCIS'. A sense of special destiny hung around the youthful prince from the beginning. His birth was inevitably marked by prolonged celebration, and with an unaccustomed lavishness James made his baptism in August 1594 at Stirling Castle the occasion for elaborate pageantry to assert his new confidence and pride in the House of Stuart.

In the presence of the assembled nobility of Scotland and visiting ambassadors, the infant prince was taken from his 'bed of estate' (which was 'richly decored, and wrought with brodered worke, containing the story of Hercules and his Travels'), elaborately baptised, then presented to King James, 'who addubbed him Knight. He was touched with the spur by the Earl of Mar; thereafter the King's Majestie presented a ducall crowne on his head, and then was proclaimed, by Lyon King of Arms, "The Right

Excellent High, and Magnanime, Frederick Henry; Henry Frederick, by the grace of God, Knight and Barron of Renfrew, Lord of the Yles, Earle of Carricke, Duke of Rosay, Prince and Great Steward of Scotland."' The banquet which followed was interrupted by a Blackamoor who entered the hall pulling a chariot with chains of pure gold:

Upon this chariot was finely and artificially devised a sumptuous covered table, decked with all sorts of exquisite delicacies and dainties of patisserie, frutages and confections. About the table were placed six gallant dames, who represented a silent comedie: three of them clothed in argentine saten, and three in crimson saten; all these six garments were enriched with togue and tinsel of pure gold and silver, every one of them having a crowne or garland on their heads very richly decked with feathers, pearles and jewels, upon their loose hair *in antica forma.*

In the first front stood dame Ceres, with a sickle in her right hand, and a handfull of corne in the other; and upon the outmost part of her thigh was written this sentence, 'Fundent uberes omnia campi,' which is to say, the plenteous fields affoord all things.[1]

Fecundity stood next to her, then Faith, Concord, Liberalitie and Perseverance, and together they served the banqueting company, who no doubt assimilated their virtues with their gifts. The chariot should have been drawn in by a lion, to symbolise the royal nature of these virtues, but the beast was omitted at the last minute for fear that it might get out of hand and spoil the feast, and a Blackamoor indiscriminately substituted.

The next spectacle to interrupt the banquet was an artificial ship, some eighteen feet long and forty feet high to the masthead, upon an artificial sea, with Neptune and his consort Thetis on board, accompanied by singing sirens:

The bulke of this ship was curiously painted, and her galleries, whereupon stood the most part of the banket in christalline glasse, gilt with gold and azure; her masts were redde; her tackling and cordage was silke of the same colour, with golden pulleis; her ordinance was 36 pieces of brasse bravely mounted, and her anchors silver gilt. And all her sayles were double, of white taffeta; and her fore sayle a shippe compasse, regarding the North-Starre, with this sentence, 'Quasque per Undas,' which is to say, through whatsoever seas or waves the King's Majestie intendeth his course, and project of any rising action Neptune, as God of the Sea, shall be favourable to his proceedings.[2]

James himself had devised this pageant to celebrate his own boldness in courtship, for 'he had undertaken in such a desperate time to saile to Norway, and, like a new Jason, bring his Queene, our gracious Lady, to this Kingdome', but, 'being detained and stopped by the conspiracies of witches, and such devilish dragons', he wished to show how Neptune had aided him, and would henceforth be his constant ally. Neptune was in fact the effective cause of the happy union of James with Anne of Denmark, and therefore the natural patron of this baptismal banquet. The vessel then delivered sugar sweetmeats in the form of fishes to the tables, whilst Amphion astraddle a dolphin played his harp, the music changing then to viols and flutes, and swelling into a general consort. The feasting continued until dawn. Thereafter the entertainment of the visitors lasted for another month, with hunting, military sports and the like.

One can see from the above accounts that the royal court of Scotland was in no way provincial in the matter of entertainments, and such tableaux would have been equally appreciated in London or Paris. The personifications, or hieroglyphs as they were called, the classical trappings, the riddling devices with their Latin mottoes, could all appeal to the international throng of noblemen who had travelled to Scotland for the prince's baptism. James, after all, considered himself to be a learned monarch, and on the rare occasions when state policy in Scotland warranted it, and money was available, he could exhibit his learning and taste in spectacles of emblematic wit of a high order.

It was partly a desire to display his learning and wisdom, and partly a genuine concern for the education of his son that caused James to write his *Basilikon Doron: or His Majestie's Instructions to his dearest Sonne, Henry the Prince*, in 1599, when Henry was five years old. For the most part, this is a typical Renaissance manual for princes, reminding Henry of his duty towards God and his people, warning him of the snares of Court life and advising him on matters of public and private conduct. The book leans heavily on classical antecedents, such as Xenophon, Plato and Seneca, but the observations on Court behaviour have a strong flavour of personal experience. Several of James's special preoccupations stand out. The divine nature of kingship is immediately alluded to: 'God gives not Kings the stile of Gods in vaine', runs the first line of the introductory sonnet, which is shortly followed by the exhortation to 'learne to know and love that God, whom-to ye have a double obligation; first, for that he made you a man, and next, for that he made you a little GOD to sit on his Throne, and rule over other men'. James several times reminds his son that he may expect to rule over more than merely Scotland. He counsels him in piety and moderation, yet surprisingly for the pacific James, he also recommends strenuous military exercise and a martial bearing. Twice he compares Henry to Alexander.

James took great care of Henry's upbringing. He entrusted him to the Earl of Mar, to be brought up in his household, after the fashion of the time. He selected an effective tutor, and no doubt *Basilikon Doron* often formed the basis of instruction. By the time James received the summons to the throne of England in 1603, Henry had developed into a remarkably forward youth of a firm and already distinctive character whose temper showed signs of being both intellectual and martial. Upon his arrival in England, he had an independent household established for him by the King, at Oatlands Palace, and although only ten years old, he began to enter into the life of his new country. Now he began 'to ply his Booke hard for two or three years, continuing all his Princely Sports, Hawking, Hunting, running at the Ring, leaping, riding of great Horses, Dauncing, Fencing, tossing of the Pike, etc. In all which, he did so farre excell as was fitting for so great a Prince'.[3] He entered Magdalen College, Oxford, in 1605, though we have no indication how frequent his attendance was. Anthony Wood records the matriculation of 'the peoples darling and the delight of Mankind' in August of this year. 'The Prince began now to be considered by men of learning, as a proper patron of their works, not only for his high rank, but likewise his relish for them.'[4]

Most of the early patronage was of a literary and dramatic nature; about Christmas 1603 he had taken over the company of players known as The Admiral's Men, who had hitherto been under the patronage of Lord Howard of Effingham and who now became known as The Prince's Servants. They were based at the Fortune Theatre, and their principal playwrights were Dekker, Chettle, Drayton and Chapman.[5] Both Chapman and Drayton were to enjoy the special patronage of the Prince.

George Chapman seems to have been granted a place in the Prince's household shortly after its establishment in 1603, being retained as a 'sewer-in-ordinary', a minor post involving the supervision of dining arrangements which must have given him time enough for his literary work. He may initially have attracted Henry's attention by his play *Bussy d'Ambois*, for Henry was particularly interested in French affairs, and he began to enter into correspondence with Henri IV as early as 1606. A mutual regard developed between the two, with the French King showing a genuine concern for the friendship of Prince Henry. Although we cannot say for certain if *Bussy d'Ambois* was written before or after Chapman entered Henry's service, it would seem reasonable to suppose that Chapman continued to exploit French subjects for his tragedies during the period 1603–12 because of his patron's known sympathies in that direction.[6] Certainly the presentation of Henri IV as ideal monarch in *The Conspiracy of Byron* (1610) was calculated to complement the young Prince's admiration for the heroic qualities of the French King. The recentness of the events in these French dramas, with their combination of political analysis and philosophical reflection set in an atmosphere of noble strife, would have given them exceptional interest; moreover the tone of these plays was probably conditioned by the circumstances of their presentation. Chapman was naturally inclined to the didactic, but the fact that his works would be watched and read by the intelligent and impressionable heir to the throne who was conscientiously preparing himself for kingship must have incited him to charge his lines with politic wisdom. 'Material instruction, elegant and sententious excitation to virtue, and deflection from her contrary' flowed from his pen in these French tragedies. In *The Conspiracy of Byron*, for example, 'we find warnings placed on every page against false ambition, favourites, the pitfalls of flattery, the dangers of policy, we find instruction in the divine right of kings and the human rights of subjects; we find exhortation to reason and learning, to loyalty and friendship, to truth and justice'.[7]

In a sense, Chapman's tragedies could be said to form a brief and compendious *Basilikon Doron* in dramatic form. The preoccupation with valorous heroic figures that is such a feature of Chapman's work, the various attempts at presenting the 'complete man' of the Renaissance in such characters as Bussy and Clermont, great and integrated beings who are 'young, learned, valiant, virtuous and full mann'd', acquire a comprehensible context if we see Chapman working in the court of a young prince who himself embodied these qualities and who actively strove to create a heroic atmosphere at that court. Chapman both responded to and contributed to that atmosphere by his plays.

His most enduring contribution, however, was his translation of *The Iliad* which he undertook under the patronage of Henry, dedicating *The Twelve Bookes of the Iliads* to him in 1609, the complete *Iliads* in 1611, and the *Whole Workes of Homer* in 1616. Not surprisingly, the prefatory material attributes to the sponsor of the translation the full range of Homeric virtues and grandeur. Henry in return seems to have been a generous patron: in a petition to the Privy Council after Henry's death, the poet claimed that the Prince commanded him to proceed with his translation of Homer, and promised on its conclusion three hundred pounds, 'And upon his death bed a good pension, during my life, commaunding me to go on with the Odysses'.[8] Henry died before making satisfaction to Chapman for a work which brought illustrious associations to himself and his court, associations which did not seem disproportionate or misplaced in the eyes of contemporaries. What the translation of the Bible was to King James's court, the translation of Homer was to Prince Henry's: each was a characteristic and fitting product of the royal encouragement of learning.

In the sonnets prefixed to *The Iliads* Chapman tried to secure and enlarge his hopes of patronage by flattering dedications to prominent nobles who were in attendance on the Prince: the Earls of Southampton, Northampton, Salisbury, Pembroke, Arundel, and the Duke of Lennox, to name the most prominent. The grouping of these figures together points up a significant fact about Henry's court: the quality and distinction of the men it attracted. Although much smaller than the King's, its reputation was in many ways much higher. It was noted for its air of chivalry, for its piety, sobriety and good order. Martial exercise was frequent, yet learning was also patronised and the liberal arts flourished; no wonder that the finer spirits of Jacobean England were attracted there, and their presence gave an international lustre to the court. Much of the credit for this achievement should go to King James, for it was he who decided to give his son this early independence and who established this separate court where Henry could develop the accomplishments of a Renaissance prince. James's action was an extension of that enlightened concern for the well-being of his heir that he had already displayed in *Basilikon Doron*, and though the success of Henry's court soon contrasted advantageously with his own, James did not attempt to interfere with its operation. Undoubtedly, the freedom and authority that Prince Henry enjoyed from such a young age, the liberal atmosphere of his surroundings together with the intelligent choice of friends, counsellors and servants, must have been to a large extent responsible for the remarkable forwardness of his character and taste. When all reservation has been made for the habitual overstatement and flattery of contemporary eulogists, there can be no doubt that Henry's temperament and his powers of judgement and discrimination were astonishingly mature, and thoroughly justified the universal admiration they received. In November 1607 we find Sir Thomas Chaloner, the Prince's Chamberlain, writing to the Chancellor of the Exchequer, Sir Julius Caesar, 'that his Highness's household, which was intended by the King for a *Courtly College*, or a *Collegiate Court*, was become so great a court, that it was ready to be overwhelmed with the charge and burden of itself'.[9] In the same year John Cleland, who was tutor to Prince Henry's close friend, Sir John Harington, celebrated this courtly college in his book *The Institution of a young Nobleman*:

Without offence to either of the famous *Vniversities* here, or our *Colledges* in Scotland, for all sort of good learning, I recommend in particular the *Academie* of our Noble Prince, where young Nobles may learne the first elements to be a *Privie Counseller*, a *Generall* of an Armie, to rule in peace, & to commande in warre. Here may they obtaine his *Highnes* favor. . . . Here shall a young Noble man learne to fashion himselfe, and to have a good *entregent* (as the French men call it.) Here is the true *Panthaeon* of Great Britaine, where Vertue herselfe dwelleth by patterne, by practise, by encouragement, admonitions, and precepts of the most rare persons in Vertue and Learning that can be found: so that the very accidents of young Noble mens studies cannot be but substantial, as sympathising with the fountaine from whence they flow. Here is a glorious and laudable emulation among Peeres without fraud or envie; al striving to doe best; and to merit most his *Highnesse* favor, *stimulos dedit aemula virtus.* For exercise of the body there is none lacking, fitting a young Noble man, so that he may learne more in this one place, in one month, then if hee should run over al France and Italie, in a year; yea, his *Highnesse* Dinners and Suppers are an other Salomons table, where the wisest men of any country may come to learne of him and his attendants.[10]

Young noblemen from all over the kingdom and gentlemen of good family did indeed resort to his palace at Oatlands or at Nonsuch to accompany or serve the Prince, to learn the art of the courtier, and particularly to enjoy the martial sports of tilting, jousting and sword-play which were notably lacking at Whitehall.

When Henry was created Prince of Wales in 1610, his affairs moved on to a plane of even greater intensity. His court, which now occupied the Palace of St James, was greatly augmented, its revenues increased. The ceremonies that marked the announcement of the new honour were suggestive of the values that Henry had come to represent, and they repay study in some detail. On 31 December 1609, in the Presence Chamber at Whitehall, Henry, under the name of Moeliades, Lord of the Isles, delivered a challenge to all knights of the kingdom, summoning them to a feat of arms to celebrate the chivalric eminence of Great Britain that would take place on the last day of the Christmas festivities. Until then, Henry feasted his comrades-in-arms and challengers like a prince from *The Faerie Queene.* Upon the appointed day, the festivities began with a masque, *Prince Henry's Barriers,* by Ben Jonson in which the legendary lineage of the House of Stuart was evoked to amplify the significance of Henry's appearance in arms and his entrance into a man's estate. The setting is Arthurian; the Lady of the Lake proclaims the happiness of Britain under James who is a new and greater Arthur sprung from the ancient stock:

> Now when the Iland hath regain'd her fame
> Intire, and perfect, in the ancient name,
> And that a *monarch* aequall good and great,
> Wise, temperate, just, and stout, claimes ARTHURS seat,
> Did I say aequall? O too prodigall wrong
> Of my o're-thirsty, and unaequall tongue!
> How brighter farre, then when our ARTHUR liv'd
> Are all the glories of this place reviv'd![11]

We are told that in this general restoration of ancient virtue only Chivalry lies in decline. It must have needed little intuition to recognise that this was

Henry's cue, but before he is introduced King Arthur appears, discovered as a star above who works his influence on British history. He reminds the spectators that Merlin's ancient prophecies have now been fulfilled, that a British king of Arthur's line sits on the throne, and the union of the Isle has been achieved. Now a greater prince shall be revealed whose accomplishments shall be unparalleled:

> Proceed in thy great worke; bring forth thy knight
> Preserved for his times, that by the might
> And magicke of his arme, he may restore
> These ruin'd seates of vertue, and build more.
> Let him be famous, as was TRISTRAM, TOR,
> LAUNC'LOT, and all our List of knight-hood: or
> Who were before, or have beene since. His name
> Strike upon heaven, and there sticke his fame.
> Beyond the paths, and searches of the sunne
> Let him tempt fate; and when a world is wunne,
> Submit it duly to this state, and throne,
> Till Time, and utmost stay make that his owne.

But first this paragon must be led in by the learned Merlin, Merlin the magus, for Henry is here being presented as a Renaissance prince in whom learning and arms are harmoniously combined, 'For armes and arts sustaine each others right'. The climax arrives, and the Prince appears:

> The heavens, the fates, and thy peculiar starres,
> MELIADUS, shew thee; and conclude all jarres.

Meliades, or Moeliades as Henry spelt it, was a figure from Arthurian romance, the lover of the Lady of the Lake; Lord of the Isles was of course part of his style as heir to the Scottish throne. But Henry chose the name Moeliades for his appearance in the myth-world of masque and pageant for its inner meaning, because it was an anagram of *Miles a deo*, or Soldier for God,[12] a name which emphasised his Christian zeal to use his arms in the service of God, and indicated a kinship with the Red Cross Knight of *The Faerie Queene*. In this masque, the frequent mention of Moeliades in connection with St George, the patron of the Order of the Garter, underlined the Protestant aspect of Henry's persona. In choosing this name, Henry was deliberately evoking associations of chivalric romance that had no reference to the rather degenerate court of King James; instead, as some recent books have pointed out,[13] these associations harked back to the knightly glamour that surrounded Queen Elizabeth and indicated Henry's intention of connecting himself with that tradition of chivalric patriotic idealism that bonded the aristocracy to the Queen in the late reign. But implicit in the 'Miles a deo' concept is a hint of the political role that Henry seems to have cherished for himself: the resolver of the religious dissensions in Europe by the force of virtuous arms. This was the grand design that many people, including Prince Henry, believed that Henri IV was embarking upon at the time of his assassination. By different means, this was also a policy of James I, who saw himself as the peacemaker of Europe, only he attempted to 'conclude all jarres' in religion through his marriage strategy, linking his children to Protestant and Catholic partners, overcoming religious discord by dynastic alliances. Since the present masque serves to herald Henry's entrance into this world as a martial hero, it is proper to expect that it should contain some hints as to how Henry foresaw his future career as a soldier prince; the ideas we have suggested here would seem to be the clues to his intentions. Jonson was presumably following a carefully prepared scenario which may have been devised by Henry himself. Nowhere else in Jonson's work does he make use of Arthurian material, indeed he wrote against it on several occasions, so one suspects that on this occasion he was working closely to royal orders.

There is much recitation of the military prowess of England's rulers in the past, with reminders that the end of war is a just and lasting peace. The presence of Prince Henry causes the spirit of Chivalry to revive, and she declares the Barriers open. Barriers was a sport where contestants on foot on opposite sides of a waist-high barrier attempted to overthrow each other by pike and sword. It was extremely unusual for a masque to devolve into military sports, rather than dancing, but this was the note that Henry wanted to set for this new phase of his life. From Stow's *Annales* we learn 'the Prince performed this challenge with wonderous skill, and courage, to the great joy and admiration of all the beholders. . . . These feates of armes with their triumphall shewes began before ten o'clock at night, and continued there untill the next morning, being Sunday: and that day the Prince feasted all the combattants at St. James.'[14]

The festival of the Barriers seems to have been very much of Prince Henry's own contriving. The ceremonies that accompanied his actual investiture as Prince of Wales in June 1610 were under the control of the King and Queen, and accordingly were more conventional. Henry made his triumphal entry into London from Richmond via the river, so the theme for the pageantry was therefore acquatic. This was an appropriate tribute to the prince of an island nation; it may also have been a recognition of his close interest in nautical matters, in navigation, the navy and the command of the sea.[15] When he reached Chelsea, he was greeted by a water pageant presented by the Lord Mayor, Aldermen and Companies of London featuring Neptune and his court. Neptune, we are told, had a special fondness for 'Britayne, which himself termed to be "insula beata," and which he has bestowed upon his best affected son, Albion'.[16] The Lord Mayor, 'attended with sea-monsters, conducted the Prince on his joyfull passage to the Citie'. On the occasion of the investiture itself, there were so many state ceremonies to be observed that there was little time for masquing. The one masque that was performed was the Queen's masque, *Tethys Festivall*, Anne's tribute to her son. The poet she chose for this work was Samuel Daniel, an odd choice—one wonders why Ben Jonson was not asked. Daniel, who was in Anne's service as a Groom of the Privy Chamber, had a modest reputation as a poet, but had had only one previous experience of writing for a masque. The success of *Tethys Festivall* was almost entirely visual, thanks to Inigo Jones's spectacular designs; poetically and thematically it was rather insipid—watery, one might almost say. Tethys, Neptune's consort (or Thetis, as she had appeared in Henry's baptismal pageant), here danced by Queen Anne, 'attended with thirteen Nymphs of severall Rivers', honoured the Prince and presented him with a rich sword and scarf. The device of the river nymphs was probably borrowed from *Poly-Olbion* which Drayton was currently writing for Prince Henry. The matter of the sword offered by Tethys is the most evocative action in the masque, and the most symbolically potent:

> And therewithall she wills him, greete the Lord
> And Prince of th'Iles (the hope and the delight
> Of all the Northern nations) with this sword
> That she unto Astraea sacred found,
> And not to be unsheath'd but on iust ground.[17]

Astraea, the goddess of Justice, was fabled to have left the earth at the end of the golden age, not to return until a new golden age begins. In her book *Astraea*, Frances Yates has reconstructed the process by which the cult grew up in the late sixteenth century of 'Elizabeth–Astraea as the empress of the world, guardian of religion, patroness of peace, restorer of virtue'. The image of the just virgin presiding over a world of purified religion and national prosperity was one of the central concepts of Elizabethan court iconography, and had been extensively exploited by artists, poets and pageant makers in the last two decades of her reign. Now, in 1610, the invocation of the sacred name and the passing of Astraea's sword to the new Prince of Wales indicate that Prince Henry was consciously trying to revive the semi-magical aura of golden majesty that had surrounded Elizabeth and transfer it to himself.[18] In this respect, *Tethys Festivall* relates back to *Prince Henry's Barriers* where Henry had cast himself as the continuer of the Elizabethan chivalric tradition. Taken together, the two masques suggest that Prince Henry saw himself as the true successor to Elizabeth's potent imaginative cult of the monarchy that had done so much to consolidate the power of the crown.

The Elizabethan associations that Henry recreated around himself were further emphasised in the next masque in which he danced: *Oberon, the Faery Prince*, performed on 1 January 1611. The very title proclaimed the inheritor of the traditions of the Faery Queen. The Oberon of the title alludes not to Shakespeare's theatrical elf but to the Oberon who is introduced in the genealogy of the princes of Faerieland in *The Faerie Queene*, Book II, Canto X. This figure was another Henry, for Spenser's 'mightie Oberon' shadowed Henry VIII in allegorical disguise. The fiction of the fairy chronicle as invented by Spenser to show the lineage of Gloriana–Elizabeth referred specifically to the House of Tudor and emphasised the Welshness of the Tudor line. Hence Oberon was an appropriate persona for Henry as Prince of Wales.[19] But the atmosphere of Henry's world of Faerie, as projected by Jonson and Inigo Jones, was no longer that of Spenserian romance: it had become a composite of medieval and classical forms. Jonson opens the masque with satyrs taken from Virgil, and Silenus, in a moonlit scene of rocks and woods, awaiting the arrival of Oberon. Oberon's castle in the rocks is gothic, yet with classical Italianate decoration, and it opens to reveal an entirely Italianate palace within. When Oberon is revealed, he is dressed as a Roman emperor, and moves in a chariot, yet he comes from Faeryland to pay homage to 'Arthur's Chair', occupied of course by King James. The verse then swells into praise of James as ideal monarch, perfect, just and true, and honours once again the Stuart myth that James is the long prophesied second Arthur who has restored the British line and unified the land. In Spenser the Faery genealogy of Queen Elizabeth is given as a mythic parallel to the 'historical' descent of Elizabeth from Brutus and Arthur, so Jonson is following Spenser here. The masque was commissioned by Prince Henry and closely overseen by him, so the mingling of classical and medieval elements that it contains may be seen as a deliberate and approved policy, a visual statement of suggestive images that express the traditions he wished to exploit in his public life. Since the masque was presented entirely to a Court audience, and since an important function of the masque was to present royal figures under ideal forms revealing the profoundest attributes that inspired and sustained them, we may regard *Oberon* as being a significant tactical display of Prince Henry's ideology.

For an elaboration of this ideology, we have to turn to Prince Henry's court as it was re-established on an enlarged scale after his creation as Prince of Wales, in order to see how, through his royal actions and patronage, he built up the image of splendid Renaissance prince on the Italian model, yet also cultivated the tradition of chivalric knighthood. The latter emphasised his continuity with the patriotic Elizabethan ethos that strengthened the affection and allegiance of the aristocracy by appealing to known and successful patterns of romantic monarchism, the paradigm of which was King Arthur faithfully served and revered by his entourage of knights, a pattern that had been recreated with immense effect around Elizabeth, and which the handsome young Henry, the Faery Prince, the son of Arthur/ James, was attempting to transfer to himself. The image of the Renaissance prince, on the other hand, set an unprecedented model of antique virtue and heroism before the English Court. The running together of these two strains of imagery is most easily demonstrated by contrasting the two depictions of Prince Henry by Isaac Oliver, painted between 1610 and 1612. One, a large oil, shows the Prince as a chivalric figure in armour upon horseback against a romantic background; the other, the miniature in the Fitzwilliam Museum, presents him entirely in the antique manner, in profile against a shell niche, dressed as a Roman emperor. One might cite also the woodcut dedicated to Prince Henry in Peacham's *Minerva Britanna* (1612), showing a fully-armed knight pricking across a plain like a perfect illustration to the opening of *The Faerie Queene*.

The cultivation of a taste for classical forms, which effectively composed the new modernism in Northern Europe at this time, is most evident in the presence amongst the Prince's servants from late 1609 onwards of Inigo Jones, who was already emerging as the foremost exponent of the Italianate movement in England. His principal employment was in designing the costumes, scenery and machinery for Henry's masques. In his first commission, the *Barriers* of 1610, the scene of ruin with which the masque opened was the most comprehensive classical panorama that English eyes had gazed on. A composite spectacle of Roman architecture in decay, it combined the grand sweep of some Coliseum-like building in ruins with a pyramid like that of Caius Cestius, an obelisk, a half-fallen triumphal arch, pillared arcading of temples, and a type of Trajan's Column, all unified in Jones's great innovation, single point perspective. This was described as the decayed house of Chivalry. To the modern reader Chivalry evokes a medieval setting; to Elizabethan historians, however, chivalry first flourished in these islands among the Britons, and the British line of kings from Brutus to Arthur was contemporary with the age of Rome. Inigo Jones was the first to realise the architectural consequences of this history, and Ben Jonson draws attention to their belief that the architecture of the age of Chivalry must have been Roman in style:

> Those *Obelisks* and *Columnes* . . .
> That strooke the starres, and rais'd the *British* crowne
> To be a constellation. . . .
>
> More truth of *architecture* there was blaz'd
> Then liv'd in all the ignorant *Gothes* have raz'd.
> There *Porticos* were built, and seats for knights
> That watchd for all *adventures*, dayes and nights
> The *Nieces* [niches] filld with statues, to invite
> Young valures [valours or worthies] forth, by their old formes to fight.
> With arkes triumphall for their actions done,
> Out-striding the Colossus of the sunne.
> And *Trophaee's*, reard, of spoyled enemies,
> Whose toppes pierc'd through the cloudes, and hit the skies.[20]

As the reviver of Chivalry, Henry/Meliades ought properly to be the reviver of antique architecture as well, but the building in which he is discovered, although called a Portico, a self-consciously Italian title, is a strange hybrid structure, part classical part gothic, a temple with a cupola, yet with gables, and a quite unclassical spikiness overall. It is an undeniably 'romantic' construction, one that an Elizabethan audience would have found congenial, and it no doubt facilitated the transition of Prince Henry and his colleagues from the scene of the masque to the combat at the Barriers which immediately followed, and which was an exercise in a romance tradition, not an antique feat of arms.

The Investiture Masque, *Tethys Festivall*, was evidently dominated by a grand spectacle of architectural display: Daniel admits this to have been the truly memorable part of the masque, in his preface to the reader:

But in these things wherein the only life consists in shew; the arte and invention of the Architect gives the greatest grace, and is of most importance: ours, the least part and of the least note in the time of the performance thereof; and therefore have I inserted the description of the artificiall part, which only speakes M. Inago Jones.

There follows an elaborate description of the scenery which parades an architectural vocabulary that must have been as exotically new in 1610 as Jones's theatrical devices:

First at the opening of the heavens appeared 3 circles of lights and glasses, one with in another, and came downe in a straight motion five foote, and then began to moove circularly: which lights and motion so occupied the eyes of the spectators, that the manner of altering the Scene was scarcely discerned: for in a moment the whole face of it was changed, the Port vanished, and *Tethys* with her Nymphes appeared in their severall Caverns gloriously adorned. This Scene was comparted into 5 Neeces, whereof that in the middest had some slender pillowes of whole round, and were made of moderne architecture in regard of roome: these were of burnisht gold, and bare up the returnes of an Architrave, Freeze, and Cornish of the same work: on which, upon eyther side was a Plinth, directly over the pillers, & on them were placed for finishings, two Dolphins of silver, with their tailes wreathed together, which supported ovall vases of gold.

Betweene the two pillers on eyther side were great ornaments of relievo: the Basement were two huge Whales of silver.[21]

There is very much more detail in the same vein; one is left in no doubt that Inigo Jones was using these court spectacles as occasions to work out in wood and plaster his command of neo-classical forms, and incidentally to accustom the aristocracy of England to the conventions of the new architecture.[22]

Jones had had little experience of building in stone before he entered Prince Henry's service, although it seems very probable that he had designed the south front of Hatfield House for Sir Robert Cecil by early 1610.[23] By May 1610, Prince Henry had appointed him Surveyor of the Works, but unfortunately there is no known building that can be attributed to him during the two years of his Surveyorship. Possibly he was employed on the extensions to St James's Palace that Henry undertook, but no designs survive. As Surveyor, he must have been considered as a practising architect; we know that Henry was interested in the modern Italian styles that Jones virtually alone in England had mastered; what may well have happened is that Prince Henry decided to go for the real thing, for by June 1611 we hear that an Italian architect, Constantino de Servi, has been summoned from Florence to provide designs for 'fountains, summer-houses, galleries and other things on a site in which his Highness is most interested'.[24] Again, no details survive of work done, but Henry's evident interest in furthering the cause of the modern architecture of Italy in England is witnessed by Robert Peake's dedication to him in 1611 of his translation of Serlio's *Booke of Architecture*, the first Renaissance treatise on architectural theory to be put into English.[25]

Where did Henry develop this taste for Italian architecture? There was not much informed knowledge of it at the English court. Presumably his meetings with ambassadors helped stimulate his taste, particularly those from the Republic of Venice, which had close relations with England, and in whose state so much of the finest modern building was to be found. Most Italian architectural theory, moreover, was based on the principles laid out by the Roman architect Vitruvius; the modern works could therefore be seen as essentially classical architecture of the Augustan period. We know that Prince Henry liked to present himself as a Roman emperor—the costume in *Oberon*, for example, or the miniature by Oliver—so a predilection towards a classical architecture would be in keeping with this aspect of his royal persona. Again, in European terms, it was not a surprising taste for a prince of the age, although unusual in England.

Another revived Roman art that attracted Henry was the art of moving waters: fountains and hydraulics. He drew to his Court in 1610 the remarkable French engineer and garden designer Salomon de Caus, who was recommended by the French Ambassador, and who was to make the gardens at Richmond one of the marvels of England, a northern Tivoli. In March 1610 he was given a yearly pension of £100, which placed him amongst the most highly paid of the Prince's servants, only Constantine de Servi and Abraham Van Niselt, a Dutch military engineer, receiving more with £200 apiece.[26] De Caus also taught the Prince mathematics. As Frances Yates has pointed out, de Caus was a master of those mechanical marvels that delighted the Renaissance imagination: fountains that could play musical tunes, water organs, and speaking statues, interest in which had been aroused by the recovery of old texts describing such marvels performed by Hero of Alexandria and his school.[27] He was a close friend of Inigo Jones, being drawn to him by a common interest in the revival of Vitruvius, and between them they commanded most of the skills that Vitruvius stated the true architect should possess: the arts and sciences based on number and proportion, music, perspective, painting and mechanics. Vitruvius had asserted that architecture was the supreme art, to which these other arts and sciences should contribute. Jones directed his attention to architecture and to the subsidiary but related matters of theatrical design, perspective and mechanics; de Caus specialised in garden design, which in the Renaissance was closely related to architecture, dependent also on proportion, perspective, geometry, and on employing the mechanical arts for the management of the waters. Where the casual eye saw delightful, balanced panoramas in a Renaissance garden, the learned, intellectual eye saw unified diversity, the harmony of right proportion, green mathematics. 'Eupompus gave splendour to art by numbers', wrote Ben Jonson; between them, Inigo Jones and Salomon de Caus were capable of giving such splendour to the domains of Prince Henry's court. Unfortunately, Henry died before such a powerful combination as Jones and de Caus could achieve much, but we may gain some idea of de Caus's ambitions by looking at the extraordinary gardens he created in the service of the Elector Palatine at Heidelberg, where he went after Prince Henry's death, and which were deservedly regarded as one of the wonders of the modern world. In dedicating his book *Les Raisons des Forces Mouvantes* to Princess Elizabeth in 1615, de Caus reminds her of her brother's profound interest in the intellectual aspects of the garden arts that he had so successfully cultivated at Heidelberg. De Caus had already dedicated a book on optics to Prince Henry in 1612, *Le Perspective, avec la Raison des Ombres et Miroirs*, in which he had acknowledged the favourable encouragement of his projects, and had asserted his commitment to Vitruvian principles in architecture and design.

One of the marks of a Renaissance Prince was connoisseurship in painting and other works of art. Elizabeth and James had no particular interests in this area, whereas Prince Henry developed this faculty from an early age. Already we hear of plans for Inigo Jones to build a gallery for his collection in 1611. In the same year the Venetian ambassador reported that the Prince 'is paying special attention to the adorning of a most beautiful gallery of very fine pictures, ancient and modern, the larger part brought out of Venice. He is also collecting books for a library he has built.'[28] The principal painter associated with the Prince's household was Robert Peake, whom we have already met as the translator of Serlio. He had formed his style in the 1580s, and was a talented and fashionable painter who executed at least a dozen surviving portraits of Prince Henry that trace his changing features from childhood to maturity. Peake's style changed too, growing less stiff and angular, yet it always remained a recognisably Elizabethan manner, with the standard poses and props. Not surprisingly, Henry's growing sensitivity to painting prompted him to seek out a foreign painter with a more modern manner, and a more subtle palette; his choice fell on the Dutch painter Michiel van Miereveld, from Delft.[29] In mid-1611 he began negotiations with this painter, who expressed eagerness to come, but who temporised until the opportunity faded away. Eventually it was Miereveld's pupil Daniel Mytens who arrived in England under the patronage of Henry's friend Lord Arundel in 1618; he, together with Queen Anne's painter Paul van Somer, effected the transformation of style and modernisation of taste in portraiture that Prince Henry had desired to bring about.

Isaac Oliver, the miniaturist, was also attached to the Household. Miniatures were always in demand in the Court world, as mementoes, or tokens of allegiance or service; they also gratified the age's delight in intricate craftsmanship and curious detail. Two superb portraits by Oliver demand attention: the one, already mentioned (in the Fitzwilliam Museum), showing Henry as a Roman emperor in the bold concise manner of an antique cameo; the other (in the Royal Collection) a larger work in a softer style,

Isaac Oliver, portrait miniature of Prince Henry

where the Prince appears almost as the reincarnation of Sir Philip Sidney, noble, intelligent, alert, in magnificently chased armour, wearing the sash and medal of St George, while in the background are the tents and preparation of war. To Oliver also has been attributed the large oil painting of Prince Henry on horseback against a mysterious soft Venetian landscape which remains one of the most powerful images of the Prince's courtly figure.

Meanwhile, besides being painted, the Prince began to seek out paintings for his own collection. When Sir Dudley Carleton went as Ambassador to Venice in December 1610, he had been charged to acquire fine paintings for the Prince as the occasion arose. In the Netherlands Sir Edward Conway, the Governor of Brill, was his agent. Foreign states recognised his enthusiasm: at the time of his investiture the Dutch States presented him with a series of sea pictures; the Venetian state also sent paintings as gifts. In 1612 the Grand Duke of Tuscany sent him an outstanding group of twelve Renaissance bronzes from the workshop of Gianbologna. We know too that the Prince had a Cabinet of Medals that drew international admiration.[30]

The overall impression is of an emerging connoisseur and virtuoso, the harbinger of a new era of taste, indeed the creator of a new aesthetic climate in England. He died before his patronage could become decisive in its effects on the arts, but his taste and influence survived in the person of his close friend and fellow collector the Earl of Arundel, and above all in his brother Prince Charles, to whom his collections passed.

Other aspects of Prince Henry's court show the quality of his intellectual ethos, and prove the truth of his assertion that he would be surrounded by 'none but extraordinary men.' For languages, Henry's teacher was John Florio, the translator of Montaigne and the compiler of various well-known Italian word books, as well as a link back to the circle around Sir Philip Sidney. His music was provided by men such as Antonio Ferrabosco, John Bull and Thomas Campion. He was evidently very responsive to music, and pleased with his consort, for letters about the Prince frequently mention his fondness for hearing it play. As his tutor Ferrabosco wrote in dedicating his *Ayres* to him: 'to a Composition so full of Harmony as yours, what could be a fitter Offring?'

Henry concerned himself too with the foundation of another necessary attribute of a Renaissance prince, a great library. In 1609 he had purchased the library of one of his tutors, John Lord Lumley, a learned nobleman who was spellbound by the antiquity and distinction of his own family, and who had been the only notable collector of paintings during Elizabeth's reign. His library was considered to be second only to Sir Robert Cotton's in importance. He had inherited much of it from his father-in-law, Henry FitzAlan, Earl of Arundel, who in turn had acquired many of the books and manuscripts from Cranmer's library. Arundel had also gathered up many treasures from the monasteries after the Dissolution, when 'manuscripts flew about like butterflies'. Lumley had consolidated this library by careful collection, and Henry continued to expand it. He established it at St James's Palace under the care of Edward Wright the mathematician, and made it available to the scholars who frequented his Court. After his death it passed, like the rest of his collections, to his brother Charles, and eventually became an important part of the Royal Library, and ultimately part of the British Museum Collection.

Henry made a show of encouraging scholarship, and was consequently deluged by writers seeking his patronage. Ben Jonson remarks in the letter to Henry prefixed to *The Masque of Queenes*, 1609, that 'Your favour to letters, and these gentler studies, that go under the title of Humanitye, is not the least honor of your wreath', and ostentatiously states that the Prince has requested him to elaborate the learning hidden in the masque by providing annotations, explanations and amplifications. Nothing could have been more flattering to Jonson, who was notoriously proud of his learning, so both this masque and *Oberon* were published with formidable apparatus and marginalia that fully compensated for the light transience of the poetry in performance.

Similar learned annotations, following Jonson's precedent, perhaps, can be found in Michael Drayton's *Poly-Olbion*, dedicated to Prince Henry in 1612. The author's friend John Selden provided them, to prove that the fictions of the poetry were raised on deep foundations, and to ballast the lightness of the verse. Drayton was associated with the Prince's Players, and by this channel had gained the Prince's ear and patronage, receiving a small pension of £10 per annum. The poem is what Drayton called a 'Chorographicall Description and historie', in many ways a poetic equivalent of Camden's *Britannia*, showing the natural beauties of the counties, their curiosities and customs, the whole held together by the device of river nymphs and river songs. The history that Drayton was committed to was that of Geoffrey of Monmouth, the British history of Brut, and the familiar descent of the Tudors from the ancient British line. As such, it celebrates the current royal house, and is properly dedicated to the Prince, described as Britain's 'best hope and the world's delight'. An illustration of Prince Henry is prefixed to the book. It shows him in half-armour executing a push of pike, as in a combat at the barriers. The martial pose was suggestive in 1612, but it was certainly not related to the pastoral content of Poly-Olbion. It ties in more with the Oliver miniature of approximately the same date showing the Prince in the camp of war. Both images express a growing expectancy about Henry's first move in the international arena: was he going to lead a Protestant army against the Hapsburg powers? Although James's policy was one of conciliation, many restless noblemen trained in arms yet frustrated in achievement would have welcomed a campaign, which would probably have enjoyed popular support. Henry had developed a reputation as a vigorous Protestant leader, firmly anti-Catholic (he would

permit no Catholics in his household), and the implications of this stance
pointed to military actions in the not too distant future.

This feeling is further borne out in another book dedicated to the Prince
in 1612: Henry Peacham's *Minerva Britanna*, where Henry's emblem is a
fully-armed knight in warlike pose, with the injunction beneath:

> Thus, thus, young HENRY, like Macedo's sonne,
> Oughtst thou in armes before thy people shine.

and goes on to assure him

> That whether TURKE, SPAINE, FRAUNCE, or ITALIE,
> The RED-SHANKE, [Scottish Highlander] or the IRISH rebell bold,
> Shall rouze thee up, thy Trophees may be more
> Than all the HENRIES ever liv'd before.

The books dedicated to a man of state do after all tell us something about
his public image. They do indicate the expectations authors have of their
patrons, they suggest the main intellectual lines of a man's mind. They
appeal to known tastes, or attempt to stimulate probable interests. There is
felt to be some harmony between a subject of a book and its recipient. Therefore the insistence on certain themes and images may be taken as a pointer
to contemporary hopes and expectations.

Other books dedicated to Henry in 1612 indicate how energetic Protestants were looking to him to take the initiative against the strengthening
power of European Catholicism. Samson Lennard, a soldier who had fought
with Sidney at Zutphen, now turned translator, prefaced his translation of
Philippe de Mornay's *The Mysterie of Iniquitie: that is to say, the History of
the Papacie*, with the appeal 'that I may live to march over the Alpes, and to
trayle a pike before the walls of Rome, under your Highnesse Standard. It
was my first profession, oh that it might be my last. The cause is God's,
the enterprise glorious. O that God would be pleased, as he hath given you a
heart, so to give power to put it in execution.' The anonymous translator of
Edmond Richer's *A Treatise of Ecclesiastical and Politike Power* urges Henry
to action against 'that monster' of Rome: 'Up then, brave Prince: the eyes
of all Christendom are now cast upon you, to see you begin; you shall not
want friends and followers.' John Brinsley the puritan divine tenders the
Prince his book *Ludus Literarius* with the comment

> And what is it, which might more advance you in the eyes and hearts of all the people of
> your most noble Father's Dominions, then if now from your first yeares, you begin to be the
> blessed instruments of the Almightie, of an everlasting benefite to the present and all
> succeeding generations, whereby you might knit all hearts more surely unto the holy God.

Dr Robert Abbot, the brother of the Archbishop of Canterbury, had addressed his *True Ancient Roman Catholic* (1611) to the Prince with the zealous hope that

> your princely name may more and more grow great, and may be a terror to that self-exalting kingdom and monarchy of the great Capitolian priest, at length to work the utter ruin and confusion thereof. Which as we believe not to be far off, so we hope, that in that glorious revenge of the cause of Almighty God, your Highness shall have a chief and an honourable part; and that God will strengthen your arms, and give edge to your sword, to strike through the loins of all them, that are the supporters of that antichristian and wicked state.

William Fennor, another dedicated anti-papist, generously offered his life in the cause, in the prefatory letter of his bigoted book *Pluto his Travails, or, The Devils Pilgrimage to the Colledge of the Jesuits.*[31]

Of course many of these writers were no doubt projecting their enthusiasm on to Prince Henry from the security of their studies, but it is very probable that the Prince's own demeanour encouraged such dedications. He had always been noted for his piety, which was not simply a matter of show: he led a regular Christian life, and insisted that his Court follow suit.[32] It was this high standard of morality coupled with firm good order that helped give his Court such a high reputation all the time it was in existence. Henry retained twenty-four chaplains, who preached in rotation. His principal chaplain and adviser was Joseph Hall, later to be bishop of Exeter, then Norwich, to whom Henry had been attracted by his book of Meditations; a moderate and firm Anglican. Henry, as we have noted, required all members of his Court to be communicating Protestants. As he grew older, his zeal strengthened, and he grew more resolute in his opposition to his father's plans for a marriage with one of the Catholic princesses of Europe. He warmly approved his sister's marriage to the Protestant Elector Palatine, and by mid-1612 he was announcing that he would accompany the couple back to Heidelberg to seek a wife among the Protestant principalities of the North.

In one other way did Henry run athwart his father's intentions, and this was in regard to Sir Walter Raleigh, who had been confined to the Tower since 1604 on charges of treason. Their friendship dated from about 1608, when Henry sought him out for advice on shipbuilding methods; their mutual interest in naval matters drew them together. From his prison, Raleigh became a sort of unofficial councillor to the Prince, writing for his benefit *The Prince, or Maxims of State*, a terse compendium in the manner of Machiavelli of the arts and difficulties of government, a work which is taut with the experience of a disillusioned observer of monarchs and states.

He urged Henry to strengthen the Navy in his *Observations concerning the Royall Navy and Sea-Service*, a book full of close practical detail on the making and manning of ships that is obviously directed at a man who knew his way around a dockyard, as well as having a voice in state councils. He also wrote for the Prince *A Discourse of the Invention of Ships*, which contains his assessment of the relative balance of sea power amongst the European countries, with his reasons for enlarging the size of the merchant marine. Apart from these considerations of state policy, Raleigh offered his opinions against the proposed match of Henry with a princess of Savoy in a tract that must have been very welcome to the Prince.

Raleigh also communicated his enthusiasm for schemes of colonisation in the New World. Henry became significantly involved with the Virginia Company. By 1609 he was investing in the venture; by 1611 he had sent out a colonising party who founded a town called Henrico, near present-day Newport News. The Virginia Company made plans for a university to be established there, and a college for the conversion of Infidels, a combination of learning and piety very characteristic of Henry, but the project and the colony foundered in an Indian massacre in 1622. Henry had eastern interests too: in July 1612 the East India Company came under his protection in terms which suggested a desire to spread Christianity in Asia as well as to trade there. In 1612 also, a voyage in search of the North-West Passage was made under his patronage. In all these plans the experience of Sir Walter Raleigh could be turned to account. Clearly Prince Henry felt the injustice of Raleigh's imprisonment, and worked for his release, but James on this question was adamant, rejecting all intercession. Although it is doubtful if Henry ever expressed the opinion often attributed to him that 'no other king but his father would keep such a man as Sir Walter in such a cage, meaning the Tower', one imagines that the sentiment was fairly accurate. In befriending Raleigh, Henry was once again displaying that tendency to associate himself with the spirit of the high Elizabethan age when enterprises of great pith and moment contrasted markedly with the present subdued state of national policy under James.

Raleigh had ample time for writing in the Tower, so it is not altogether surprising that he undertook the largest subject imaginable, *The History of the World*. Begun for his own satisfaction in 1606, it gradually became directed to Prince Henry, who came in Raleigh's eyes to represent its ideal reader and judge. This huge folio is a providential history of the nations, showing God's hand moulding the course of events, and revealing God's judgements among the kingdoms of the earth. It opened in Paradise, and was to close in England. It traced the history of the Jews in immense detail, for there the operations of the divine spirit were most evident. All other nations provided a theatre for the moral drama of history, but the Jews in the beginning of time and the English in the latter days principally attracted Raleigh, for both were chosen people dwelling under the eye of God. As a royal actor soon to come upon the scene, Prince Henry stood in need of instruction in the morality play of world history, and this instruction provided Raleigh with a significant role even though he lay in prison. 'It was for the service of that inestimable Prince Henry that I undertook this work', runs the Preface. That Henry read and discussed it seems clear from the author's admission that he had to expand and alter the work at royal request, for he states that he had been 'directed to enlarge the building after the foundation was laid, and the first part finished'. We know that the book was entered in the Stationer's Register as ready for printing on 15 April 1611, but its publication was deferred, presumably so that additions and alterations could be made to accommodate the Prince's observations. In the event, it was not published until 1614, when, Raleigh laments, 'It is now left to the world without a Master'. The first part had ended with the splendid apostrophe to Death as the ultimate agent of divine justice that touches man more powerfully than all God's words:

O eloquent, just, and mighty Death! whom none could advise, thou hast persuaded; what none hath dared, thou hast done; and whom all the world hath flattered, thou hast cast out of the world and despised; thou hast drawn together all the far-stretched greatness, all the pride, cruelty, and ambition of man, and covered it all over with these two narrow words, *Hic iacet.*

These words were ironically prophetic, for by the end of 1612 Prince Henry had 'interest in nothing but in the gravel which fills his mouth', and had gone to his long home. With him faded Raleigh's hopes, and ambition to continue the History. When he finally published it in 1614, he added a melancholy tailpiece expressive of his dejection: 'besides many other discouragements persuading my silence, it hath pleased God to take that glorious prince out of the world to whom [these histories] were directed, whose unspeakable and never enough lamented loss hath taught me to say with Job, *Versa est in luctum cithara mea, et organum meum in vocem flentium.*'33

In October 1612 Henry fell ill of a fever, which steadily worsened. The arrival of the Elector Palatine for his marriage with Princess Elizabeth threw the court into festivities in which Henry participated with hectic vigour, but he was forced to take to his bed, where he suffered the appalling ministrations of the most learned doctors in the land.34 After incessant bleedings and purgings he died on 6 November. A detailed account of his illness and autopsy was written by Sir Theodore Mayerne, his principal physician, from which modern medical authorities are persuaded that the Prince died of typhoid fever, which was active in London at that time.[35]

On 7 December, the funeral procession of some two thousand mourners moved from St James's Palace to Westminster Abbey in a black pageant of sorrow that reminded many of the funeral of Sir Philip Sidney, twenty-six years before. The column was headed by the customary body of poor men clad in black gowns, expressive of the dead man's charity, then a great number of servants of the attending nobles, then the whole of the Prince's household in ascending order of importance, punctuated by standards, regalia, and riderless horses covered in black, with escutcheons, representing the Prince's many titles. Next came the gentleman of the Palatinate in 'unexpected suits of woe', followed by Prince Charles's household. The gentlemen of England grew more numerous, the knights more frequent, the heralds came closer together, then a great mass of barons and bishops preceded the achievements of Prince Henry; then 'The corps of the Prince, lying in an open chariot, with the representation of him invested with riches of state of purple velvet, furred with ermines; his cap and coronet on his head, and his rod of gold in his hand. At his feet within the chariot sat Sir David Murray, the master of his Wardrobe.' A canopy of black velvet was carried over the hearse, together with ten bannerets about the body. The Garter King of Arms walked behind, heralding the Chief Mourner, Prince Charles, who was followed by the Elector Frederick. There followed the principal earls of England, and counts of the Palatinate. The guard closed the rear. The King was too broken to attend, and had withdrawn from London.[36] At the Abbey, the Archbishop of Canterbury preached the funeral sermon, at the conclusion of which the officers of Henry's household solemnly broke their white staves of office over the coffin, and the assembly dispersed. The coffin remained in state in Westminster Abbey for some days, before being buried in Henry VII's Chapel. This choice of sepulchre was expressly made by King James, who had determined to use the chapel as the burying place for his line, thus emphasising even in death the relationship between the Stuarts and the founder of the Tudor dynasty. Amazingly, in one of the great ages of funerary sculpture in England, no monument was erected to the Prince. We do not know why. Eventually, James I would lie in the same chapel, equally uncommemorated.

At the end of the year came the formal dissolution of the Prince's household, when Dr Hall preached a farewell sermon to 'the Family of Prince Henry', as the household termed itself. From the tone of that sermon one senses how privileged and happy the members of that family considered themselves: it radiates a sincere conviction that service under the Prince of Wales had been a brief golden age. 'We have lived in the eye of a Prince, whose countenance was able to put life into any beholder. How oft hath that face shined upon us, and we have found our heart warm with those comfortable beams.' The time had come for them all to make their own way in the world once more: 'We are all now parting from one another, and now is loosing a knot of the most loving and entire fellowship that ever met in the court of any Prince.'37

There may have been no memorial to the Prince in alabaster or brass, but in poetry there was an unprecedented outpouring of formalised grief. Again, one has to look back to Sir Philip Sidney's death for a comparable moment in literature, yet the mourning of poets for the Prince was far more widespread. Even the death of Queen Elizabeth had prompted relatively few elegies, for the poets were more anxious to greet the new king. But Henry was the prince of patrons in his time, whose affection for poetry and learning was so well known, and the natural tragedy of his death combined with the disappointment of all poets and artists at the loss of the new Maecenas. Over fifty elegies were printed between 1612 and 1614, including four anthologies from the universities of Oxford and Cambridge, and two volumes of funeral sermons.38 Donne, Chapman, Campion, Webster, Tourneur, Heywood, William Drummond, William Browne, Henry King, Giles Fletcher, George Wither, Sir John Davies, Sir Edward Herbert all contributed their elegies, yet for all the brilliant poetic intellects that treated the subject, no poem written on this occasion has had an enduring fame.39 Several themes recur again and again: the cruelty of fate, the blow to the cause of Protestantism, and Christianity in general (many poems lament that there will be no war against Rome, or crusade against the Turks), the loss to learning, the inscrutable providence of God, and the hoary platitude that Henry was too good for earth, and had to be transplanted to heaven. Many speculated about the great question that hung over the Prince's abbreviated life: what would his policy in Europe have been, for it seemed inconceivable that Henry would have remained inactive for long.

In Donne's poem, for example, the dense obscurity clears momentarily as he faces this question, and hints that in some quarters millenarian hopes rested on the Prince, that he might have achieved the culminating peace of the world that would stretch into eternity:

> Was it not well believ'd, till now, that *Hee,*
> Whose *Reputation* was an *Extasie*
> On neighbour States; which knew not Why to wake

> Till *Hee* discoverd what wayes *Hee* would take:
> For Whom what Princes angled (when they tryed)
> Mett a *Torpedo*, and were stupefied:
> And Others studies, how Hee would be bent;
> Was His great *Father's* greatest Instrument,
> And activ'st spirit to convey and tye
> This soule of *Peace* through CHRISTIANITIE?
> Was it not well believ'd, that *Hee* would make
> This *general Peace* th'eternall overtake?
> And that *His* Times might have stretcht out so far
> As to touch Those of which they *Emblems* are?

This is an extreme statement of visionary hopes, but it does reveal the intensity of expectation that hung upon the career of a politically significant figure in an age when all action or promise of action was interpreted in an atmosphere charged with religious speculation. Everything was a portent or a sign which cried out for interpretation. Donne, as the most intelligent and theologically adept of the elegising poets, is utterly perplexed by the death.

> Look to me *Faith*; and look to my *Faith*, GOD;
> For, both my *Centres* feel this *Period*.

For explanations, he is forced to fall back upon platitudes: he concludes that Henry's death is a punishment visited upon a sinful generation; the world does not deserve the hopeful times that Henry's life promised; men must suffer for their sins and errors, so Henry's death is a sign of God's continuing displeasure:

> Therefore *Wee live*: though such a Life we have
> As but so manie *Mandrakes* on his Grave.

Even faith cannot fathom the mystery of the death, and the poem evades a resolution by a sideways flight of speculation about the composition of the soul.

Among the many elegies, Thomas Campion's stands out for its imaginative power, for its sensitive combination of public and private grief. He wrote a sequence of poems, *Songs of Mourning*, which were set to music by Giovanni Coprario, the italianised John Cooper who had been Prince Henry's lutenist and music teacher. The sequence is dedicated to the Elector Frederick as an act of consolation; as Campion says, 'Quod seperest, nimios nobis omni arte dolores / Est mollire animum, spes meliora dabit' (What remains is the courage to soften excessive grief by all our art, and then hope will give us better things).[40]

One would very much like to know the circumstances in which this sequence of words and music was presented at Court. The directness of address is such that they must have been given in the presence of the royal family, before the wedding of Elizabeth and Frederick on 14 February 1613. The intimacy of tone and the fact that the accompaniment was a single lute or viol suggest a small private audience. Campion in the opening lines of the elegy professes to be a priest presiding over the rituals of grief:

> For I will open to your free accesse
> The sanctuary of all heavinesse
> Where men their fill may mourne, and never sinne:
> And I their humble Priest thus first beginne.

In this first elegy, with its evocation of Prince Henry's presence, Campion's verse achieves an almost Shakespearian power:

> And like a well-tun'd chime his carriage was
> Full of coelestiall witchcraft, winning all
> To admiration and love personall.
> . . .
> When Court and Musicke call'd him, off fell armes,
> And, as hee had beene shap't for love's alarmes,
> In harmony hee spake, and trod the ground
> In more proportion then the measur'd sound.
> How fit for peace was hee, and rosie beds!
> How fit to stand in troopes of iron heads,
> When time had with his circles made complete
> His charmed rounds! All things in time grow great.

The description of his activities endows him with a vitality perpetuated by poetry over death:

> But our young *Henry*, arm'd with all the arts
> That sute with Empire, and the gaine of harts,
> Bearing before him fortune, power, and love,
> Appear'd first in perfection, fit to move
> Fixt admiration; though his yeeres were greene,
> Their fruit was yet mature: his care had beene
> Survaying India, and implanting there
> The knowledge of that God which hee did feare:
> And ev'n now, though hee breathlesse lyes, his sayles
> Are strugling with the windes, for our avayles
> T'explore a passage hid from humane tract,
> Will fame him in the enterprise or fact.
> O Spirit full of hope, why art thou fled
> From deedes of honour? why's that vertue dead
> Which dwelt so well in thee?

There is no answer, and the poet, addressing now the surviving Charles, turns to the speechless consolation of a dirge:

> To whose eternall peace wee offer now
> Guifts which hee lov'd, and fed: Musicks that flow
> Out of a sowre and melancholike vayne,
> Which best sort with the sorrowes wee sustaine.

The following poems in the sequence are directed to the other members of the royal family. They do not attempt to explain, mythologise or palliate Prince Henry's death: they express an unfeigned grief and dissolve into sad music. The beautiful opening line to the Count Palatine—'How like a golden dreame you met and parted'—conveys the sweet sadness of all these personal poems. The sequence ends with two public poems, one 'To the Most disconsolate Great Brittaine', the other 'To the World'. This last sums up the sentiments of the great majority of poems written upon the Prince's death:

> O poore distracted world, partly a slave
>   To Pagans sinnefull rage, partly obscur'd
> With ignorance of all the meanes that save;
>   And ev'n those parts of thee that live assur'd
> Of heav'nly grace, Oh how they are devided
> With doubts late by a Kingly penne decided!
>   O happy world, if what the Sire begunne
>   Had beene clos'd up by his religious Sonne!
>
> Mourne all you soules opprest under the yoake
>   Of Christian-hating Thrace: never appear'd
> More likelyhood to have that blacke league broke,
>   For such a heavenly prince might well be fear'd
> Of earthly fiends. Oh, how is Zeale inflamed
> With power, when truth wanting defence is shamed!
>   O princely soule, rest thou in peace, while wee
>   In thine expect the hopes were ripe in thee.[41]

Prince Henry is viewed against the dominant anxieties of the time: the threat to Christendom from the Turks, the unending disputes about the true religion, even amongst Protestants themselves, the sense of England's impotence, and of her enemies' advantage, now that Henry is dead. The hope placed in the young survivors, the 'thine' of the poem, seems weak in comparison with Henry's widely acknowledged promise.

Notes to Chapter Three

1   'Ceremonial of the Baptism of Henry, Prince of Scotland', in John Nichols, *The Progresses of Queen Elizabeth*, London 1823, vol. III, pp. 353–69.

2   *Ibid.*

3   Sir Charles Cornwallis, *The Life and Death of our late most incomparable and heroique Prince, Henry, Prince of Wales*, 1641, p. 7.

4   Thomas Birch, *The Life of Henry Prince of Wales*, London 1760, p. 44.

5   E. K. Chambers, *The Elizabethan Stage*, Oxford 1923, vol. II, p. 186. We hear of them playing seven times before Henry in the winter of 1604.

6   After *Bussy d'Ambois* came *The Revenge of Bussy d'Ambois*, *The Conspiracy of Byron* and *The Tragedy of Byron*.

7   N. D. Solve, *Stuart Politics in Chapman's Tragedy of Chabot*, Ann Arbor, Mich. 1928, p. 17.

8   Sidney Dobell, 'Newly Discovered Documents of the Elizabethan and Jacobean Periods', *The Athenaeum*, 1911, I, p. 433.

9   Birch, p. 97.

10   Quoted in E. C. Wilson, *Prince Henry and English Literature*, Ithaca, N.Y. 1946, p. 52.

11   *Prince Henries Barriers*, in *Ben Jonson*, ed. C. H. Herford and P. & E. Simpson, Oxford 1941, vol. VII.

12   According to Drummond of Hawthornden in his poem 'Teares on the Death of Moeliades', 1613.

13   See Frances Yates, *Astraea*, 1975, and *Shakespeare's Last Plays*, 1975. Also Roy Strong, *The Cult of Elizabeth*, 1977.

14   John Stow, *Annales*, continued by Edmond Howes, 1615, p. 897.

15   From an early age Prince Henry had been interested in the arts and crafts of sailing. In 1604 James had caused a small vessel to be built 'for the amusement of the Prince, and his instruction in the business of shipping and sailing, for which he afterwards showed a strong inclination' (Birch, p. 38). This commission brought Henry in touch with Phineas Pett, one of the King's shipwrights, with whom he maintained a friendship until his death, taking him into his service, and always respecting his advice. *The Autobiography of Phineas Pett*, ed. W. G. Perrin, in *Publications of the Navy Records Society*, LI (1918), contains an unaffected account of Prince Henry's dealings with Pett.

16   See the account of the pageant 'Londons Love to the Royal Prince Henrie', in John Nichols, *Progresses of James I*, 1828, vol. II, pp. 326ff.

17   *Tethys Festivall*, in *The Complete Works of Samuel Daniel*, ed. A. B. Grosart, London, 1885, vol. III.

18   See Roy Strong, *The Cult of Elizabeth*, London 1977, pp. 189–90.

19   See Greenlaw's observations in the Variorum Spenser. 'By *Fairy* Spenser means *Welsh*, or, more accurately, *Tudor*, as distinguished from the general term British. He looks on England as Britain, ignoring, for the purpose of the poem, post-Conquest history. The Tudor dynasty, therefore, brings back the ancient British line, and one purpose of the poem is to celebrate this fact in compliment to the Queen. But Gloriana, the Faerie Queene, is *Elizabeth Tudor*. The old British spirit, the real England, [is] represented in Prince Arthur.' *The Works of Edmund Spenser*, ed. Greenlaw, Osgood

and Padelford, London 1966, vol. II, pp. 453–4.

The significance of the name Oberon also indicated Henry's legitimate descent from Henry VII (Elficleos, the father of Oberon) and associated him with the authority and dominion of Henry VIII.

20   *Prince Henries Barriers*, in *Ben Jonson*, ed. Herford and Simpson, vol. VII, pp. 37–40, 56–63.

21   *Tethys Festivall*, in *The Complete Works of Samuel Daniel*, ed. Grosart, vol. III, p. 307.

22   It is possible, for example, that the romantic castle in mixed gothic and classic that featured in *Oberon* might have inspired the Little Castle at Bolsover, begun by Charles Cavendish, who was associated with Prince Henry's circle, in 1612.

23   See Lawrence Stone, 'The Building of Hatfield House', in *Archeological Journal* CXII, 1956, pp. 100–28.

24   John Harris suggests that this site was Richmond, in *The King's Arcadia*, London 1973, p. 43.

25   See R. Wittkower, 'English Literature on Architecture', in *Palladio and English Palladianism*, London 1974. There had been John Dee's précis of Vitruvius in *Elements of Geometrie* (1570), and Henry Wotton was to publish *Elements of Architecture* in 1624, but the next standard Italian treatise to be published was Vignola in 1655.

26   See Birch, pp. 466–7.

27   See Frances Yates, *The Rosicrucian Enlightenment*, London 1972, p. 11, from which this account of de Caus's activities is derived. See also the discussion of de Caus in Roy Strong, *The Renaissance Garden in England*, London 1979.

28   *Venetian State Papers* 1610–13, p. 106. Quoted in Roy Strong, *The English Icon*, London 1969, p. 56.

29   Miereveld was described by Peacham in his *Compleat Gentleman* as 'the most excellent painter of all the Low Countries'.

30   See the letter from John Chamberlain to Sir Dudley Carleton, 19 November 1612, in *The Letters of John Chamberlain*, ed. N. E. McClure, Philadelphia, Pa. 1939.

31   For an account of the dedications to Prince Henry in 1612, see E. C. Wilson, *op. cit.*, pp. 106–16.

32   E.g. 'He ordered boxes to be kept at his three houses, St. James, Richmond and Nonsuch, for the money required of those, who were heard to swear; which money was distributed to the poor.' Birch, pp. 85–6.

33   'My harp also is turned to weeping, and my organ into the voice of them that weep.'

34   See Birch, pp. 333–60 for an account of the Prince's last illness.

35   Theodore Mayerne, *The True Account of the Illness, Death . . . of Henry, Prince of Wales*, 1612. Printed in *Opera Medica*, ed. J. Browne, 1701.

36   See the contemporary account of the funeral in Birch, pp. 522–9.

37   'A Fare-well Sermon, preacht to the Familie of Prince Henry', in *The Works of Joseph Hall*, ed. J. Pratt, 1808, vol. V.

38   See 'Elegies and other Tracts issued on the Death of Henry, Prince of Wales, 1612', in *Publications of the Edinburgh Bibliographical Society* VI, 1906, pp. 132–58.

39   The principal elegiac forms and dominant themes of these poems have been analysed by Ruth Wallerstein in 'The Laureate Hearse' in *Studies in Seventeenth Century Poetic*, Madison, Wis. 1950. See also E. C. Wilson, *op. cit.*, pp, 144–68.

40   *The Works of Thomas Campion*, ed. Walter R. Davis, New York 1970, p. 116.

41   The reference in line 6 is to King James's reply to Cardinal Bellarmine, *Premonitions to all most mighty Monarchs, Kings, Free Princes, and States of Christendom,* 1609.

[4]
The wedding of Princess Elizabeth

King James's daughter, Princess Elizabeth, did not attract a great deal of literary or artistic attention until the great moment of her marriage to Frederick, Elector Palatine, in 1613. Her early life had been uneventful. As was common with children of the great families of the land, she had been brought up in another household, that of Lord and Lady Harington, who had been kindly mentors and had educated her intelligently. It was not until 1608, when she was twelve, that she came to Court, where she rapidly developed a strong affection for her brother Prince Henry, whom she had hitherto hardly known. Henry thoroughly approved of their father's decision to marry her to Frederick, who though young was widely regarded as the leader of continental Protestantism. He was the grandson of William the Silent, the liberator of the Netherlands, and the principal lay elector of the Holy Roman Empire. Prince Henry with his own marked Protestant zeal welcomed the prospect of an alliance with a kindred spirit, while Parliament and people approved the marriage as a firm sign that James was developing a forward policy of Protestant commitment in Europe.

In response to this general enthusiasm, celebrations were planned on the most lavish scale, and Prince Henry himself had a hand in contriving the fireworks and the river battle which were to be the principal public events, and both of which contained religious themes that suggest Henry's own preoccupations. Henry's sudden death in November 1612 plunged the Court into the profoundest mourning, but since the Elector and his retinue were already in England, the wedding could not be too long delayed. Official mourning lasted only a month, and the marriage and public festivities were arranged for February 1613. Then at last the great water battle took place on the Thames. It represented a conflict between Christian and Turkish ships, including an attack on a great Venetian 'argosy' or merchant ship that was spectacularly saved by a Christian fleet, 'with the drums, trumpets, flutes and guns filling the ayre with repercussive acclamations' all afternoon long, until a Christian victory was assured.[1] The fireworks next evening emphasised the Protestant aspect of the marriage. The hero of the piece was 'the great unresistable Champion of the World, and uncontrollable Patron, St. George', who defeated a hellish magician, a dragon and a giant in order to free the Lady Lucinda from enthralment. The subject is close to that of Book I of *The Faerie Queene*, where English-Protestant St George defeats the Papal magician figure Archimago, routs the giant

Princess Elizabeth and Frederick, Elector Palatine, engraving by Elstrack

Orgoglio or Pride, and destroys the great dragon who represents the devil and all his works, to secure the release and companionship of Una or Truth. The spectacle was at once popular and allusive, just as St George was both a popular saint featuring in mummers' plays and folk pageants, and a courtly champion of chivalric Protestantism as patron of the Order of the Garter. The Elector Frederick himself had just been made a member of that order. For the London crowds there were entertainments such as 'An artificiall Fireworke . . . seene flying in the ayre like unto a Dragon, against which another vision appeared, flaming like St. George on horseback, brought in by a burning enchanter, between which there was fought a most strange battell continuing a quarter of an hour or more; the Dragon being vanquished, seemed to rore like thunder, and withall burst into pieces and so vanished'. For the more knowing members of the audience there was the memory of Prince Henry's association with the cult of St George as part of his Protestant policy, to which the present marriage formed a complement. The evening burnt itself out with 'flakes of flashing fire and explosions, with always rackets flying and reports thwacking'.[2]

The wedding itself took place on Valentine's Day 1613, at Whitehall, where the couple were married by Archbishop Abbot according to the rites of the Church of England, the service concluding with an anthem of benediction by John Bull. The political nature of the marriage, anti-Papal and anti-Hapsburg, was acknowledged by the absence of the ambassadors of the Hapsburg powers, Spain and the Spanish Netherlands, while the Dutch, French and Venetian ambassadors attended. Queen Anne, who had been a Catholic since about 1600 and who inclined towards Spain in her modest political views, relented in her dislike of the marriage only at the last moment and came to the ceremony in state.

To celebrate the wedding three masques were given, one by a group of lords at Court, the two others by the Inns of Court. As Ben Jonson was abroad at this moment, other poets had a chance to show their powers, in alliance with Inigo Jones's scenic inventions. *The Lords' Masque*, whose principal sponsors were the Earls of Salisbury and Montgomery and Lord Hay, was written by Campion and performed on the night of the wedding. In it, Orpheus, the creator of inspired music, releases Entheus, or Poetic Fury, from the cave of madness, in order that his 'celestiall rage' and 'excelling rapture' may 'create / Inventions rare, this night to celebrate'. Entheus conjures up Prometheus or Celestial Fire, and the three 'help to induce a courtly miracle'. Prometheus reveals a heaven of eight great stars which Inigo Jones contrived to 'moove in an exceeding strange and delightfull maner'. The stars dance for joy, as they were reputed to have done on

Easter Day, or when Beatrice was born. This rare phenomenon was rapturously viewed by the English Court, who were the more enthralled when the stars were transformed into the eight masquing lords. Then four female statues were revealed: the creations of Prometheus which envious Jove had turned to stone. Now Jove relents, and moved by Orpheus' music and Entheus' poetic power, he fills them with life and love, and the masquers carry them off into a dance; four more statues then appear, and are awakened into a dance of love, which then enlarges to embrace the audience, 'and first of all the Princely Bridegroom and Bride were drawne into these solemne Revels'. Thus divine love for mankind, expressed through the two harmonies of poetry and music, reveals itself auspiciously on this nuptial night.

But all is not done. This is a royal and international marriage, whose consequences stretch far out into the future.[3] At the conclusion of the dances the scene changes again to become 'a prospective with Porticoes on each side . . .; in the middle was erected an Obeliske, all of silver, and in it lights of severall colours; on the side of this Obeliske standing on Pedestals, were the statues of the Bridegroome and Bride, all of gold in gratious postures'.[4] It is a scene of prophecy, for a Sybil enters, and miraculously pulls the huge obelisk forward, and utters in Latin her vision of the future. The learned might know what to expect, for in that much used source-book of emblems and motifs, Cesare Ripa's *Iconologia*, from which so many English masques derive their devices, 'a gold-clad figure with an obelisk or pyramid represents "The Glory of Princes" '[5] and their immortality. So it is of the glory of these princes that the Sybil speaks. Elizabeth is hailed as 'the mother of kings, of emperors. Let the British strength be added to the German: can anything equal it? One mind, one faith, will join two peoples, and one religion, and simple love. Both will have the same enemy, the same ally. . . . Peace will favour them, and the fortune of war will favour them; always God the helper will be at their side.'[6] The masque then turns from compliment to politics, applauding the Anglo-German union as the beginning of a new Protestant power on the continent that may one day take over the Empire itself with the help of God, a prophecy that began to materialise in 1619 when Frederick accepted the throne of Bohemia and became a potential candidate for the Imperial throne.

The night following the wedding saw the presentation of the Masque of the Middle Temple and Lincoln's Inn, arranged by Chapman and Jones. The thematic content of this masque was slender, its success consisting mainly in sheer extravagance of costume and excellence of dancing. After a comic anti-masque of baboons attired as fantastical travellers, the principal masque is introduced by the Princes of Virginia, who are drawn to England by the news of the wedding. They sing a hymn of worship to the setting sun, and they are then invited to change their worship to the rising sun, King James:

> of your fit devotion turn the events
> To this our Briton Phoebus, whose bright sky
> (Enlightened with a Christian piety)
> Is never subject to black Error's night.

Chapman is evidently exploiting the topicality of the Virginia plantation schemes, and the English ambition to convert the Indians to their brand of Christianity. Such a theme would have appealed to Prince Henry, who was interested in such projects, but it had a limited relevance to Elizabeth and Frederick, although it might have veiled an anti-Spanish attitude, for there were fears of a Spanish attack on Virginia at this time, and the present marriage was a distinctly anti-Spanish contract. The American princes bring with them the god of Riches, and sing several songs in honour of the royal couple. Fortune has decided to settle in England too, a not entirely appropriate gesture, as Elizabeth and Frederick were going to live in the Palatinate. The whole spectacle was introduced by an Italian fantastico, who seems a total irrelevance to the production. Chapman's invention here creeps very close to the ground indeed.[8]

The Gray's Inn and Inner Temple Masque a few days later, written by Francis Beaumont to subjects devised by Francis Bacon, was altogether more coherent. It began with a water pageant across the Thames, which served to introduce the fluvial theme of the masque, the marriage of the Thames and the Rhine. The gods preside over the symbolic wedding, assisted by water nymphs. Then, in honour of the event, the Olympian knights, the chief masquers, appear to revive the Olympian Games, an occasion which must have provided brilliant opportunities for mimic dancing. As in *The Lords' Masque*, statues are brought to life by Jove, and by a dance to the music of love, a conceit that suggests the revivifying power that this marriage exerts over its beholders. The masque ends with a delightful prayer that the young couple may triumph over time in their happiness:

> I would these paire when they are layd
>   And not a creature nigh 'em,
> Could catch his scythe as he doth pass,
> And clip his wings, and breake his glasse,
>   And keep him ever by 'em.[9]

Historically, when the Olympic Games were held, universal peace prevailed throughout the Greek world, so the theme acts as an augury for the prosperous times of Frederick and Elizabeth. It may also be intended as a compliment to King James, who watched the masque, on his avowed policy as peacemaker. Beaumont's masque is purely festive and celebratory, unlike Campion's, where the final prophecy, with its intimations of future struggle and empire, and its acknowledgement of enemies, speaks of matters that were prominent in all the participants' minds, and recognises the essentially political–religious nature of the marriage.

Beaumont's dramatic talents were also in request at the Court during the Christmas revels that preceded the marriage, for *Philaster*, which he wrote in conjunction with Fletcher, was twice played then. The reasons for the popularity of this pastoral romance at this moment may be found in its happy-ever-after plot, which ends with the marriage of the faithful lovers, Princess Arethusa and Prince Philaster, who triumph over schemes for more disagreeable alliances, and also in the relevance of the plot to political circumstances antecedent to the Palatine marriage. *Philaster* seems to have been written in 1609, when James was toying with the idea of a Spanish marriage for Prince Henry, a plan that was extremely unpopular in the nation at large, and which Beaumont and Fletcher seem to have been covertly criticising in the play, where the Calabrian King tries to force his daughter into an unwilling match with a Spanish prince, only to be outwitted so that Arethusa marries the man of her desires.[10] James had dropped his plan, although it was to surface again for Prince Charles in the 1620s, but the choice of the play for two performances during the betrothal festivities in 1612–13 suggests that it expressed a feeling of dangers averted and emphasised the exceptional good fortune of Elizabeth in finding against the odds a husband to whom she was affectionately drawn, and who was a firm anti-Spanish figure. The tone of the play has some affinities with the latent hostility to Spain in Chapman's wedding masque. The ending of the play, where the King joins the hands of his daughter to her beloved and says,

> Enjoy, Philaster,
> This Kingdom, which is yours, and after me
> Whatever I call mine. My blessing on you;
> All happy hours be at your marriage-joys
> That you may grow yourselves over all lands
> And live to see your plenteous branches spring
> Where ever there is sun

> (V.v.216–23)

achieves a mood of graciousness most appropriate to the betrothal time.

For the celebrations during the winter of 1612–13 some twenty plays were given at Court by the King's Men, which was Shakespeare's company.

These plays included *Much Ado*, both parts of *Henry IV*, *Julius Caesar*, *Othello*, *The Winter's Tale* and *The Tempest*. It has long been felt that the masque in *The Tempest* was interpolated by Shakespeare in order to celebrate the betrothal of Elizabeth and Frederick, and it was probably played before them on or around 27 December 1612, which was the betrothal night. The action of *The Tempest* suited itself to such an occasion, for it contains a beautiful island princess, daughter of a supremely wise father, who is visited and loved by a handsome young prince from over the seas, and eventually betrothed to him. The interlude in Act IV shows how adroitly masque can function as an expression of ideals that human behaviour aspires to, and that enhance the rituals of society. The vision induced by Prospero is a specific exercise of his magical art: the spirits that he conjures up present the 'insubstantial pageant' of the masque, but just as the spirits belong to a higher level of human consciousness, beyond whose threshold Prospero has passed, so do the meanings of the masque relate to a higher level of understanding, expressing the ideas that give shape and purpose to the rite of marriage. Iris, the presenter of the masque, is the figure of the rainbow, the bridge between earth and heaven, and the pledge of God's favourable aspect towards mankind; as such she was a fitting goddess to usher in the betrothal celebrations (and had already been so used by Jonson in his masque *Hymenaei* for the marriage of Lady Frances Howard and the Earl of Essex), for lawful marriage and the procreation of new souls is the time when the earthly cycle of life intersects with the divine, a notion with which Spenser closed his *Epithalamion* to his own bride:

> And ye high heavens, the temple of the gods,
> . . .
> Poure out your blessing on us plenteously,
> And happy influence upon us raine,
> That we may raise a large posterity,
> Which from the earth, which they may long possesse
> With lasting happinesse,
> Up to your haughty pallaces may mount.

Iris joins with Ceres, the goddess of nature's fertility, to offer a celebration to Juno, whose aspect here is that of Juno Pronuba, the goddess of marriage; the three figures together form a hymeneal triad expressing the ideal condition of marriage. Iris informs us that Venus and Cupid, the sensual and mischievous aspects of love, are far from the scene, 'Cutting the clouds towards Paphos'. Juno and Ceres then pronounce a blessing (in incantatory octosyllabics that are frequently employed for prophecy in this period), which in desiring happiness and plenty also foresees an ideal world in which there is only Spring and Autumn, freshess and fulfilment:

> Spring come to you at the farthest
> In the very end of harvest.

(IV.i.114–15)

There is no winter of death in this vision; instead there is a glimpse of the golden age returned in which the seasons of Spring and Autumn are simultaneous. Ferdinand's comment at this moment underlines the point:

> Let me live here ever;
> So rare a wonder'd father and a wise
> Makes this place Paradise.

(IV.i.122–4)

The verse moves easily between classical and Christian reference; the golden age becomes the earthly paradise presided over by the 'wise father'. Played at Court before James, Ferdinand could turn here to the King who was also a wise father and (in his own estimation) God's viceroy, ruling over the paradise of England. It was an essential part of the masque's function to evoke such elevated associations, and a Court audience in 1612 would well know how to catch these allusions. Iris then summons the nymphs and reapers to begin the masque dance, pastoral as befits the earthly paradise. It is indeed 'a most majestic vision, and / Harmonious charmingly', for the concord of the dance and the paradisal allusions have revealed the mystery of which the rites of betrothal and marriage are but outward forms.

In the case of *The Winter's Tale*, the wooing of Perdita by Florizel must have taken on fresh significance when played before Elizabeth and Frederick, as it could be made to mirror their courtship and express the hopes for a brilliant future now vested in this couple after the recent death of Prince Henry, who could be poignantly identified with the precocious young Mamilius, the heir to Leontes's throne who dies so suddenly in the play.[11] Like *The Tempest*, *The Winter's Tale* contains elements that acquired a new relevance with the turn of events in the winter of 1612, and the actions of the younger characters in particular would have been very suggestive. One wonders also whether the presentation of *The Winter's Tale* at Court in the Christmas season might have suggested the motif of reanimated statues that appeared both in Campion's *Lords' Masque* and in Beaumont's masque for Gray's Inn, for each of these masques uses the device to express the revitalisation of the world by love.

Frances Yates has recently argued that *Cymbeline* too, like *The Tempest*, was adapted for performance during the season of festivities for the marriage, notably by the addition or alteration of the masque-like vision of Jupiter that occurs in Posthumus's cell. She has plausibly proposed that *Cymbeline*, based as it is on British history, dealing with a king who has two sons and a daughter—the sons being revealed as chivalric princes dwelling in Wales in a rocky cave which is reminiscent of the setting of Prince Henry's masque *Oberon*—and concluding with the establishment of a great peace, appears to contain a great deal of thematic material related to 'the glorification of King James and his children'.[12] The suggestion is that Shakespeare added Posthumus's vision of Jupiter and the sybilline riddle to enhance the play for performance at Court as a dramatic encomium on the royal children, but that the sudden death of Prince Henry destroyed the balance of the play and rendered it too painful to perform. The vision contains the prophecy of an imperial future which was a common trait of many of the wedding tributes, and which carried a special force when uttered in the context of the Anglo-German alliance. The interpretation of this vision at the end of the play is left to the soothsayer Philarmonus, whose role is similar to that of the Sybil at the end of Campion's masque; he speaks of the translation of empire to the west, and specifically to the British race of the line of Cymbeline/James, for the vision

> foreshow'd our princely eagle,
> Th'imperial Caesar, should again unite
> His favour with the radiant Cymbeline
> Which shines here in the west.

$$(V.v.471-4)$$

There is a prominence of cedar imagery in the prophecy, which makes it very probable that it refers to King James and the prosperous future of his house. Philarmonus's final speech celebrates the achievement of the great Jacobean peace which is seen as a heaven-ordained event, evidence of the Providence that watched over James:

> The fingers of the pow'rs above do tune
> The harmony of this peace.

Another of Shakespeare's plays which appears to have very strong connections with the marriage festivities is his last work, *Henry VIII*. As R. A. Foakes, the editor of the New Arden edition, points out, 'A play on the downfall of Wolsey, the last great Catholic statesman of England, on the rise of Cranmer, and the birth of "that now triumphant Saint our late Queene Elizabeth" would have been very appropriate' for a marriage which was popularly seen as furthering the Protestant cause in Europe, and extending the Reformation, and which also assured the perpetuation of Protestant values by Queen Elizabeth's young namesake. 'For many, the occasion revived memories of the palmy days of the great Queen: Princess Elizabeth was following her namesake in her support of the true religion, if not in getting married.'[13] The ceremonies attendant on the birth of Elizabeth form the culmination of the play, and in the last scene the Garter King of Arms (the heraldic agent of St George), invokes a blessing on the child: 'Heaven, from thy endless goodness, send prosperous life, long and ever happy, to the high and mighty princess of England, Elizabeth' (V.iv.1–3), a blessing that would have had a direct relevance to the present if we assume that Shakespeare's play was occasioned by the royal wedding. Foakes suggests that the instances of high pageantry which are a marked feature of *Henry VIII*, such as those at Anne Boleyn's wedding and the christening scene, as well as the masque given at Wolsey's house and the Gentleman's enthusiastic commentary on the coronation procession at IV.i, may all reflect the ceremonies of the marriage itself.[14]

At the end of this play of pageantry, politics and religion, Cranmer pronounces a prophecy over the young princess Elizabeth. We have already seen how prophecy was a characteristic of masques of state significance; the presence then of Cranmer's prophecy in *Henry VIII* may help confirm that the play was designed to form part of the festivities in 1613, although there is no extant record of its performance then. As Cranmer utters his prophecy about the glorious reign of Elizabeth and her blessed peace, he sees through time a vision of the Jacobean age:

> Nor shall this peace sleep with her, but as when
> The bird of wonder dies, the maiden Phoenix,
> Her ashes new-create another heir,
> As great in admiration as herself,
> So shall she leave her blessedness to one
> (When heaven shall call her from this cloud of darkness)
> Who from the sacred ashes of her honour
> Shall star-like rise, as great in fame as she was,
> And so stand fix'd. Peace, plenty, love, truth, terror,
> That were the servants to this chosen infant,
> Shall then be his, and like a vine grow to him;
> Wherever the bright sun of heaven shall shine,
> His honour and the greatness of his name
> Shall be, and make new nations; he shall flourish
> And like a mountain cedar reach his branches
> To all the plains about him. . . .
>
> (V.v.39–54)

The new phoenix is of course King James, but by natural extension it refers to his children, and in particular Princess Elizabeth, who by virtue of her name was often considered to be the inheritor of the old Queen's spirit; indeed, it was a commonplace of courtly compliment to stress their successive identity.[15] Queen Elizabeth herself had frequently been imaged as a phoenix for her uniqueness and her solitary state, and the image transferred easily to the young princess in whom poets hoped that the royal virtues would be reborn.[16] The play then ends with a note of Protestant affirmation that was a hallmark of most of the spectacles arranged for the Palatine marriage, a note that must have been extremely pleasing to the ear of King James, whose policy was now at the peak of popularity.

It was as a phoenix that John Donne chose to celebrate Elizabeth in the most attractive of the wedding songs written for this occasion, his 'Epithalamion'.[17] Donne probably had a personal motive in addressing Elizabeth because she had been the youthful companion of his friend and patron, Lucy Harington, later Countess of Bedford, whose parents had been the Princess's guardians. Donne exploits the traditional belief that the birds of the air mate on St Valentine's Day, and that Valentine is therefore the Bishop of the Air,

> And all the chirping Choristers
> And other birds are thy Parishioners.

Admist a great chorus of birdsong the phoenix Elizabeth is seen winging to her marriage with that logical impossibility, another phoenix, Frederick. Elizabeth is bidden to her wedding, is transformed into a star en route, and shines forth a message of change to mankind:

> Up then faire Phoenix Bride, frustrate the Sunne,
> Thyself from thine affection
> Takest warmth enough, and from thine eye
> All lesser birds will take their Jollitie.
> Up, up, faire Bride, and call,
> Thy starres, from out their severall boxes, take
> Thy Rubies, Pearles, and Diamonds forth, and make
> Thy selfe a constellation, of them All,
> And by their blazing, signifie,
> That a Great Princess falls, but doth not die;
> Bee thou a new starre, that to us portends
> Ends of much wonder; and be Thou those ends.
>
> (29–40)

In the context of 1613, those 'Ends of much wonder' must have been political, referring to men's expectation of the powerful new political and religious union that was created by this marriage. Donne hyperbolically proclaims that it will bring a new age into being: 'May all men date Records, from this thy Valentine.' But the larger issues are only hinted at, and the epithalamion dwells affectionately on the lovers' happiness, and concludes with a charming genre scene which reminds us how little privacy Jacobean lovers had, isolated in their tented bed within a crowded room:

> Others neare you shall whispering speake,
> And wagers lay, at which side day will breake,
> And win by observing, then, whose hand it is
> That opens first a curtaine, hers or his;
> This will be tryed to morrow after nine,
> Till which houre, wee thy day enlarge, O Valentine.
>
> (106–12)

Elizabeth and Frederick departed for the Palatinate in April 1613. From Dover Elizabeth wrote a fond farewell letter to her father, in which she lamented that they would probably never see each other again, a striking reminder of the relative immobility of princes in those days.[18] Just before the departure, Phineas Pett the royal shipwright launched a new vessel which was aptly christened 'The Phoenix' in honour of the Princess and which promptly joined the small fleet that accompanied the couple across the Channel.[19] Elizabeth and Frederick sailed in Prince Henry's recently launched flagship 'The Prince Royal', the most advanced English vessel afloat, which caused a great stir when it arrived in Holland. Its figurehead was a splendidly carved George and Dragon, an expression of Henry's militant Protestantism which also seemed a fit emblem for the young couple on whom so many religious and political hopes rested. The premier Earl of England, the Earl of Arundel, and his Countess were in attendance, along with Lord and Lady Harington, participating in the tumultuous welcome offered to the party in the Low Countries and in Heidelberg, where the entry was one of exceptional magnificence. The future of the Palsgrave Frederick seemed lustrous indeed: if the rather weak Prince Charles died, he would become King of England; an imperial destiny was possible within the Holy Roman Empire; in the event, he was invited to become King of Bohemia in 1619. No wonder then that prophecy played such a part in the entertainments presented to the couple. But ceremonial prophecy is by its nature optimistic, and no poet or dramatist foretold the catastrophe that followed on Frederick's acceptance of the Bohemian throne in 1619, nor could anyone foresee the invasion of the Palatinate in 1620, which turned Elizabeth and Frederick into the most distinguished refugees of the Thirty Years' War.

Notes to Chapter Four

1 John Taylor, 'Heaven's Blessing and Earth's Joy', 1613, printed in Nicols, *Progresses of King James*, 1828, vol. II, p. 529.

2 *Ibid.*, Vol. II, pp. 529–30.

3 The political consequences of the marriage matured a century later, when George I, who was descended from Elizabeth and Frederick, ascended the throne of Great Britain.

4 *The Works of Thomas Campion*, ed. W. Davis, New York 1970, p. 259.

5 *Ibid.*

6 *Ibid.* (translation from the Latin).

7 *The Plays and Poems of John Chapman*, ed. T. M. Parrott, London 1914, vol. II, p. 178.

8 For an altogether more admiring view of this masque, see D. J. Gordon's 'Chapman's *Memorable Masque*' in *The Renaissance Imagination*, Berkeley, Cal. 1975, where he explores the intellectual background to the work and makes a case for its inner coherence.

9 Francis Beaumont, *The Masque of the Inner Temple*, ll. 356–60, in *A Book of Masques*, ed. T. J. B. Spencer and S. Wells, Cambridge 1970.

10 See *Philaster*, ed. Andrew J. Gurr, The Revels Plays, London 1969, Introduction pp. xxvi–xxix, and li–lix.

11 The audience must have been moved by the unhappy coincidence of Prince Henry's death and the death of Mamilius, although the dramatic circumstances of *The Winter's Tale* had of course no counterpart in life.

12 Frances Yates, *Shakespeare's Last Plays: A New Approach*, London 1975, pp. 41–59. This book proposes a number of connections between the representation of hopeful children in the Last Plays and the members of the royal family.

13 *Henry VIII*, ed. R. A. Foakes, New Arden Edition, London 1958, Introduction, p. xxx.

14 *Ibid.*

15 The identity of the two Elizabeths is extensively elaborated in William Leigh's 'Queene Elizabeth Paralleled in her Princely Vertues', 1612, and emphasised in John King's 'A Sermon at Whitehall upon . . . the Marriage of the Lady Elizabeth', 1614. See also Robert Allen's 'Teares of Joy Shed at the Departure of . . . Fredericke and Elizabeth', 1613.

16 For the phoenix imagery associated with Queen Elizabeth, see Frances Yates, *Astraea*, London 1975, pp. 58–66.

17 The country became a nest of singing birds chanting spousal verses; the Oxford anthology, *Epithalamia sive Lusus Palatini* (Oxford 1613) alone contained 242 poems, but, as in the case of Prince Henry's death, little verse of merit appeared on this obligatory occasion. Anagrammatists as usual were busy discovering Elizabeth's destiny in her name: 'Elizabeth Stuart, Princesse—I secure best Palatine's rest' is the most conclusive of the revelations.

18 It is a measure of Princess Elizabeth's education that she habitually corresponded with her brother Henry in French, and with her father in French, Italian, and sometimes in English. Her relations with her husband were conducted in French.

19 See *The Autobiography of Phineas Pett*, ed. W. G. Perrin, London 1918, p. 104.

[5]
Thomas Howard, Earl of Arundel

By descent, Thomas Howard, Earl of Arundel, should have been Duke of Norfolk, but the title had been placed in abeyance when his grandfather was executed in 1572, accused of treason against Queen Elizabeth by plotting to bring in Mary, Queen of Scots. Thomas's father, Philip Howard, was consequently reduced in title to Earl of Surrey, until the death of his maternal grandfather in 1580 brought him the ancient title of Earl of Arundel. He did not long enjoy its honours or estates, for he soon fell heir to the Queen's traditional suspicion of his family, and he was imprisoned for much of his life on an unsubstantiated charge of treason. Under particularly oppressive conditions he maintained a resolute Catholic faith, so that his death in the Tower in 1595 was considered by his co-religionists as a species of martyrdom. Philip's wife, Anne Dacre, a northern heiress reduced to poverty by the forfeit of her estates to the Crown on religious grounds, was equally staunch in her Catholicism, offering protection to many clandestine Jesuit priests, including Robert Southwell and Father Gerard, in the rural mansions where she was obliged to live. In this secluded and strictly pious atmosphere, far in the country and deep in royal disfavour, she raised her son Thomas, who was born in 1585.

We know very little of his early years, until he presented himself at Court at the beginning of the new reign, with high hopes of favour from the son of the Queen whose cause had ruined Arundel's family and lost them their titles and estates. James received him cordially, confirmed him in his titles of Earl of Arundel and Surrey, but made no move to restore him to the Dukedom of Norfolk, nor did he offer to return the forfeited lands, allowing them rather to be absorbed by more powerful branches of the Howard family, the Earls of Northampton, Suffolk and Nottingham. None the less, as Earl of Arundel Thomas Howard ranked as premier Earl of England.[1] He consolidated his position by his marriage in 1606 to Aletheia Talbot, a daughter of Gilbert, Earl of Shrewsbury, grand-daughter of Bess of Hardwick, and god-daughter of Queen Elizabeth. Aletheia's two elder sisters were married to William, Earl of Pembroke, and to the Earl of Kent, and with them she was co-heiress to the Talbot fortune. Thus fortified by this new access of wealth and kindred, Arundel launched himself into Court life. We find him as one of the principal masquers in Jonson's *Hymenaei*, presented on 5 January 1606 to celebrate the marriage of the Earl of Essex to Frances Howard, Arundel's cousin, and thereafter for the next few years he participated actively in the entertainments at Court. Increasingly he was attracted into Prince Henry's circle, and from 1607 onwards he seems to have been in regular attendance on the Prince. Although there was a difference of nine years between them, their tastes and interests were very similar and it is probable that the older Arundel was instrumental in drawing out the artistic tastes of the young Prince, acting as a cultural mentor as well as a knightly companion.

One has the impression that Arundel found the sober and disciplined conditions surrounding Prince Henry much more sympathetic than James's busy and intriguing Court. Arundel's temperament was haughty and austere; his secluded upbringing and the consciousness of his high ancestry promoted a certain aloofness which intensified as he grew older. He had few close friends, and sought intellectual companionship rather than social conviviality. He was a man of integrity in a reign not noted for high principles at Court; he was a statesman rather than a politician, an aristocrat rather than a courtier. Even his dress marked his distance from his peers, for he is shown in all his portraits in sober and subdued clothes, or in plain armour, looking more like a Venetian senator than a Jacobean courtier. Clarendon, who was no friend to him, observed that

he was generally thought to be a proud man, who lived always within himself, and to himself, conversing little with any who were in common conversation; so that he seemed to live as it were in another Nation; . . . it cannot be denied that he had in his person, in his aspect and countenance, the appearance of a great man, which he preserved in his gate, and motion. He wore and affected a Habit very different from that of the time, such as men had only beheld in the Pictures of the most considerable Men; all which drew the eyes of most, and the reverence of many towards him, as the Image, and Representative of the Primitive Nobility, and Native Gravity of the Nobles, when they had been most Venerable.[2]

Such a man belonged naturally to the Court of Prince Henry; their friendship was close, and had the Prince lived, Arundel would doubtless have been one of his principal advisers.

The Earl of Arundel is generally considered to be the foremost connoisseur of the arts in Stuart England, but where did he acquire his knowledge and how did his tastes develop? One stimulus to his collecting must have come from his great-uncle, John Lord Lumley, who had inherited the great Tudor prodigy house Nonsuch Palace from his father-in-law, Henry Fitzalan, Earl of Arundel, and had turned it into the nearest approximation to an art gallery in Elizabethan England. Most of the collection consisted of portraits, and of these the great majority depicted the innumerable ramifications of Lumley's family tree;[3] others were of famous historical figures or notable contemporaries, but with a few exceptions the subjects were more important than the artists to Lord Lumley. The whole, however, formed a deliberate, organised and valued collection assembled with far greater care and intelligence than was evident in any other Elizabethan house. Lumley possessed several statues, of an unspecified nature, probably portrait busts; he also collected books on a scale exceptional in his age.[4] As the nearest surviving relative of Lord Lumley, Thomas Howard must have expected to inherit a good part of these collections, but when Lumley died in 1609 he left all his possessions to his second wife, who dispersed most of them over the years, and sold the library to Prince Henry, so that very few items eventually came into the hands of Lord Arundel, although she did leave him an important group of Holbein portraits, including Erasmus and Sir Thomas Wyatt. However, the existence of this large collection in a related branch of his family must have served to sharpen the Earl's sense of pleasure in the visual arts. The most decisive influence in the formation of his taste would appear to have been Inigo Jones. A virtually inescapable figure at Court because of his superintendence of the masques, Jones possessed a knowledge of modern Italian and French taste and theory in the arts that was almost unique in England in the first decade of the seventeenth century, and he was happy to communicate this knowledge to those who were willing and anxious to patronise. He had been trained as a painter, and now professed architecture; he had travelled widely in Europe. He had a strong intellectual and scholarly interest in the subjects he treated, not just a mechanical brilliance in invention. Jones would have been the only man capable of fostering and informing the range of taste developed by both Arundel and Prince Henry, and it would be plausible to imagine that Arundel as the elder of the two benefited first from Jones's experience.

In April 1613 Arundel was appointed to accompany Henry's sister, the Princess Elizabeth, back to Heidelberg after her marriage to the Elector Palatine. On this occasion we find Inigo Jones in his train, and once the formal duty of escorting the young couple to their home had been fulfilled, the Earl and Countess set off privately for Italy, with Jones as their companion. The combination was a potent one for the future of English taste in the arts, for this journey marked Arundel's growth to maturity as a connoisseur and confirmed his preference for the Italian manner, while it enabled Jones to study the ancient and modern buildings of Italy at first hand, furnishing himself with a working vocabulary of design that he would exploit for the rest of his career. The development of architecture in England during the seventeenth and eighteenth centuries, and the shape of the great collections of the English aristocracy, were conditioned by the results of this tour. It was the first time that an English nobleman had travelled to Italy explicitly to examine the art and architecture of the country, and on his return Arundel was to make full use of his new knowledge and his new acquisitions to establish an unprecedented style of living, a cultivated neo-classicism that was to be the forerunner of so many aristocratic life-styles in the eighteenth century. The party made for Venice, for a variety of reasons: the Venetian Republic was on friendly terms with Great Britain; there was a distinguished British ambassador in Venice in the person of Sir Dudley Carleton, who could provide competently for their reception; within the state lay Padua, whose medicinal waters had already benefited the Earl in 1612 when he had made a journey there to recover his health (he suffered from consumption in his younger years); most significantly of all, the state of Venice contained the finest buildings by the leading modern architects of Italy (Palladio, Sansovino and Scamozzi), and the glories of the sixteenth-century Venetian school of painters, dominated by Titian, Tintoretto, Giorgione and Veronese, were still fresh and radiant in the city itself. The Arundels were splendidly received by the Doge and Senate in a series of banquets and festivals, after which they retired into private life to pursue their own interests, inspecting the buildings and visiting the collections of the great families.

As far as buildings were concerned, Andrea Palladio (1508–80) was the definitive exponent of modernism, and his book, *I Quattro Libri dell' Archi-tettura* (1560), was the most luminous architectural treatise of its age, and one that was to have immense influence on architecture in England and in America, in subsequent centuries. Inigo Jones kept a diary in his own copy of this work (now in the Library of Worcester College, Oxford), and from it we learn that by 23 September 1613 he and the Arundels had reached Vicenza, the *locus classicus* of Palladianism. Palladio's architecture, based on the study and measurement of ancient Roman models and guided by the principles set down by Vitruvius in the first century A.D., was one of the last expressions of Renaissance humanism in Italy. It emphasised the supreme importance of symmetry and the harmony of proportions, proportions that were related on the one hand to the ideal dimensions of the human figure, and on the other to the fundamental mathematical ratios established both by the division of the musical scale and by the spacing of the planets, so that a Palladian building represented a statement in stone of basic cosmic harmonies related to the human frame, dressed in the dignity of the Roman orders, and serving a social function. Palladio, like other Renaissance architects before him, mixed antiquarian research and revival with a philosophical argument justifying architecture as the supreme union of the arts and sciences, a revelation (to the initiated) of platonic ideas ordered into a formal structure by mathematical discipline. His practice was so assured, so varied, so versatile, so lively in fact, that his appeal was irresistible. Vicenza then as now was an exhibition ground and seminary of architectural ideas: palaces, villas, loggias, a basilica, and the superb Teatro Olimpico were all to be found within the circuit of this small town. The adaptability of Palladio's style was remarkable, and the impact of this serene and noble Italian modernism on Jones and Arundel, used as they were to the gothic jumble of London, must have been overwhelming. Some of the notes that Jones made seem to have been intended to catch Arundel's imagination and cause him to build in a grand signorial fashion at home: for example, 'On the piaza, over against ye Bassilica is the Captaynes house and a great lodge, the room aboufe this lodge is adorned with Paintings in ye roofe of Paulo Verro; and there is a small cornish for ye hangings, another payntedd, betweene which ar armor, halbards and suchlyke, aboufe quadros paynted.'⁵ The Englishmen were even able to purchase some of Palladio's drawings and designs from his pupil Scamozzi, whom they met in Venice, and who also sold them a large number of his own drawings. The great tradition was so near at hand that one can understand why Jones felt himself to be a vital extension of it when he returned home.

From the Veneto the party moved south to Florence and Siena. Florence seems to have made remarkably little impression on them, for there is scarcely any reference to the town and its treasures in Arundel's letters or in Jones's notes. The great attraction was Rome itself, where they spent the winter of 1613–14, even though the city at this time was out of bounds for English travellers, as the city of Anti-Christ and the source of so much political and religious enmity to England. The licence to travel, which was the Englishman's permit to leave his country, specifically excluded Rome from his peregrinations. There was a small community of Englishmen in Rome, almost entirely Roman Catholics who had gone to the source of their faith, and anyone who went there was automatically suspected of un-English activities. Since the Howards had been a notoriously Catholic family, their presence in Rome was disturbing to Carleton, the ambassador in Venice, part of whose function was to report back on the movements of his countrymen in Italy. He wrote to London:

The Earle of Arundel and his Lady have spent many days in [Rome]: which I could not believe uppon advertisements from thence, until I had spoken with some who had seen them there. I heare of no English who did much resort unto them but Toby Mathew and George Gage, neither of any course they took for other purpose than the satisfying of curiosity; yet the quality of their persons being so much above other travellers, I held it my duty to give this advertisement.[6]

Mathew and Gage were both zealous Catholics, but they were also lovers of art who later acted as agents for Arundel and Buckingham, so we may assume that their meetings were cultural, not seditious; still, it was obviously difficult for Carleton to be entirely sure that the Arundels were in Rome for its art and not its religion. The avid pursuit of antiquities was the real justification for their presence there, and it proceeded with visits to the ruins, where Jones filled a sketchbook with drawings and notes on the buildings, and compared the engravings in books he had bought with the original subjects. Here, as in Vicenza, Jones undertook a systematic study of architecture in all its parts that was to ensure the thorough command of classical forms that would distinguish his constructions in England. Arundel's enthusiasm led him to obtain a licence to dig and to begin his own excavations, an unprecedented activity for an Englishman. He was rewarded by the discovery of a number of statues, of some Roman consular family, apparently, which he had crated up and sent back to England. From this time dates the Earl's lifelong passion for classical statuary, a taste which he introduced into England. As Henry Peacham wrote in his *Compleat Gentleman* in 1634, 'To [his] liberal charges and magnificence, this angle of the world oweth its first sight of Greeke and Roman Statues, with whose admired presence he began to honour the Gardens and Galleries of Arundel House about twentie yeares agoe, and hath ever since continued to transplant old Greece into England.'[7] The Italian custom of adorning noblemen's palaces with antique statues conferred a prestigious distinction on their owners which must have impressed him, and in England, where Roman literature and history formed such an important part of a gentleman's education, the sight of original Roman sculpture, in contrast to the slightly languid and mannered figures that passed for Roman sculptures in the engraved title-pages of Elizabethan books, was to bring a new force and clarity to Englishmen's understanding of the ancient world.[8]

After Rome, Arundel's party continued on to Naples, where they visited more temples. They returned to Rome via Tivoli and Trevi, when Arundel was summoned home by the death of his great-uncle, the Earl of Northampton, who had willed him his great house at Greenwich and much land besides. While Jones made a final visit to Venice and Vicenza, the Earl resumed his full state, and proceeded home via Turin and Paris, arriving in London in November 1614, having spent nineteen months abroad.

Not surprisingly, the Earl soon embarked on a programme of building, under Inigo Jones's supervision. Extensive alterations were made to the Greenwich house, of which we know nothing, as it burnt down in 1617; the reconstruction that interests us took place at Arundel House, situated between the river and the Strand, to the east of Somerset House. This had been the London seat of the Bishops of Bath and Wells, acquired by the Earls of Arundel in the sixteenth century, lost under Elizabeth, and regained by Thomas Howard in 1607. It was a typical late medieval complex of courtyards, halls and lodgings, which are preserved for us in Hollar's engravings of the 1630s. Arundel now added an extension unique of its kind in England, a long two-storied gallery leading down to the Thames, designed by Inigo Jones and built on purpose to contain the Earl's collections, the statuary on the upper floor, the paintings on the lower. Two companion paintings by Daniel Mytens from 1618 (now in the collection of the Duke of Norfolk) provide the only surviving views: the Earl, soberly dressed in a furred gown, wearing the George and Garter, turns his long dispassionate, aristocratic face to the viewer, and points with his marshal's baton into the sculpture gallery, an elegant, restrained hall, styled completely in an early sixteenth-century Italian manner, open at the far end where an arch leads through to a balcony over the river. The statues, raised on plinths, include public figures, a Diana, a Minerva and a cupid, and appear to be of excellent quality. The Countess is seen sitting before the lower gallery, which is lined with portraits and which leads out into a formal garden terminating in a pergola. These two paintings present the Arundels as a new type of Englishman, able to invite comparison with the sophisticated cognoscenti of the continental aristocracy.

The building activities that followed Arundel's return from Italy were made possible by the extra income from the Northampton legacy, and by the demise in 1616 of Lady Arundel's father the Earl of Shrewsbury, whereupon a great inheritance flowed in to her. The Earl's income was now some £25,000 annually. The year 1616 was a good one for the collections also, for the Earl of Somerset, condemned for his part in the Overbury murder, was required to forfeit his paintings (including works by Tintoretto and Veronese, a Titian, and drawings by Leonardo), which King James then presented to the Arundels. At the time of his disgrace, Somerset had also been in the process of arranging a purchase of Venetian paintings from Sir Dudley Carleton, which Carleton now offered to Arundel, who bought all twelve. Carleton also made him a gift of an antique head of Jupiter, in a gesture that was clearly meant to strengthen his connections with the Earl to ensure his advancement when he returned to political life in England. (The very fact that Somerset had a collection of paintings at all is a sign that leading courtiers were now expected to profess an interest in the arts; a decade earlier this would have been unlikely, but the example of Prince Henry and Arundel had worked an enduring change, so that even an uncultivated upstart like Somerset felt obliged to conform to the rising taste.) In this same year too, Lord Roos, the grandson of Lord Burleigh, left England on a mission to Spain and gave Arundel the statues he had just brought back from Italy.

The Arundel Collection was building up fast, money was coming in to support and expand it, while the Earl's star rose higher at Court. In July he was made a member of the Privy Council, and in preparation for the creation of Prince Charles as Prince of Wales in November 1616, the Earl was restored to the office of Earl Marshal of England, which had been hereditary in the Norfolk branch of the Howard family, and which entitled him to preside over all the chivalric ceremonies of the Court.⁹ The year ended with the Earl receiving Holy Communion in the King's chapel at Christmas. This significant gesture declared to all his adherence to the Church of England, and settled for good any suspicions of his allegiance to Catholicism. In fact, Arundel's religion had hitherto been invisible. His letters reveal him as a man who possessed a personal piety, undifferentiated by creed. Though his upbringing was Catholic, as was his wife's, their children were baptised into the established Church; he did not frequent Catholic chapels, nor did he often associate with known Catholics; indeed, his friendship with Prince Henry would have been inconceivable if he had displayed Catholic sympathies. His Italian journey had taken him to Rome but not into the Roman Church. His secretary Edward Walker wrote of him that 'he was in Religion no bigot or Puritan, and professed more to affect moral virtues than nice questions and controversies'.¹⁰ It is probably fair to say that he regarded theological entanglements with indifference, and maintained the central Christian beliefs in harmony with a strictness of conduct that amounted to a form of Christian Stoicism. One would imagine that his acceptance of the Anglican communion represented an act of allegiance to the Crown rather than to the Church, for he owed much to King James, and remained always a firm monarchist.

Collecting was one aspect of Arundel's career as a connoisseur, patronage was another: in keeping with the princely nature of his regime, he sought to create art as well as collect it. In 1618 he brought over the Dutch artist Daniel Mytens, who executed several portraits of the Earl before passing into the service of the King. More important for the future of English painting, Arundel was making attempts to attract Van Dyck from Antwerp, and late in 1620 the painter arrived in London. Although he came to England under Arundel's auspices, Van Dyck was rapidly taken up by the King and given a pension, but he then left the country, apparently to perfect his manner in Italy. He was not to return until 1632. Contact with Van Dyck may first have come about through the Countess, who had sat for her portrait to Rubens, Van Dyck's master, early in 1620 when she had passed through Antwerp.[11] Her meeting with Rubens resulted in the first portrait of an English subject by that master, an indication of the English slowness to establish relations with the major painters of the age. Rubens celebrated the Countess in his finest baroque manner: she is seated before an Italianate baldacchino, attended by jester, dwarf and dog, at the centre of a world charged with energy. The swirl of twisted columns, the billowing of the cloth of state, the rippling muscles of the dog, the flow of the Countess's gown all project the characteristic grand animation of Rubens's vision of nobility. The contrast between this painting of 1620 and Mytens's 1618 portrait of the Countess seated before her picture gallery, formal, grave and static, marks a significant advance in English taste, and we may remember that Mytens himself, with his sophisticated poses and his command of perspective, represented a great advance on the stilted manner of early Jacobean portraiture. Once again, the Arundels stood in the vanguard of new values in art. Rubens did not come to England until 1629, upon a diplomatic mission touching peace between England and Spain, when he was much in the company of Arundel, and an admiring visitor to the galleries. The King took advantage of his presence to commission the designs for the ceiling of the Banqueting House, but there was also time for Rubens to paint the Earl of Arundel in full armour—a reminder that the arts of peace were not the exclusive concern of England's foremost nobleman.

Rubens professed himself amazed at the richness of the Earl's collections, with every justification, since they were indeed outstanding. We may advance a little, and assess the contents by means of the inventory drawn up in Amsterdam in 1655, after the death of the Countess there, when the collections had already declined from their zenith through sale and the hazards of exile.[12] Some six hundred paintings are listed, almost entirely from the Italian, German, Flemish and Dutch schools, consisting mostly of portraits and religious and mythological subjects, landscapes being scarcely represented at all. (Landscape had a low intellectual status in England in the seventeenth century, as it lacked the moral elevation and instruction that history, religion or mythology offered.) The collection was dominated by the

Venetian painters, and by Holbein. According to the 1655 inventory—which of course reflects a mid-seventeenth-century view of attributions, many of which would now be considered excessively optimistic—there were some thirty-six paintings by Titian, nineteen Tintorettos, seventeen Veroneses, sixteen paintings attributed to Giorgione, a dozen or so Raphaels, eleven Correggios, and a remarkable twenty-five pieces by Parmigianino, five Leonardos (including a Leda and a Beheading of St John) and forty-three paintings by Holbein. Holbein had painted many of the Howards in the great days of their political ascendancy in the reign of Henry VIII, so there may well have been an element of family sentiment in Arundel's fondness for his work. We get a glimpse of these works in their original setting, and a sense of the intense pleasure they occasioned, from the German connoisseur and painter Joachim von Sandrart, who visited England in 1627 and was made welcome at Arundel House:

From the garden one passed into the long gallery of the house; where the superlative excellence of the works of Hans Holbein of Basel, held the master's place. . . .

The far-famed Earl of Arundel, who spared neither gold nor silver if anything by Holbein was to be had, brought together a whole gallery of paintings by that master; as well as complete books of his sketches. . . . The Earl . . . showed him in addition, several times, a very small book, likewise executed by this noble hand, containing on twenty-two pages the whole story of the Passion. Here again, all was carried out as finely and carefully as in pure miniature. Amongst other things, the figure of the Redeemer was each time introduced in the form of a monk habited in black. On one occasion, when discussing this book with the Knight Inigo Jones . . ., the King's famous architect, he conducted Sandrart to the King's Cabinet, where he showed him, amongst other things, a book full of the designs of this artist in pen and ink.[13]

It is details like these that persuade us that Arundel was a genuinely knowledgeable collector, who did not simply collect art for the status and distinction it conferred (as, one suspects, did Buckingham), but who had a close working sense of the masterpieces he possessed, who understood the difficulties and achievements of artists, and took pleasure in studying technique and in discussing the beauties and rarities of his collection with practising artists as well as with gentlemen connoisseurs. Rubens, who had come to know him well, called him 'one of the four evangelists, and a great upholder of our art'. A telling sign of his serious appreciation of art was his great collection of old master drawings. Drawings appeal strongly to the private pleasure of the possessor: they are not for ostentatious display or for public advertisement; they allow one to trace the quick workings of the imagination at first hand and they show the flurry and thought of experiment out of which the deliberate work emerges; they enable one to enjoy the mastery of technique in a fragment, in a mere outline of a hand or face; they hold a vision that often fades in the finished piece. To collect drawings with the passion that Arundel did is to know about art from the inside and to respond to its creative energies. We have seen how he acquired the architectural drawings of Palladio and Scamozzi. These were merely a beginning. He also possessed some incomparable Holbeins, several drawings by Raphael and a distinguished group of sketches by Parmigianino. The volume of Leonardo drawings now at Windsor was once in Arundel's hands. Perhaps the greatest genius with a pen or pencil was Dürer, to acquire whose works the Earl was almost willing to bankrupt his posterity. In later years he became an ardent hunter of Dürers, and on his embassy to the Emperor in Germany in 1636 he was haunted by dreams of what he might discover as he passed through the towns where Dürer had worked.

Arundel certainly knew the pleasures of the chase. His principal agents in the search for paintings and antiquities, the Rev. William Petty and Sir Thomas Roe, were people of the first importance to him. Roe went out to Constantinople as Ambassador in 1621, and just as Arundel had taken every care to use Sir Dudley Carleton's position in Venice to his own advantage, so now he cultivated Roe, urging him to search for Greek statues, inscriptions and manuscripts. Roe himself knew relatively little of such subjects, but was very willing to bend his attention to his patron's requests. Greece of course was under Turkish domination at the time, and virtually unexplored in the matter of antiquities. Roe quickly put a man in the field on the Earl's behalf, and was soon able to report:

Concerning antiquities in marbles, there are many in divers parts, but especially at Delphos, unesteemed here; and, I doubt not, easy to be procured for the charge of digging and fetching, which must be purposely undertaken. It is supposed that many statues are buried, to secure them from the envy of the Turks; and that, if leave obteyned, would come to light, which I will endeavour as soon as I am warme here.

Coynes will be had from Jewes, but very deare when enquired for. Two are given me by Dominico to present to your Lordship, which I have delivered to Antony Wood, captain of the Rainbow; the one gold, is of Alexander; the other is brasse, and very antient, of a Queen of Servia, with hieroglyphicks now unknowne. I have also a stone taken out of the old pallace of Priam in Troy, cutt in horned shape: but because I neither can tell of what it is, nor hath it any other bewty, but only the antiquity and truth of being a peece of that ruined and famous building, I will not presume to send it you; yet I have delivered it to the same messenger, that your Lordship may see it and throw it away.

At Scio I found divers rare peeces of white corall, the gatherings of a dead English Gentleman, in the hands of our Consull; which, because I thought they would well affect you for: fountaines (your Lordship's curiosity being unlimitted) I advised him to send, which I think you shall receive by this shipping. What other services I can doe your Lordship, I will not fail.[14]

By 1624 the Duke of Buckingham was beginning to use Roe for identical purposes; to counter this formidable competition, Arundel sent out his trusted and knowledgeable servant, William Petty, who was one of his chaplains, and whose piety was less in evidence than his skill in charming works of art from their resting places. He it was who suggested prising the ancient statues from the Golden Gate at Constantinople, causing Sir Thomas Roe as Ambassador a world of trouble in bribes and cajolery before the operation was stopped by popular discontent, as the statues had a superstitious significance regarding the city's fate. Roe's letters to the Earl are full of Mr Petty's adventures as he journeyed round the coasts of Turkey and Greece:

Mr Petty hath advised mee, that retorning from Samos, where hee had gotten many things, going to Ephesus by sea, hee made shippwrack in a great storme upon the coast of Asia; and, saving his owne life, lost both all his collection of that voiadge, and his commands and letters by mee procured, desiring mee to send him others, or else, that hee can proceed no further. Hee was putt in prison for a spy, having lost in the sea all his testimonyes; but was released by the witness of Turks that knew him. From thence he recovered Scio, where hee furnished himselfe againe; and is gone to the place where hee left his boate to fish for the marbles, in hope to find them, and from thence to Ephesus; and this is the last newes I heard from him.[15]

and again:

I am informed hee hath gotten many things rare and antient. Ther was never man so fitted to an imployment, that encounters all accidents with so unwearied patience; eates with Greekes on their worst dayes; lyes with fishermen on plancks, at the best; is all things to all men, that he may obteyne his ends, which are your lordships service. He is gone to Athens, whither also I have sent; and from thence promiseth mee to visitt this citty, wher I shalbee glad to enterteyne him, and to know the history of his labours. . . . I have sent three servants togither to Tassos, Cavalla, Philippi, and all the coast of Thrace; followed Mr Petty to Pergamo, and Troy; am digging in Asya; and to fulfill the proverb, turning of all stones. Somwhat I hope to gett, to save my creditt; but I dare not write to his grace untill I am in possession; so often I have beene by Greekish promise deceived.[16]

Books too fell into Mr Petty's cunning hand. Roe laments in a letter to the Archbishop of Canterbury that

Mr Petty, a woorthy gentleman and learned, employed hither by my lord of Arundell for antiquities, by my meanes had admittance into the best library knowne of Greece, where are loades of old manuscripts; and he used so fine arte, with the helpe of some of my servants, that hee conveyed away 22. I thought I should have had my share, but hee was for himselfe: hee is a good chooser, saw all, or most, and tooke, I thincke, those that were, and wilbe of greate esteeme. Hee speaketh sparingly of such a bootye, but could not conteyne some time to discover, with joy, his treasure. Historyes some, Ephraim and Manasseth, two Greeke fathers, Phocion, Eusebius, and some other names that I have forgott. When hee returnes, I make no doubt he will communicate, and contribute to the publique good; for I esteeme him a woorthy man. I meant to have a review of that library; but hee gave it such a blow, under my trust, that since it hath beene locked up under two keys, wherof one kept by the townsmen that have interest or oversight of the monastery.[17]

Ephesus, Pergamon, Troy, Corinth, Samos, Scio: the long tentacles of Arundel's curiosity touch them all. English voices are heard on the classical sites; the crude excavations that prefigure centuries of archaeological activity begin. Arundel was far ahead of his time in combing Greece and the eastern Mediterranean for classical statuary, for it would not be until the late eighteenth century that English collectors would begin to explore that part of the world for works of art. His adventurousness was well rewarded: much of the statuary unearthed in the east was authentically Hellenistic, rather than Roman work, and of a high quality. Besides several fine torsos and busts, the finds included part of the frieze from the Great Altar of Pergamon, an altar dedicated to Hermes and Demeter, and the head of a bronze statue of a poet, a work of magisterial power, known as the 'Arundel Homer' and now in the British Museum.

Even at this stage there is a certain intelligence present, for Arundel was as much interested in antique inscriptions as in statues, and specifically charged his agents to look out for them. Roe remarked that Buckingham wanted only intact statuary, but the Earl found fragments valuable because they had a partial beauty that his mind could perceive as well as his eye: this sensitivity, like his fondness for drawings, points to a more sophisticated taste than his contemporaries possessed. Roe was able to cheer Buckingham in 1626 with the news that 'Mr Petty hath raked together 200 pieces, all broken, or few entire'.[18] When the marbles bore inscriptions, Arundel was alert to their scholarly value, that one inscribed stone might be worth a gross of battered statues. Just after Christmas 1627 a major consignment of marbles gathered by Mr Petty arrived at Arundel House. Sir Robert Cotton the antiquary was extremely excited by them and by the Greek inscriptions they bore; he rushed off to his friend John Selden, the master of ancient tongues, and urged him to begin the work of translation at once. Selden was fired by the idea, gathered two learned friends, Patrick Young, the King's Librarian, and Richard James, and together they met next day at dawn to begin the decipherment.

The result of this activity was Selden's *Marmora Arundelliana*, published in 1628, an account of the inscriptions which attempted to establish their historical context. It was the first direct study of classical archaeological material by an Englishman, a notable piece of scholarship for its time. Written in Latin, it spread the fame and importance of Arundel's collections around Europe and enhanced his reputation for eminence in the world of learning, a reputation that he was anxious to establish.

The Earl deliberately gathered learned men around him, and his friends, who were principally antiquarians, included the leading scholars of the age. Selden, 'that great living library of learning', was one of the most intimate: his prodigious abilities encompassed Roman and British history (in his annotations to Drayton's *Poly-Olbion*), genealogy and heraldry (in *Titles of Honor*), religious history and canonical law (in *A History of Tithes*), comparative religion and philology (in *De Dis Syriis*), Greek and Roman epigraphy (in *Marmora Arundelliana*), and English and international law and jurisprudence. Sir Robert Cotton was another friend whose scholarly temperament harmonised with the Earl's. Cotton owned the finest private library in England, one especially rich in charters and Anglo-Saxon and medieval manuscripts; he was a philologist, a historian, an Anglo-Saxon scholar and a numismatist, as well as being, like Selden, a leading Parliamentarian. A generation older than these men was William Camden, the greatest of the Elizabethan historians, and the true progenitor of antiquarian studies in England. As Headmaster of Westminster School, he would have taught Cotton and also Arundel, who seems to have received part of his education there.[19] Their friendship continued until Camden's death in 1623. Then there was William Lisle, who was a pioneer in Anglo-Saxon studies, a subject he had entered into in order to learn the doctrinal position of the Saxon Church. He published a number of bilingual texts that did much to help the revival of Old English, which was essential to the research of this group of men, interested as they all were in the early history of Britain. Another outstanding scholar closely associated with Arundel was Francis Junius. He was a native of Heidelberg, and had studied under the philologist Vossius; he developed into a brilliant student of Anglo-Saxon and the Teutonic languages. Arundel became his patron, offering him the post of Librarian at Arundel House, where Junius pursued his researches indefatigably, reputedly working from 4 a.m. to 8 p.m. with a two-hour break for food and recreation. Junius shared his patron's love of painting, too, although in a characteristically scholarly way, and published in 1637 an account of painting in the classical world, *De Pictura Veterum*, which he translated as *The Painting of the Ancients*. He also asserted in this book the humanist dimension of the artist's profession, to which he ascribed considerable philosophic stature. In his early years with the Arundels, Junius acted as tutor to the children, and he remained close to the family for some forty years, ultimately going with them into exile. Henry Peacham, man of letters, minor artist and even lesser poet, also served as tutor in the household, and his much reprinted *Compleat Gentleman* must reflect the cultivated pattern of life at Arundel House. Also enjoying the Earl's friendship and patronage were Sir Henry Spelman, a specialist in Church history and ecclesiastical law, William Oughtred, the foremost mathematician of Stuart England, and William Harvey, who was Arundel's physician. The Earl employed the Venetian Francesco Vercellini as his Italian Secretary, who dealt with his Italian correspondence, and who was a connoisseur of the arts in his own right. And of course Inigo Jones was in frequent attendance. Culture and scholarship made all these people welcome to the Earl, who was much more accessible to intellectuals than to politicians, and the presence of such men made Arundel House a centre of advanced learning in London, a miniature academy in effect with its own library and collections.

The death of King James in 1625 brought to an end the prosperous phase of Arundel's public career. It seems strange that Charles, who shared many of Arundel's tastes, should not have continued the friendship begun by his father. The Duke of Buckingham may well have had a role to play in this alienation, for his influence strengthened in the new reign, and he and Arundel were mutually antagonistic. In 1626 the King's coolness towards the Earl hardened into active hostility when Arundel's eldest son, Lord Maltravers, secretly married Lady Elizabeth Stuart, thus thwarting Charles's own plans for her. Unjustly holding Arundel responsible for this marriage, Charles sent him to the Tower and deprived him of his regular apartments at Court. The House of Lords soon exerted pressure to release him, but it was not until mid-1628 that Arundel was received back into royal favour. By 1632 he had regained his place in public life, and was appointed by Charles to an Embassy to Holland to escort home the recently-widowed Queen of Bohemia.

In 1636 a far more important mission was entrusted to him: the Earl was chosen by King Charles to undertake an Embassy to the Emperor Ferdinand to try to persuade him and the Imperial Electors, who were due to meet at the Diet of Ratisbon, not to ratify the treaty of Prague which would confirm the Duke of Bavaria in the possession of the Upper Palatinate which he had seized from Frederick, Elector Palatine, King Charles's brother-in-law, in 1623. Frederick had died in exile in 1632, and his widow Elizabeth, naturally but unrealistically, hoped that she could claim the Palatinate for her eldest son. The probability of a Catholic Emperor denying the claims of a Catholic duke to the Palatinate in favour of a young Protestant prince, after some fifteen years of religious warfare, was nil. Charles, too impoverished to field an army in support of his sister's claims, resorted to the futile expedient of diplomacy and Arundel was dispatched on the unrewarding mission. For him, the compensation was the opportunity to prospect for works of art along the route, and to see the great Imperial collections in Vienna and Prague.

The journey began well: a particular stroke of good fortune enabled him in Nuremberg in May 1636 to buy the famous Pirckheimer Library, which had been created by Willibald Pirckheimer, the wealthy Renaissance humanist who was a lifelong friend of Albrecht Dürer and who had helped to form the artist's interests in the Greek and Roman classics, in philosophy and archaeology. Dürer himself helped to buy books for Pirckheimer in Italy. He had provided illustrations to Pirckheimer's own writings, and had illuminated many of the books in the library, as well as providing them with portrait miniatures, emblematic designs and engraved bookplates.[20] This, then, was the library of a learned humanist and scholar, who had been educated in Italy and had developed an exceptional breadth of taste; it was full of very early printed editions, which are amongst the most beautiful of books, and also contained valuable manuscript material. By the time of Arundel's visit to Nuremberg, the library had come into the hands of an indifferent descendent, Hans Imhoff, who was anxious to sell in the hard times of the Thirty Years War. He wrote that his advisers 'recommended to take the good opportunity, which may never repeat again' and to sell to the Earl. They pointed out that the library was very old, many of the books, especially the manuscripts, illegible, and that such books were available either in new editions or in better ones, much easier to read than 'the uncomfortable' old books and of far greater contemporary use.[21] Arundel bought the library for the very low price of 330 thaler, with Imhoff lamenting at the formidable bargaining power of the Earl. In his confidential letters to Petty, Arundel does not mention the deal, and it is quite possible that in the hasty circumstances of the purchase he was not aware of the full scope of the treasures he had bought. Given his passion for Dürer, he must have been overwhelmed when he eventually examined the books in London to discover that he had become the owner of at least eight books with illustrations by the master (mostly Italian incunabula of Greek texts); in addition there were some autograph letters from Dürer to Pirckheimer and a fragment of his diary covering his journey to the Low Countries. Arundel also bought the copperplate of Dürer's etching of Pirckheimer. Amongst the manuscripts was one of the book of Genesis which Francis Junius estimated to be 'the oldest Greek manuscript in England, and perhaps in Europe',[22] now in the British Museum.[23] Later in the journey, the Bishop of Würtzberg unexpectedly presented Arundel with a Dürer madonna. This windfall of items by Dürer was augmented shortly after Arundel's return home to

England when Daniel Mytens, who was now acting as an agent for Arundel in the Low Countries, put him in the way of six books by Dürer which appear to have been volumes of manuscripts and drawings. Arundel had very rapidly become a major collector of Dürer.

In Cologne, the Earl invited into his service the Bohemian artist Wenceslaus Hollar, who would soon be the principal illustrator of the treasures of the Arundel Collection, and who would also become the most memorable recorder of the landscapes, towns and society of seventeenth-century England. Hollar was an etcher of considerable brilliance who had left his native Prague some nine years previously, and had worked as an illustrator for various German publishers before he had the good fortune to join Arundel's household. He had built up a modest reputation as a topographical artist, specialising in the long panoramic views of cities and landscapes that he had learnt from Matthew Merian, the Frankfurt engraver and publisher whose books and prints of European towns were widely circulated and much prized. But Hollar personally had a great admiration for Dürer, and his technique as a draughtsman and water-colourist owed a great deal to Dürer; it may well have been this quality in his work that attracted Arundel's attention, for one can well imagine him patronising an artist in that tradition. Hollar immediately became the visual recorder of the expedition, producing a long series of watercolours of the embassy's journey down the Rhine, one of the most sensitive and attractive groups of landscapes of the century.[24]

Through the peaceful scenes of the Rhineland we see the English mission in their broad barges, looking like miniature Noah's arks, drifting slowly down the river, flying the flag of St George for safe passage, the low roofs of the cabins crowded with curious Englishmen gazing at the strangeness of the German landscape. Past the spiky medieval villages and squat fortresses, past ornate palaces and high-roofed monasteries they drift, sometimes lavishly received, sometimes rebuffed, and sleeping mostly on board their barges. But the tranquil scenes that Hollar records offer no sense of the devastation and misery that prevailed in so many of these towns after years of war. The destruction of vineyards and harvests, and grim weather, had produced a famine so great that cannibalism had become endemic in the region.[25] The relief that the Earl distributed was often a cause of minor riots as starving mobs fought for the food. William Crowne, a young gentleman in the Ambassador's retinue, kept a diary of the mission's journey which he published in 1637 and which contains some harrowing descriptions of the conditions in the towns they passed through, including dying populations, bodies scraped out of graves for food, and the omnipresent threat of murder and plague. On one occasion he records how meat for the Earl's supper was cooked one night in the burning remains of a house, which next day they discovered had been set on fire because it harboured the plague. Near Nuremberg, two of Arundel's attendants were abducted and savagely murdered.[26] In such circumstances the Earl's perseverance in making excursions to palaces and churches where paintings and curiosities might be seen or even bought amounted to exceptional bravery in the cause of art.

The Earl met with the Emperor twice, at Linz and at Ratisbon (now Regensburg). He was most courteously welcomed, but he received no satisfaction for the English proposals concerning the Palatinate, only an elaborate dismissal. Between the two meetings he chose to spend the time in travel from Linz to Vienna along the Danube, then to Prague, the old Imperial capital, and finally to Augsburg. The viewing of the Emperor Rudolph's immense collections at Prague must have been the cultural peak of the whole journey. With the exception of the Vatican, the palace at Prague was the greatest treasure house in the world, with an incomparable gallery of paintings, particularly strong in the sixteenth-century artists of Italy and the North, and with a remarkable array of cabinets of curiosities containing those 'objects of virtù' so dear to the collectors of the late Renaissance: elaborately wrought articles of gold and silver, precious stones, natural wonders, monstrosities and oddities, astronomical instruments, decorated armour from many countries. Rudolph had a passion for fantastic clocks which he collected, commissioned or designed and which clearly fascinated the English party, for Crowne describes them at some length in his diary. Against all these wonders, the strange beauty of the new world provided a memorable contrast, for the Holy Roman Emperors had been the recipients of many gifts from the Americas. The sheer indiscriminate, exhilarating variety of Rudolph's collections represented the culmination of an older tradition, whereas a stricter principle of taste governed the Earl's collecting habits: greater connoisseurship within a narrower range, more sophistication and refinement. He was assembling a collection in the modern sense, in comparison with which the imperial collection was more like a museum.[27]

All the time the negotiations were going on with the Emperor, Arundel was thinking about his collections, maintaining contact with his agents, writing in particular to Mr Petty in Rome, urging him to acquire certain statues, and trying unsuccessfully to make arrangements for the purchase of a fallen obelisk in the Circus Maxentius, the same obelisk that Bernini would later use as the centre-piece to his fountain in the Piazza Navona. He also added another painter to his train, Henry van der Borcht, primarily a portrait painter, whom he now sent to Italy to study and improve his art by acquaintance with the best models, and to acquire judgement of paintings under Petty's direction. 'I will have him only attend to design well, and be bred to see and observe paintings and designs well, that he might be fit another day to take to our pictures and collection of designs at Arundel House, he being apt to love and understand matters of art.'[28]

The aesthetic fruits of Arundel's embassy to Germany became evident after his return to England at Christmas 1636. The latest accessions gave a new richness to the collection, which the Earl now felt was sufficiently important to be described to European cognoscenti. Hollar was set to work to etch its masterpieces with a view to publishing an illustrated account of the paintings—a primitive sort of catalogue, in fact, that would extend the fame of the collections, enlarging on the fame that Selden's book had already brought to the marbles. In the next few years Hollar produced a stream of etchings of the Earl's pictures, each with the little motto 'ex collectione Arundellianiae' neatly written at the bottom of the print. The Holbeins were the most prominent. Although they were never made up into a book, these prints must have circulated widely and in large numbers, to judge by the quantity that have survived. Engraving was a compendious way of transmitting knowledge of paintings, and Hollar's scrupulously etched prints must have benefited many gentlemen in England and abroad by introducing them to inaccessible works of art and by enabling them to form an inexpensive collection of reproductions for their own pleasure and instruction. In 1600, let us say, there would have been no demand for such matters amongst educated Englishmen, but the growing exposure to continental culture by travel, the cultivation of the arts in the peaceful and superficially prosperous reign of James, and the example so successfully given by the Earl of Arundel himself had created a climate in which taste for the fine arts was becoming an expected part of a gentleman's education.

In the cultivated atmosphere of Arundel House Hollar had time to follow his natural inclination towards topographical art, and he began to draw and etch those distinctive views of London which provide the finest record of what the city looked like before the Great Fire. In 1637 he published a magnificent panorama of Greenwich, which marked an epoch in the art of this country, for it was the first mature English landscape piece. Hollar was effectively the originator of the landscape tradition in England. In a country where painting was almost synonymous with portraiture, landscape had scarcely existed except as a rudimentary background for figure painting. Some few artists, usually Flemish or Dutch, had indeed made forays into the English scene—painters such as Antonius van den Wyngaerde, Joris Hofnagel, or Claude de Jongh—but their occasional compositions were not sufficiently numerous to create a tradition. Nor was there much demand amongst English gentlemen for landscape compositions: we have seen how few there were in Arundel's collection, for example. Hollar, however, had been trained in an important European topographical tradition, and in the course of his long residence here, and with his responsiveness to the character of the country, he was able to establish the genre and help create an enduring taste for landscape here by means of a long succession of varied prospects in a mature and sensitive style, of which Greenwich was the first. The sustained excellence of his work, coupled with his distinctive, delicate manner, provided a basis for a consistent treatment of landscape that was perpetuated to the end of the century by followers such as Francis Place, Francis Barlow, and David Loggan. The Greenwich print was dedicated to the Queen, whose principal residence lay there, but the dedication suggests that Hollar was trying to attract attention and patronage in the royal circle. The print, which would be on sale at a London stationer's, also served to announce the presence in this country of a new and remarkable artist, one indeed who had no rival in the medium (for etching was virtually unknown in England) or in the genre.

Hollar's finest landscapes are of scenes on Arundel's estate at Albury in Surrey, which was the Earl's favourite country residence. The old, half-timbered manor house, shrouded by great trees, was picturesque and peaceful, and provided the Horatian pleasures of the country life after the pressures of existence at Arundel House on the Strand. Hollar etched a number of views of the manor and of the surrounding countryside with a delicacy and freshness that place them in the highest class of landscape art. They epitomise the harmony and calm of the English countryside in 'the white time of peace' before the Civil Wars. Hollar's talents were recognised at Court, and he was made drawing master to the Prince of Wales, a considerable distinction when one considers that he was appointed by the most aesthetically sensitive of English monarchs. Nevertheless, although he had an entrée to the Court, Hollar remained at Arundel House for as long as the Earl remained in England.

Hollar for all his abilities was an important minor artist working in minor genres; he was completely overshadowed by Van Dyck, whose presence in England so radically changed the fashionable style of portraiture. Van Dyck's relations with King Charles are discussed in another chapter, but for Arundel the painter executed several commissions. One of them, showing him in full armour, with his grandson Thomas Howard, was sent to Mr Petty in Rome in 1635 to serve as a model for a sculptured bust by Bernini.[29] (This was at the same time that the King sent his triple portrait by Van Dyck for

Bernini to use as the basis for a bust.) No record of such a sculpture survives, but it is characteristic of Arundel that he should seek to be portrayed by the leading sculptor of the age.

The most interesting of the Van Dyck images is the so-called Madagascar portrait, a double portrait of the Earl and Countess, painted in 1639, of which several versions exist. The picture records a remarkable aberration in Arundel's career. Earlier that year he had been made Commander of the Army against the Scottish Covenanters, but after the failure of that expedition he had returned to London, and plunged unexpectedly into a scheme for the colonisation of Madagascar. Prince Rupert had initiated the idea in 1636, but had been dissuaded; Arundel now took up the project with enthusiasm. The island was unexploited, its climate was reputed to be excellent (a relevant consideration for the Earl, whose health was never robust), the financial advantages of colonisation were thought to be impressive, the element of adventure was no doubt alluring. Still, that the premier Earl of England should propose to depart for a remote, savage island in the Indian Ocean was bizarre in the extreme. One might suggest that he had scented the approach of Civil War in England, that he regarded his recent ill-advised expedition against Scotland as a sign of worse things to come, and that he had decided to withdraw from the country. Whatever his motives, the King approved, a prospectus was issued, financial support was solicited, ships were commissioned, then silence descended on the

Van Dyck, the 'Madagascar' portrait of the Earl and Countess of Arundel

venture. We do not know what caused the collapse of the scheme, but its very existence was ominous. In Van Dyck's painting, which must have been done while the scheme was still in prospect, the accoutrements project a new image of the Arundels. The Countess holds an astrolabe and a pair of compasses, instruments of navigation and most unexpected attributes for a woman, but suggesting her learned grasp of scientific matters and her active participation in the enterprise. In one version Francis Junius stands behind the Earl, the representative of the world of scholarship with which the Arundels wished to associate themselves. Junius's right hand holds a manuscript; the other rests on a bust of Homer. The Earl, wearing armour beneath his ermine, points to the island of Madagascar on a globe. The implication would seem to be that the arts and sciences, philosophy and learning, military skill and courtly manners, are about to be transported to this island beyond Africa, a mission of civilisation into the wilderness.

In 1641 the Earl grew more involved in the increasing turmoil of English politics. As Lord High Steward he presided over the trial of the Earl of Strafford, and perhaps it was his association with that trial which moved the King to turn down Arundel's subsequent petition to be restored to the Dukedom of Norfolk. Dejected, he asked leave to travel, and Charles asked him and the Countess to accompany Marie de Medici, the Queen Mother, who had been visiting the English Court, to Cologne. Next year, in February 1642, the King requested Arundel to accompany the Queen and Princess Mary to Holland, where the Princess was to live with her new husband, William of Orange. It was a similar task to that which he had undertaken for Princess Elizabeth nearly thirty years before, but this time there was little of the buoyancy and optimism of that first progress: the political scene was grim, Arundel was ageing. The King asked him to stay on in Holland to resolve some unfinished business with the marriage treaty, and with the outbreak of Civil War in England in 1642, Arundel chose to live in exile.

The Arundels settled in Antwerp in 1643. A large part of their collections, excluding the marbles and much of the library, was carried across to them. Two years later, the Earl went south to his beloved Padua, for reasons of health, and there, in September 1646, he died. The Countess remained in Holland until her death in 1654. The splendid collections were largely dispersed, becoming one of the more notable casualties of the Civil War in the world of fine arts. The Countess sold off certain smaller items, medals and intaglios, for her maintenance in exile; after her death the Arundels' only surviving son Lord Stafford sold some of the paintings to the Spanish ambassador in London, others to the collector Jabach in Paris, and many of the finest works to the agent of the Archduke Wilhelm in Brussels. So the first great English collection of paintings was broken up and flung back into European circulation. The marbles and the library had a more fortunate destiny: in 1667, John Evelyn prevailed on Henry Howard, Arundel's grandson, to present the inscribed stones to the University of Oxford, after Evelyn had grown distressed by the neglected state into which they had fallen. The sculptures were carried off in various directions, but the great majority were eventually given to the same University in 1755,[30] and were finally housed in the Ashmolean Museum in the nineteenth century. Evelyn was also instrumental in persuading Henry Howard to bestow the Arundelian library on the Royal Society, with the exception of the books of heraldic interest, which were given to the Royal College of Heralds. So the most scholarly aspects of the collections were saved, but the central glory, the paintings, departed.

Arundel had been a culturally isolated figure from the 1630s onwards. Apart from his wife and eldest son, who certainly shared his concern for the arts, he had few familiars. Cotton died in 1631; Selden lived on, though increasingly drawn into political debate. Above all, King Charles should have been a natural companion as a lover of the arts, but Arundel's diffidence and respect for majesty prevented intimacy. His secretary remarked that 'he knew and kept greater distance towards his Sovereign than any person I ever observed'.[31] But in his last years on the continent the Earl discovered a disciple after his own heart: John Evelyn. Presumably Arundel knew the Evelyn family from the closeness of their manors at Albury and Wooton; at any rate, the young Evelyn (he was born in 1620) was on familiar enough terms to be frequenting Arundel House in 1641 and having his portrait painted by Van der Borcht. In October of that year the Earl invited him to join his party for a week of sight-seeing in the Low Countries. They came together again in Venice in 1645, where they inspected palaces and churches and viewed collections; the Earl asked Evelyn to accompany him on a visit to Mantua, where they saw the curiosities and antiquities of the town, and appreciated in particular the ducal gardens there. Evelyn went to study at Padua, where their friendship deepened, and on his departure for England in April 1646 the Earl, who was now in decline, gave him detailed notes in his own hand of the curiosities to be seen on the return journey. These Remembrances, as Evelyn called them, are a testimony to the Earl's intense pleasure in the visual arts and his satisfaction at having found a young Englishman who was apt for learning. In a sense, the Remembrances were a cultural will, for John Evelyn was in effect the real inheritor and preserver of Arundel's taste. Although he had no great fortune with which to accumulate treasures, yet his advanced connoisseurship in the arts, the internationalism of his taste, and the freedom from religious and nationalistic prejudice in his appreciation of painting and architecture, were all qualities that were encouraged and intensified by his association with Arundel. Moreover, Evelyn's books on architecture, engraving, painting and collecting, published after the Restoration, as well as his own busy presence in so many intellectual and social circles, did much to disseminate the values of the Arundel ethos across a broad section of Restoration gentry. Of course, the continental exile of many leading Royalists during the Civil War had done much to increase a civilised consciousness of the arts, bringing Englishmen into a fuller appreciation of the intellectual and aesthetic pleasures furnished by the visual arts. The vision of the civilised life that recognised the arts as the fullest expression of nobility of spirit—or *virtù*, as the Italians called it—was first perfected by the Earl of Arundel, yet by the end of the century it was generally shared by the aristocracy of this country and had profoundly conditioned the way in which its leisure was expended. One can well understand why Horace Walpole called Arundel 'the father of vertù in England'.

Sir Edward Walker, Arundel's secretary and his first biographer, suggested that if the Earl had a fault it was the excessive expenditure of money on his collections, coupled with a certain negligence towards the sources of his income, but then he justified the Earl's practice by reminding the reader that the collections were ultimately for 'the Glory and Ornament of his Country'. This is an important point, for together with the Earl's deep concern for the dignity and authority of the aristocracy,[32] the grandeur of his collections represented a design to realise an ideal of princely magnificence which had long prevailed amongst Italian and French dukes and cardinals, but was alien to England. Arundel's internationalism also assisted the emergence of this new type of English nobleman, for his ambassadorial journeys and private travels provided an unprecedented display of English authority and culture in Europe.

In many ways, the Earl's devotion to collecting was a substitute for religion. His passionate commitment to the arts was comparable to the commitment to Catholicism in the two preceding generations of his family. Arundel appears as the forerunner of the great secular-minded aristocrats of the eighteenth century, who conceived that taste, judgement and scholarship are allied to conduct and morality, and who believed that the imaginative control of paint, marble, precious stone or metal by the artists of pagan Greece and Rome, of Catholic Italy, or Protestant Germany expresses a common aspiration to beauty and intellectual delight. In short, Arundel was a great Humanist. We have noted that his secretary observed that 'he professed more to affect moral virtues than nice questions or controversies', and in his later years he seems to have turned more and more to Stoicism as a personal creed. Its appeal must have been very strong in the disintegrating years of the 1630s and 1640s. The Earl seems to have had an especial regard, amounting even to veneration, for the antique busts of the Stoic Emperor Marcus Aurelius and his wife Faustina. About 1637 he acquired the Roman head believed to represent Seneca, which Rubens had previously owned and included in his painting 'The Four Philosophers'.[33] One might argue that the austere bearing that seemed such a notable feature of his public and political life was a deliberate exercise of the fundamental Stoic virtue of *gravitas*.[34]

A splendid baroque mythologisation of the Earl's death exists in the form of a spectacular etching by Hollar, after a design by the Dutch artist Cornelius Schut: 'The Apotheosis of the Earl of Arundel', dedicated to the Countess, and presumably executed in 1646. In the midst of an extraordinarily busy scene of death, the Earl, in armour, sits reflectively upon his tomb as Time and Death attempt to drag him away; higher than Time, charioted Fame sounds her trumpet over the Earl. The air swirls with putti, pulling him towards Fame. Below the Earl, the reeling figures of Painting and Sculpture, accompanied by a distraught Minerva, protest against his taking off. Personifications of Hope and Faith lie downcast beside Love. The foreground of the scene is strewn with treasures from the Earl's collections: paintings by Holbein, a drawing by Raphael, books, medals, coins, statuettes, and bronzes. By the figure of Sculpture lie two marble heads which appear to be those of Marcus Aurelius and Faustina, the Stoical mentors of the Earl and Countess (these two heads were added by Hollar to the original design of the Apotheosis).[35] The whole animated scene occurs within the confines of a Roman circus, a semi-circular wall with niches containing sculpture, surmounted by a balustrade crowned with torches, the fires of life, one of which is obliterated by Time's glass. Behind Time and Death stands an obelisk, a conventional Renaissance symbol marking the end of life, as in a Roman circus it marked the end of the race.[36] This may well be an allusion to the antique obelisk that Arundel had wished to bring from Rome to England. The etching is particularly interesting for its depiction of the tomb that Arundel specified in his will to be built at Albury, but which was never erected. It was to have been of 'white marble or brasse', designed by the Italian artist Francesco Vanelli; the pose of the Earl, seated and gazing heavenward in a mood of contemplation, was a singular one by the conventions which prevailed in English funerary sculpture at the time. By his side a lion, symbol of fearlessness, holds his

ILLVSTRISSIMÆ ET EXELLENTISSIMÆ   HEROINÆ ALETHEIÆ MARTIÆ.

Talbotorum gentis Salopiæ Comitis heredi ... uxori unice et unice dilectæ, peregrinationum omniumq̃, fortunarum fide et ... diffisse Comiti THOMÆ HOWARDI *Ill.mi et Ex.mi Arundellæ Surriæ et Norfolciæ Comitis Angliæ Comitum Superem ... miræq̃ Regni Marescalli Nobilissimæ gentis Howardæ primipis, Baronis Howardi Mowbray etc. Nobilissimiq̃ aureæ Per ... [Or]dinis Sodalitii Equitis Doctorum hominum fautoris bonæumq̃, artium instauratoris, huic artis Pictoriæ cordiali eius amore cui Suis ... om[ni]us in umbolas dentum luctum ac Mæcenatis sui à mortis temporisq̃, oblivione sana artumque Gentis defendentibus æternas æn ... Iucius observantiæ et gratitudinis ergo in vivam memoriam et pietatis in defunctum* I. M. D. D.   *Ioannes vander Borcht sculpsit*

Cornelius Schut Inventor   *Wenceslaus Hollar fecit*

'The Apotheosis of the Earl of Arundel', etching by Hollar after a design by
Cornelius Schut

escutcheon with its many quarterings. The chaste sarcophagus is in the
finest seventeenth-century Roman manner, announcing the advanced taste
of its incumbent even in death.

Arundel's will is memorable for its practical benevolence and for the
characteristic decorum that it imposed on his beneficiaries even from beyond

the grave. He requested that:

> I desire . . . that some House might bee built vpon Our ground neere the Churchyard at Alebury, where Six honest vnmarried men might bee honestly and well fedd and cladd, and have good Comoditie of Bookes to study with, and convenient roomes to make all Distillations, phisickes, and Surgerie, to bee given for ever to the poore for Charitie, and no money to bee taken for it, for the number of Six I name in gratitude to Almighty God, who gave Six Sonnes to my deare wife and mee. . . . I would have all their Cloathes Ash Coloured. As also I could wish (if it might bee) those of my Family might mourne for mee only in Ash Colour, in respect it is the Colour of Ashes into which my flesh is to Dissolve.[37]

But the hospice was never built, the monument never erected, for the vast culture of the Earl had been achieved through immense expenditure which far outran even his vast income, with the result that the scale of the Earl's operations ultimately ate into his estates, for land had to be sold to settle the huge debts he had incurred. The very grandeur of the Earl's position that the arts enhanced was threatened by the sheer expense that those arts demanded.

Notes to Chapter Five

1   At this time there were no English peers above the rank of Earl except the Marquis of Winchester, who took no part in public life.

2   Clarendon, *The History of the Rebellion*, Oxford 1705, pp. 55–6.

3   Lord Lumley was so obsessed with the antiquity of his genealogical lines that King James once remarked, 'I didna' ken that Adam's ither name was Lumley!'

4   See E. Milner, *Records of the Lumleys of Lumley Castle*, 1904, pp. 94–100. Also, for an account of the contents of the collection, see 'The Lumley Inventories' in the *Proceedings of the Walpole Society*, VI, 1918, pp. 15–35, and D. Piper, 'The 1590 Lumley Inventory', *Burlington Magazine* XC, 1957, pp. 224–31.

5   Quoted in D. Mathew, *The Jacobean Age*, London 1938, p. 135.

6   Quoted in Mary Hervey, *The Life, Correspondence and Collections of Thomas Howard, Earl of Arundel*, Cambridge 1921, pp. 83–4.

7   Henry Peacham, *The Compleat Gentleman*, 1634, p. 107. Most of the statues were displayed in the gardens of Arundel House. The novelty of this arrangement can be gauged from Bacon's first sight of the collection: 'Sir Francis Bacon coming into the Earl of Arundel's garden, where there were a great number of ancient statues of naked men and women, made a stand, and as astonished, cried out "The Resurrection!"' (*The Letters and Life of Francis Bacon*, 1862–74, vol. VII, p. 177).

8   This more accurate sense of classical form is evident in the work of the sculptor Nicholas Stone as he assimilated the lessons of the Arundel marbles in the second and third decades of the century.

9   The title of Earl Marshal of England was not solely and permanently vested in Lord Arundel until 1621.

10   Edward Walker, 'A Short View of the Life of Thomas Howard', in *Historicall Discourses*, 1705, p. 222.

11   A letter from the Earl's secretary Vercellini to his master about the progress of the Rubens portrait indicates that overtures to Van Dyck were being made in 1620. See Hervey, p. 175.

12   This inventory may be found printed in full in Hervey, pp. 473–500.

13   From Joachim von Sandrart, *Teutsche Academie*, 1675, passage translated in Hervey, p. 256.

14   Letter of 27 January 1625, quoted in Hervey, p. 266.

15   Letter of 20 October 1625, Hervey, p. 273.

16   Letter of 28 March 1626, Hervey, p. 274.

17   Letter of 8 April 1626, Hervey, pp. 275–6.

18   Letter of November 1626, Hervey, p. 270.

19   See Hervey, p. 15.

20   See E. Panofsky, *The Life and Art of Albrecht Dürer*, Princeton, N.J. 1971, pp. 7–8.

21   Quoted and translated by F. Springell, in *Connoisseur and Diplomat*, London 1963, p. 107.

22   Letter from Francis Junius to Sir William Dugdale, 28 January 1656, in W. Hamper, *Life, Diary, and Correspondence of Sir William Dugdale*, London 1824, p. 299.

23   Cotton Otho B. vi.

24   These drawings may be found reproduced in M. V. Kratochvíl, *Wenzel Hollar: Reisebilder*, Prague 1966.

25   See C. V. Wedgwood, *The Thirty Years War*, London 1961, p. 400.

26   See 'The Diary of William Crowne', printed in Springell, pp. 54–135.

27   For an account of the Imperial collections, see R. J. W. Evans, *Rudolph II and his World*, Oxford 1973.

28   Letter from Arundel to Petty, 20 September 1636. Quoted in Springell, p. 101.

29   See the letter informing Petty of his intentions in Hervey, p. 391.

30   See D. E. L. Haynes, *The Arundel Marbles*, Oxford 1975.

31   Walker, p. 222.

32   Arundel's revival of the Earl Marshal's Court to judge of matters of chivalry, title and precedence was a sign of his concern to strengthen the integrity of the aristocracy in a period when royal caprice was endangering its authority and reputation.

33   See Michael Vickers, 'Rubens' Bust of Seneca?' in *Burlington Magazine* CXIX, 1977, pp. 643–5.

34   It has been so argued by K. Sharpe in *Faction and Parliament*, Oxford 1978, pp. 209–44.

35   See Michael Vickers, 'Hollar and the Arundel Marbles' in *Städel Jahrbuch*, Munich, VII, 1979, pp. 126–32.

36   *Ibid.*

37   See Hervey, pp. 460–1.

[6]

The Duke of Buckingham as collector and patron

The rise of George Villiers from obscurity as a country gentleman to national pre-eminence as the inseparable companion and favourite of the King astonished and disconcerted his contemporaries. He first caught the King's eye in 1614, and thereafter honours flowed to him irresistibly, for the King's affection towards him never wavered. He became the royal cupbearer in 1614, he was made a Gentleman of the Bedchamber and knighted in 1615, appointed Master of the Horse and created Knight of the Garter in 1616.[1] In the same year he was made a Viscount, then advanced to Earl of Buckingham in 1617, and sworn in as Privy Councillor. 1618 saw him made Marquis. He became Lord High Admiral in 1619. The ultimate advancement came in 1623, when he was created Duke of Buckingham, the only duke in the peerage of England. What interests us here is the cultural style adopted by a man who suddenly found himself equal with princes and endowed with bewildering amounts of money.

As his position became assured, around 1616–17, and he began to gather around him the household proper to a great man, his interests turned to collecting paintings and statuary, for by this time the size and diversity of such collections were looked upon as a gauge of greatness in England. Initially, Buckingham seems to have been a prototype of Sir Visto in Pope's epistle 'Of the Use of Riches' who suddenly decides to 'have a Taste' and precipitately sets about acquiring the correct components. Buckingham was fortunate, however, in attracting to his service at a very early stage a refugee Huguenot called Balthasar Gerbier, whom he employed on account of his command of French, Dutch and Spanish, and because he had a 'good hand in writing, skill in sciences such as mathematics, architecture, drawing, painting, contriving of scenes, masques, shows and entertainments for great princes'.[2] Gerbier became Buckingham's mentor in aesthetic matters, and was largely responsible for educating his patron into an informed appreciation of painting and sculpture. As Buckingham's friendship with Prince Charles deepened into intimacy, the Prince took over the direction of his taste, but Gerbier remained an invaluable adviser and agent for many years.

Gerbier's primary responsibility was for the Duke's collection, and he was an indefatigable pursuer of rarities who seems to have delighted in the challenge of difficult negotiations. A letter of his to Buckingham, sent from France in 1624, conveys something of his acquisitive zeal, and also gives an idea of what could be achieved with persistence and ready money:

I mentioned, in my former letter . . ., the large and rare paintings in possession of a person called President Chevallier, who has also some antique heads in marble and in bronze, the whole neither to be sold nor to be given away without some scheme; but I have sworn to myself, as I did about the Prelate of Venice, that we must have them or I lack invention, for, as they are the ornament of a handsome house in France, they must be jewels at York House. . . .

. . . During the time I have been in Paris, I have not passed one hour without searching after some rarity; and I should have stayed there but four days, had it not been, as I thought, very necessary that I should find out all that there is in Paris; and I never could have thought that they had so many rare things in France, all which are to come into your hands at your happy arrival. I beg your Excellency yet to read the other sheet, and you will there see three rare pictures of Michael Angelo [and] Raphael. It is, my lord, because since my last I have found at the house of the Bishop of Paris three of the most rare pictures that can be. The first is a St. Francis, a good-sized painting, from the hand of the Cavalier Ballion, as good as Michael Angelo Carazoago [Caravaggio]; and the other a picture of our Lady by Raphael, which is repainted by some devil who I trust was hanged; but still it is so lovely, and the drawing is so fine, that it is worth a thousand crowns. There is another picture of Michael Angelo Buonarroti; but that should be seen kneeling, for it is a Crucifixion, with the Virgin and St. John—the most divine thing in the world. I have been such an idolater as to kiss it three times, for there is nothing that can be more perfect. It is a miniature. I have a hundred thousand things to say, but I offend too much in trespassing so long upon your patience. I have met with a most beautiful piece of Tintoret, of a Danaë, a naked figure the most beautiful, that flint as cold as ice might fall in love with it. I have given twenty crowns in hand; it costs, with another head of Titian, sixty pounds sterling. I have given also twenty crowns in hand for the Gorgon's head; it costs two hundred crowns. . . . I beg of you to attack Mons de Montmorency, for he has the most beautiful statues that can be spoken of; that is to say, Two Slaves by Michael Angelo, and some others. He is so liberal that he will not refuse them.[3]

The detailed composition of Buckingham's collection probably represented Gerbier's taste more accurately than its owner's, for Buckingham seems to have regarded his collection as a brilliant possession rather than an extension of his own values and character. He did, however, share the common bias of English collectors of his time towards sixteenth-century Venetian painting, with, in his case, a particular admiration for Veronese. Gerbier was active in seeking out Venetian masterpieces, as was the English ambassador in Venice, Sir Henry Wotton, who acted as Buckingham's agent there for several years. The collection was displayed at York House on the

Strand.⁴ If the 1635 inventory of Buckingham's paintings offers a reliable guide to the disposition of the pictures within the house—and it should do, for the Duchess had a pious affection for her husband after his death, and the house did not undergo any great change, as far as we know—then we can imagine the visual impact of some of the key rooms when the collection was at its height.⁵ The Hall was dominated by one of Titian's portraits of Charles V, and 'one great piece being Scipio', presumably Van Dyck's 'Continence of Scipio'; the Great Chamber, which would have been the scene of the Duke's entertainments, was largely given over to Rubens, the greatest of the living masters: ten of his works hung there, with his great equestrian portrait of the Duke at the centre. Here were Rubens's 'Boar Hunt', two smaller landscapes, portraits, 'Christ Crucified' and 'The Torments of Hell'. A 'Diana and Calisto' by Titian also hung there. The pictures in Buckingham's closet presumably represented his personal favourites: as one might expect, there were full-length portraits of King James and Charles. Here, in one of the more private quarters of the palace, was the acknowledged gem of the collection, Titian's 'Ecce Homo', the powerful, crowded composition of Christ before Pilate now in the Kunsthistorisches Museum at Vienna. Next to it, in 1635 at least, hung 'Venus looking in a Glass' and 'Venus Sleeping and Cupid Pissing', copies after Titian. Besides two Titian portraits, this room also contained a 'Salome' by Leonardo, a Virgin by Andrea del Sarto, Tintoretto's 'Woman taken in Adultery', and pieces by Giorgione and Correggio. Even when we make allowance for erroneous attributions so common in the seventeenth century, this was an impressive cluster of paintings. Buckingham's Veroneses were exhibited in the Gallery. There were twelve of them, all but one religious in subject, hanging with a miscellaneous group of Italian and Dutch works. Only one portrait of a non-noble Englishman is recorded in the collection, and that was of Ben Jonson, by 'Blyenberke'—presumably the minor Dutch artist Abraham van Blyenberch. This picture is now in the National Portrait Gallery.

Buckingham concentrated his statuary at Chelsea House, another Villiers residence, on the edge of London. He owned more than a hundred pieces, and unlike Arundel, whose collection was composed almost exclusively of antique marbles, Buckingham bought modern as well as ancient work. His *pièce de résistance* amongst the moderns was Gianbologna's 'Cain and Abel', which Philip of Spain had presented to Prince Charles in Madrid, and which Charles gave to Buckingham on their return as a gesture of friendship. In the quest for antique statues, Buckingham followed the lead of Arundel, putting out feelers into the Levant, and, like Arundel, working through the ambassador at Constantinople, Sir Thomas Roe. Roe was first instructed to prospect for statuary on the Duke's behalf in 1624, and understandably he responded to the request from the royal favourite. Ambassadors ultimately expected lucrative promotion at home, and Buckingham was more likely to advance a man's career than Arundel, who opposed the upstart Villiers. Roe seems to have been personally well-disposed towards Arundel, but he complied with the rival request as well. Fortunately, Buckingham was not attracted by the artistically incomplete but historically significant pieces of sculpture that gave Arundel so much satisfaction, nor was he interested in inscriptions—he 'was not so fond of antiquity to court it in a deformed or misshapen stone', as he said—so Roe could continue to entertain the interests of both parties.

Although Arundel later developed into a personal and political opponent of Buckingham, he did make a significant gesture of friendship and conciliation with the favourite in 1620, when he appears to have commissioned a painting from Van Dyck for presentation to Buckingham. We know that 'one great piece being Scipio' hung in the Hall at York House, and this is assumed to be identical with the painting 'The Continence of Scipio' by Van Dyck now at Christ Church, Oxford. The subject is derived from Livy (Book XXVI, 50) and recalls the generosity of the victorious Scipio in giving freedom to a captive maiden of great beauty, whom he might have kept for his own purposes. The gratitude of the maiden's betrothed and her parents, and the modest relief of the maiden herself, make up the emotional counterbalance to Scipio's noble gesture in Van Dyck's presentation of the scene. Buckingham occupies the focal centre of the painting as the grateful fiancé, and he is dressed in contemporary costume in contrast to the classical vestments of the other figures. His central position in the role of the betrothed suggests that the painting alludes to Buckingham's marriage, which took place in the same year as the painting, 1620. This probability is strengthened by the detail of the servants bearing treasure, which, according to Livy, was intended as ransom for the maiden, but was instead offered by Scipio to the couple as a wedding gift. The painting itself, therefore, seems likely to have been intended by Arundel as a wedding present to Buckingham in 1620, and the subject had the added appeal of associating Buckingham with an elevated theme of Roman virtue. The probability that Arundel was the commissioner of the work stems from the fact that Van Dyck came to England under the sponsorship of Arundel on his first brief visit in 1620–1, and there is additional evidence in the presence of a large fragment of antique sculpture in the left foreground by the figure of Scipio. This can be identified as a marble frieze-block from the Trajaneum at Pergamon, once in the Arundel Collection and now in the London Museum.[6] The prominence of this piece surely marks Arundel's involvement with the work. 'The Continence of Scipio' is not a particularly fine composition—it belongs to an early phase of Van Dyck's career, when he was still under the powerful influence of his master, Rubens. Rubens himself had painted the same subject, and Van Dyck's painting owes its general organisation to that work, but is an inferior relative of the original treatment.[7] The rhythms of Van Dyck's painting are slack, the colours cold; the figure of Buckingham is awkwardly interposed, and the maiden lacks vitality and grace. One can understand why Van Dyck was advised to go to Italy at this stage of his career to improve his technique. Nevertheless, the 'Scipio' holds considerable interest as a product of Van Dyck's earliest relations with England, and it also provides the first instance of Buckingham's translation on to the plane of heroic or mythological activity, a treatment he would receive with some frequency during the 1620s, especially from the hand of Rubens.

Buckingham first met Rubens when he went to Paris in 1625 to escort Henrietta Maria to London for her wedding with King Charles. Buckingham caused a sensation in Paris by the extraordinary magnificence of his

Van Dyck, 'The Continence of Scipio'

Rubens, 'The Duke of Buckingham on Horseback'

costume (his wardrobe included a white satin suit sewn all over with diamonds, said to be valued at over £80,000, or over a million pounds today); his indiscreet flirtation with Anne of Austria, Louis XIII's Queen, attracted less favourable attention. With Rubens he formed a friendship that continued for the remaining years of his life, a friendship advantageous to Rubens for diplomatic reasons, and to Buckingham for artistic ones, for the Duke was eager to commission and purchase from the artist.

Buckingham seems to have suggested a commemorative painting of his embassy and of the Anglo-French marriage, for a sketch survives in the Prince of Liechtenstein's collection of an allegorical baroque tableau that seems designed as a ceiling decoration. It shows Mercury conducting Psyche to Olympus. Buckingham represents Mercury, an appropriate association, as Mercury is the patron of embassies. He brings Psyche, or Henrietta Maria, to Cupid, who is of course Charles, who in turn kneels before the deified James, receiving his posthumous approval.[8] The sketch was never developed into a painting, but it does serve to indicate how Buckingham was regarded as a member of the Stuart pantheon, and it also carries the suggestion that the marriage of Charles and Henrietta Maria was thought of in terms of the myth of Cupid and Psyche from the very beginning, a myth which was to enjoy considerable currency during their reign.

One of the earliest fruits of the relationship between Rubens and Buckingham was the marvellously sensitive portrait sketch, now in the Albertina at Vienna, which catches the handsome, confident shrewdness of Buckingham's features more compellingly than any other depiction of him. Rubens used the sketch for the great equestrian portrait of the Duke that used to hang in the Great Chamber of York House. (It was destroyed in the fire at Osterley Park in 1949.) The elemental energy that Rubens commanded at will blows through this scene where Buckingham rears his horse on a windswept beach; allegorical figures whirl in turmoil in the air, Neptune and Tethys gaze admiringly from the reeds. The painting alludes to several of Buckingham's offices. Most evidently he is Master of the King's Horse; Rubens pays tribute to his celebrated powers of horsemanship, showing him riding a Spanish genet, a breed he introduced into England, and executing the difficult manoeuvre known as a *levade*.⁹ The marine setting, with the fleet at sea, refers to his office of Lord High Admiral, and his full armour and martial baton indicate a military command, all of which details suggest that the work reached its full state of composition at the time when the Duke was commanding the combined naval and military expedition against La Rochelle in 1627. The humiliating disaster of that incompetently managed campaign is sublimely ignored in the painting, where a smiling Victory holds out her laurel wreath before the Duke. The painting was presumably commissioned in Paris in 1625, but it seems not to have been finished until after the Duke's death in 1628, for a winged figure can be seen blowing out the flame of life over the Duke's head, a last-minute addition, one assumes, as the painting left the studio. The work was unquestionably the finest state portrait of its date in England, and would set the pattern for Van Dyck's equestrian portraits of King Charles in the next decade. One further detail of the scene should be noticed: the Medusa-headed figure of Envy that is being repelled by one of the Duke's guardian powers. Envy, or more accurately resentment, was a powerful and widespread force working against the Duke, most evident in the unsuccessful attempt to impeach him in 1626, and inclusion of Envy in the painting was an honest recognition of current feeling. The Duke himself was willing to acknowledge it as well. Before he left London for his unpopular attack on France in 1627, 'the Duke gave his farewell supper at York House, and a masque unto their majesties, wherein first comes forth the Duke, after him Envy, with divers open-mouthed dogs' heads, representing the people's barking; next came Fame . . .'.[10] These symbols of negativity, such as Envy, Detraction, Discord, provided a satisfactory means of localising and exorcising the powers they represented. In an age when personification was a mode of thought, these scapegoat figures must have had considerable therapeutic value, allowing one to visualise the forces of opposition in a manageable form.

Envy appears again in the other great Rubens painting lost in the Osterley fire, the one formerly known as 'The Apotheosis of the Duke of Buckingham'. Since the Duke must have commissioned this large work for a ceiling at York House during his lifetime, it is unlikely that it represents his posthumous rise to heaven. More likely, it shows the Duke borne up to the Temple of Virtue or Honour, aided by Minerva and Mercury. Fame and the Graces assist his ascent, while monstrous Envy ineffectually snarls. Figures who probably represent Virtue and Prosperity await him on the steps of a baroque temple. The composition has obvious affinities with the ceiling of the Banqueting House that Rubens began to paint shortly after this work.

The climax of Buckingham's relations with Rubens came in 1627 when he successfully negotiated the purchase of the artist's personal collection of paintings and sculpture for £10,000. The great majority of Rubens's paintings on display at York House—there are thirty listed in the 1635 inventory—came as a result of this sale, which was the real coup of Buckingham's career as a collector. Besides a wealth of old masters and contemporary works, Rubens possessed a rich gallery of antique sculpture which he drew on to give authenticity to his historical paintings. In the same year that Buckingham acquired this collection, King Charles bought the collections of the Dukes of Mantua; these acquisitions, along with Arundel's steady purchase of paintings and sculpture, established the English Court as the leading power in the international art market, and gave Rubens ample grounds for his astonishment at the wealth of art treasures which he found in England during his visit in 1629–30, and which he describes in his letters of that period.

Being the inseparable companion of King Charles, Buckingham naturally benefited from Charles's initiative in attracting continental artists to England. Gerrit van Honthorst came in 1628. He painted several portraits of the Duke and his family, and also the large 'Apollo and Diana' which shows Buckingham presenting the Liberal Arts to Charles and Henrietta Maria. The painting is discussed in some detail in a later chapter, but here it suffices merely to note that Buckingham is cast as Mercury, the patron of the arts, bringing them into the presence of Their Majesties—a thoroughly misleading view of his position, yet one that shows how much he wished to be seen as a cultural power at the Caroline Court. This was at least the third time he had been associated with Mercury, in ambassadorial or cultural roles, yet in view of Mercury's position as the right-hand man of Jupiter, it was an entirely appropriate typing. Besides Honthorst, Buckingham also cultivated Gentileschi, whom Charles had brought over in 1626, giving him accommodation at York House, and commissioning work from him. The most famous result of these commissions was 'The Penitent Magdalen' (now in the collection of the Earl of Elgin), an elegant piece of pietism in the Caravaggio manner. Apparently, in the last three years of his life, Buckingham was beginning to take an altogether more serious and direct interest in the arts than had previously been the case.

Outside the sphere of painting and sculpture, Buckingham's involvement with the arts was slight. It is difficult to believe that he had much time for reading, and although some forty books were dedicated to him, there is no discernible pattern of subject matter that would allow us to identify the particular interests of the Duke. They form a miscellaneous assortment of history, travel, military affairs, sermons and anti-Catholic polemic, mostly by minor writers courting favour, and with few distinguished names in evidence.[11] The dedications are thickest in the years 1619–20, falling off thereafter: it would appear that Buckingham gave little encouragement to writers. Virtually the only literary commission of any significance from Buckingham was to Ben Jonson for a masque to entertain King James on his visit to Burley-on-the-Hill, the Duke's Rutland home, in 1621. The resulting masque, *The Gypsies Metamorphos'd*, proved to be James's favourite. It was King James who provided the most flattering of all dedications to Buckingham when he offered him *A Meditation upon the Lord's Prayer* in 1619, a book for the benefit of all of his subjects, but 'especially those who follow the Court', who he realises have little time for meditation. He praises Buckingham for his 'frequent hearing of the word of God', and for 'so often receiving the Sacrament', holding him up as a model of the active courtier who does not neglect his religious obligations.

Buckingham's good fortune in artistic matters continued after his death. A memorable portrait of him, lying dead in bed, exists at Castle Ashby, possibly from the hand of Van Dyck—a haunting image.[12] Although King Charles was dissuaded from giving him a state funeral and tomb, Buckingham's wife raised a magnificent monument to him in Westminster Abbey, executed by Hubert le Sueur, a work of outstanding craftsmanship and beauty, with mourning statues of Mars and Neptune, Minerva and the figure of Prosperity cast in the finest bronze, and four great jet obelisks. At the wish of King Charles, he was buried in Henry VII's Chapel, which hitherto had been reserved for royalty. Even in death, Buckingham enjoyed unprecedented favour.

Notes to Chapter Six

1   Master of the Horse was the third highest office at Court, after the Lord Chamberlain and the Lord Steward; he was responsible for the stables and the running of the Court outdoors.

2   B. Gerbier, *To All Men Who Love Truth*, 1646, quoted in G. Huxley, *Endymion Porter*, London 1959, p. 34.

3   Quoted in C. R. Cammell, *The Great Duke of Buckingham*, London 1939, pp. 358–60. (Translated from the French by Cammell.)

4   The old palace of the Archbishops of York, which had passed into the hands of the Bacon family, and with Francis Bacon's fall in 1621 it had been bought by the King, who presented it to the Duke. The Duke made some moves to modernise it, employing Gerbier, who had talent as an architect, to remodel some of the rooms and dress it in a classical facade, for which purpose much of the stone assembled for the rebuilding of St Paul's was appropriated.

5   See Randall Davis, 'The Inventory of York House Paintings in 1635' in *Burlington Magazine*, March 1907.

6   The fragment was discovered in excavations on the site of Arundel House in 1972.

7   The Rubens 'Scipio' was destroyed in 1636. An engraved reproduction survives.

8   For illustration and discussion of this sketch, see G. Martin, 'Rubens and Buckingham's "fayrie ile"', in *Burlington Magazine* CVIII, 1966, pp. 613–18.

9   Identified as such in Cammell, *op. cit.*, p. 375. The Duke's powers of horsemanship were well-known and admired. In 1618, M. Baret dedicated to him *An Hipponomie or the Vineyard of Horsemanship*.

10 Letter to the Rev. Joseph Meade, quoted in Martin, *op. cit.*, p. 617.

11 Bacon dedicated the 1625 edition of the *Essays* to him in an obvious bid to regain favour at Court. Donne offered him a sermon in 1622, the same year that William Burton dedicated his *Description of Leicestershire*, hoping for support from the county's greatest son.

12 The absence of any documented portrait of Buckingham by Van Dyck is a puzzling aspect of the artistic record. For an account of existing portraits of the Duke, see Cammell, *op. cit.*, pp. 371–85.

[7]
Inigo Jones

Without Inigo Jones the splendours of the Stuart Court would have been inconceivable. He was England's universal man—architect, mechanic, mathematician, artist, designer of sets and costumes, antiquary and connoisseur. His talents realised the architectural ambitions and theatrical fantasies of the monarchy and of leading aristocrats from the death of Elizabeth through to the Civil Wars, and in many ways he was responsible for the forms that those ambitions took, for he was virtually alone in his knowledge of the modern arts of design, and his genius was almost the sole channel by which these arts were communicated to the British Court. In the insular world of Great Britain at the beginning of the seventeenth century, excluded as it was from Europe by religious differences, there were few men who had had the opportunity of cultured travel on the continent— there were perhaps more Englishmen acquainted with the New World than with Italy—and Jones was exceptional in his experience and unique in his ability to apply it to the circumstances of Stuart England.

The details of Jones's formative years remain obscure. It is generally thought that he took service with Lord Roos, the brother of the Earl of Rutland, and travelled with him in France, Germany and especially Italy, and that in 1603 he went with the Earl of Rutland's embassy to Denmark, where he found employment with the Danish King, Christian IV. Christian thereafter seems to have recommended him to his sister Queen Anne, in whose service we find him in 1604.[1] In these early years Jones was primarily a painter, but what he saw in the courts of Europe enlarged his sense of the possible, and gave him a more exalted view of the artist's scope. In the informal education that Italy gave him, the recent architecture of the Venetian region took an important place, as did the staging of the lavish intermezzi that were the high points of the festive year in certain Italian courts. We do not know what he saw, or whether he had access to the Court of the Grand Duke of Tuscany at Florence where these spectacles reached their most sophisticated form, but he learnt enough to grasp the mechanics

CELEBERRIMVS VIR INIGO IONES / PRÆFECTVS ARCHITECTVRÆ
MAGNÆ BRITTANIÆ REGIS ETC.

Ant.van Dyck pinxit
R.V.Vorst sculp

Cum priuilegio

Portrait of Inigo Jones, an engraving after Van Dyck.

of spectacle and illusion, and the management of the interlocking art forms in these intermezzi, so that once back in England he was able to put his knowledge into practice, with ever-increasing skill, in the masques for the Stuart Court. In Italy too he must have become acquainted with the Vitruvianism that formed the context in which so much of his later development took place.

As the only surviving treatise on architecture from antiquity, Vitruvius's *De Architectura* lay behind most Renaissance discussions of theory and practice on the subject from Alberti onwards. It was not simply his instructions concerning the schemes of the various classes of building common in the ancient world nor his explanation of the orders that secured his hold over Renaissance practitioners, but his principles, and his high valuation of the architect as polymath and philosopher in stone. For Vitruvius, the composition of an architectural scheme from the total plan down to the smallest unit should be integrated by a series of mathematical ratios whose intellectual consonance would reflect the proportioned cosmic harmony of the spheres in their heavenly spacing and the microcosmic echo of that harmony in the ideal dimensions of the human body. The Vitruvian system was dependent upon the Pythagorean belief that the universe was mathematically structured according to certain key ratios that were also the source of musical harmony. The substantial form of a building raised on Vitruvian principles therefore embodies a series of mathematical concepts directed towards a philosophic end. Consequently the architect is not just a talented artisan with a gift for design, as was so often the case in sixteenth-century England, but a man of exceptional intellectual powers who should be educated in the higher arts and sciences that render the mind capable of the sublime vocation of architecture. Hence the need for a knowledge of mathematics, geometry, astronomy, music and philosophy, especially Platonic, as well as a mastery of the practical mechanical arts.[2] Such ideas had very limited currency in England in the sixteenth century, although they had been given an exposition by the hermetic philosopher John Dee in his Preface to his translation of Euclid in 1570, which Jones may have read in his formative years; in Italy, however, they formed the ethos in which architects were nourished.[3] Whatever Jones had learnt of such ideas on his first visit to Italy he was able to consolidate when he returned in 1613–14 in the company of the Earl of Arundel, for by that time he was already established as the master technician at the Stuart Court; he had been Surveyor to Prince Henry for two years, and had begun to make some preliminary essays in architecture. With Arundel he was able to move in the most cultivated Italian circles, to meet architects of the first order such as the aged

Scamozzi, to visit Vicenza, the city of Palladio, and to study in detail antique Roman buildings as well as modern constructions. As his annotated copies testify, he was also able to read the principal Italian treatises on architecture in the immediate setting of the buildings they describe. This visit was decisive in turning him to the practice of architecture and in confirming his disposition to impose Italian aesthetic values at the English Court.

But we anticipate his career. His first employment was with Queen Anne, whose avant-garde taste in the arts ought to be better recognised than it is. She initiated the masques that were the most distinctive expression of Court culture under the Stuarts, commissioning the first of them, *The Masque of Blacknesse*, in 1605, presumably after lengthy discussion with Inigo Jones over what could be achieved in the way of spectacle. Her intellectual abilities may not have been remarkable, but her taste was exacting and new. She provided Jones with his first full-scale monumental commission when she engaged him to rebuild her lodge at Greenwich, where she had already employed the Frenchman Salomon de Caus, who was introducing a wholly new concept of landscape design into England, with formal gardens, grottoes, fountains and cascades. She had a taste for painting which resulted in a modest collection at Oatlands and Somerset House; she patronised Isaac Oliver, the finest of the miniaturists after the death of Hilliard, and in 1617 she drew into her service Paul van Somer, the most advanced painter to work in England before the coming of Mytens and then Van Dyck. Van Somer's style brought a new maturity to portrait painting, by means of his sensitivity to depth and movement, coupled with an ability to integrate his figures into an atmospheric landscape. Most of Anne's patronage was motivated by her love of magnificence, but she was an active, stimulating patron, unlike James who tended to be a passive recipient of the arts and who rarely imposed high standards of taste, even though he was extremely fortunate in what he received. Inigo Jones gratified the Queen's love of splendour year after year in the annual miracles he performed for her, in which she appeared variously as an Aethiopian nymph, or Bel-Anna Queen of the Ocean, or Neptune's consort Tethys.

The costumes that Jones designed for these masques show an unexpected side of his genius, yet the very fact that he engaged in such work underlines his determination to have all the visual elements of a masque under his control. Even in normal circumstances Court apparel was notoriously extravagant, for the Court served as an exhibition centre for style and wealth, so the creation of costumes for the Queen and her ladies who were to be revealed as divine figures or ideal qualities posed a challenge that Jones tirelessly rose to. Behind his breathtaking inventions often lay learning elegantly concealed. He drew on costume books such as Cesare Vecellio's *Habiti Antichi e Moderni* to give accuracy to foreign or antique dress, and he took care to stress the symbolical appropriateness of costume to character. As an example, we may take the river nymphs in *Tethys Festivall*:

Now concerning their habits: first their head-tire was composed of shels and corrall, and from a great Muriake shell in forme of the crest of an helme, hung a thin wauing vaile. Their vpper garments had the bodies of sky-coloured taffetaes for lightnes, all embroidered with maritime invention: then had they a kinde of halfe skirts of cloth of siluer imbrodered with golde, all the ground work cut out for lightnes, which hung down ful, & cut in points: vnderneath that, came bases (of the same as their bodies) beneath their knee. The long skirt was wrought with lace, waued round like a Riuer, and on the bankes sedge and Seaweedes, all of gold. Their shoulders were all imbrodered with the worke of the short skirt of cloth of siluer, and had cypresse spangled, ruffed out, and fell in a ruffe aboue the Elbow. The vnder sleeues were all imbrodered as the bodies: their shoes were of Satin, richly imbrodered, with the worke of the short skirte.[4]

Men were given an equally gorgeous attention. The masquing lords in *Hymenaei*, for example, had their fashions

taken from the antique Greeke statue; mixed with some moderne additions: which made it both gracefull, and strange. On their heads they wore Persick crownes, that were with scroles of gold-plate turn'd outward, and wreath'd about with a carnation and siluer net-lawne; the one end of which hung carelesly on the left shoulder; the other was trick'd vp before, in seuerall degrees of foulds, betweene the plates, and set with rich iewels, and great pearle. Their bodies were of carnation cloth of siluer, richly wrought, and cut to expresse the naked, in manner of the Greeke Thorax; girt vnder the brests with a broad belt of cloth of gold, imbrodered, and fastened before with iewels: Their Labels were of white cloth of siluer, lac'd, and wrought curiously betweene, sutable to the vpper halfe of their sleeues; whose nether parts, with their bases, were of watchet cloth of siluer, chev'rond all ouer with lace. Their Mantills were of seuerall-colour'd silkes, distinguishing their qualities, as they were coupled in payres; the first, skie colour; the second, pearle colour; the third, flame colour; the fourth, tawnie: and these cut in leaues, which were subtilly tack'd vp, and imbrodered with Oo's, and betweene euerie ranke of leaues, a broad siluer lace.[5]

The anonymous taylors who executed these masterpieces deserved recognition, but none was ever forthcoming; all the acclamation was showered on Inigo Jones and the wearers. To judge by the minutely detailed accounts of dress given in the printed versions of the masques, the costumes provided some of the most prized memories of the performance. The prodigious cost of Inigo's fashions may be imagined. Often one costume would run to two or three hundred pounds, the equivalent to the annual rent from several manors, yet the King and Queen and their companions were willing to pay for their brief apotheosis, for it was irrefutable proof of their greatness to the Court, the only audience that mattered.[6]

As one surveys the long succession of Inigo Jones's costume designs, one is struck by the growing fluency of his draughtsmanship, especially noticeable during the years 1605–10, when he was moving from a rather stiff, painstaking manner to a deft animated style. Orgel and Strong, in their book on Jones's theatrical work, make the point that Jones was virtually the only Englishman of the time who could draw properly, and that much of his success at Court was based on the simple fact that he could express himself lucidly on paper.[7] There is much truth in this opinion, for he must have been constantly submitting designs for approval, and altering them to order: a quick expressiveness with pen and paint was essential. If one compares his draughtsmanship with that of Henry Peacham, who evidently prided himself on his ability to draw, one sees how exceptional Jones was. He seems to have acquired his style from Italian mannerist engravings, for his figure drawings especially, with their elongated sinuous forms, confident and elegant as they half-turn on the page, move in an exhilarating atmosphere of courtly mannerism. This buoyancy of manner continues down to the end of James's reign, after which the liveliness begins to fail and the designs become more derivative and less inventive, but during this central period Jones's drawings can compare with continental masters such as Rubens, Van Dyck or Callot.

When Inigo staged his first masque at Court he was introducing an art form that was fundamentally alien to his audience. Elizabethan masquing entertainments had tended to be a series of tableaux that took place in various parts of a hall, with few properties. The Elizabethan theatre also functioned without scenery, on a shallow stage. The illusory depth that Jones achieved in his set for *The Masque of Blacknesse* by means of single point perspective was unprecedented, and quite baffling to the spectators, who simply were not used to the optical phenomena involved. The lighting and mechanical motion that Jones introduced here were also novel—and it is a sign of his many-sidedness that he had invented the devices necessary to produce the intense focused light and machinery for the stage effects he required.

The Masquers were placed in a great concaue shell, like mother of pearle, curiously made to moue on those waters, and rise with the billow; the top thereof was stuck with a cheu'ron of lights, which, indented to the proportion of the shell, strooke a glorious beame vpon them, as they were seated, one aboue another: so that they were all seene, but in an extrauagant order. . . . These thus presented, the Scene behind, seemed a vast sea (and vnited with this that flowed forth) from the termination, or horizon of which (being the leuell of the State, which was placed in the vpper end of the hall) was drawne, by the lines of Prospectiue, the whole worke shooting downewards, from the eye; which decorum made it more conspicuous, and caught the eye a farre off with a wandring beauty. To which was added an obscure and cloudy nightpiece, that made the whole set of.[8]

This setting was revolutionary, and like many revolutions in the arts was not appreciated. There is a well-known letter from Sir Dudley Carleton complaining about the incoherence of the new staging, and Court gossip writers for the next decade often failed to respond to Inigo's magical effects because they were visually undereducated. (Orgel and Strong go as far as to suggest that for some twenty years the only person in the audience who fully appreciated the Court masques was the Venetian ambassador.)

Jones's mechanical innovations included the *scena versatilis*, or turning stage, a two-sided device which could be rotated to introduce a new scene, or reveal the masquers. This was first used in *Hymenaei* (1606). For *Oberon* (1611) he employed the *scena ductilis*, or sliding scene, a series of flats which could be pulled in and out to open up new backgrounds, and which added considerably to the sense of depth on stage. Because of the relatively large number of scene changes that the *scena ductilis* permitted, it remained the basic vehicle for the rest of Jones's career. These transformation scenes must have provided the moments of greatest wonder, especially when the anti-masque gave way to the masque proper. Entrancing displays of light and music generally covered the change, that often gave visual expression to the secret and sublime operation of majesty that was the central theme of the masques. *Hymenaei* offers a characteristic example:

Here, the vpper part of the Scene, which was all of Clouds, and made artificially to swell, and ride like the Racke, began to open; and, the ayre clearing, in the top thereof was discouered IUNO, sitting in a Throne, supported by two beautifull Peacockes; her attyre rich, and like a Queene, a white Diademe on her head, from whence descended a Veyle, and that bound with a Fascia, of seuerall-coloured silkes, set with all sorts of iewels, and raysed in the top with Lillies and Roses; in her right hand she held a Scepter, in the other a timbrell, at her golden feete the hide of a lyon was placed: round about her sate the spirites of the ayre, in seuerall colours, making musique: Aboue her the region of fire, with a continuall motion, was seene to whirle circularly, and IVPITER standing in the toppe (figuring the heauen) brandishing his thunder: Beneath her the rainebowe, IRIS, and, on the two sides eight ladies, attired richly, and alike in the most celestiall colours, who represented her powers.[9]

Flying machines of various sorts were an important part of the apparatus of wonder, and they grew steadily more ambitious, until the clouds in Jones's late masques became crowded with celestial folk—a theatrical comment perhaps on the inflation of honours, which was a notorious feature of James's reign.

Architectural setting had always been prominent in Jones's scenery, and after his return from his second Italian journey in 1615 he began to concentrate increasingly on the serious practice of architecture in three dimensions. His appointment as Surveyor of Works in that year gave new scope for such activity. He may already have been employed by Robert Cecil to design the South Front of Hatfield House, but his first documented commission was from Arundel for his houses at Greenwich and on the Strand, after which came the Queen's House at Greenwich. Here the challenge was to rebuild an old lodge that stood across the public way to the palace, and Jones's solution to the problem resulted in the first completely modern building in England—modern in this context meaning classical principles refracted through Italian practice of the sixteenth century. A Palladian villa began to rise at Greenwich, with a rusticated ground floor designed to carry a *piano nobile* flanked by loggias and pierced centrally by a Palladian window. Unfortunately, work was suspended in 1618, and the building as we know it today did not take its final shape until the 1630s, when Henrietta Maria had the villa completed to revised designs.

1619 was the *annus mirabilis* of Inigo Jones's career. In that year he designed the new Banqueting House at Whitehall and the Prince's lodging at Newmarket; he was working on Buckingham's new house at Whitehall, as well as producing masque design and supervising the pageantry for Queen Anne's funeral. He had become the complete expositor of Jacobean taste. The importance of the Banqueting House in Stuart affairs cannot be overstated. Although today it sits modestly in Whitehall overshadowed by monumental buildings of a later age, it was then the very nucleus of royal activity; what St Paul's and the Houses of Parliament were to Church and State, so the Banqueting House was to Monarchy. When it burnt down in January 1619, its rebuilding was imperative, for it was the King's hall of state, his audience chamber and his place of judgement; the masques were held here, as was that other ceremony that testified to the King's divinity, the Service of Healing. Banqueting was the least of its functions. The need for a new hall provided Jones with the opportunity to give permanent expression to those monarchical qualities which hitherto had been much proclaimed but only transiently displayed. This Banqueting House would definitively establish James as an Augustus exercising imperial sway, as a Solomon presiding in judgement; it would be a symbol of his peace and of the harmony of his rule, and it would be the Temple of the Stuart Kings. Inigo Jones therefore planned a Roman basilica, that carried imperial, judicial and religious associations, and based his design on a scheme in Vitruvius modified by Palladio.[10] The interior is a gigantic double cube, 110 feet by 55, but that stark fact cannot convey the nobility of these dimensions or the grandeur that radiates from the immaculately controlled order of the parts. Jones transformed the traditional apse of the basilica into a great coffered niche where the King sat in majesty, somewhat in the fashion that Rubens portrayed in the painting on the ceiling above. This niche would have formed the central focus of the room, integrating the King like a living statue into the architecture of the whole, and its removal, some time in the 1630s, must considerably have diminished the dramatic power of the interior scheme. Externally, the pure symmetry of the façade stood out in the heterogeneous jumble of late gothic that composed Whitehall, plainly announcing that a new age had begun.

The speed with which the Banqueting House was rebuilt indicates the urgency with which James viewed the project, for this was the time when Lord Treasurer Cranfield was trying to impose some austerity over the royal finances in order to check the King's habitual overexpenditure, and even the Queen's funeral in spring had been delayed for lack of funds. The overriding justification for this work may perhaps be found in the negotiations for a Spanish bride for Prince Charles which were thought to be on the verge of success.[11] If this happened, James would soon be receiving a Hapsburg princess at his Court, and he would have achieved his ambition of becoming the pivotal figure in European politics, allied to both Protestant and Catholic powers, thus bringing closer his cherished aim of a general peace assured by Stuart dynastic policy. A king in such a position needed a palace that would be an appropriate theatre for his great acts. Even as it was going up, James had it painted as the background to a state portrait by Paul van Somer, in a surprising break with the traditional rich cloth of state that James preferred in his pictures: the new Banqueting House was an invaluable extension to the royal identity. The prospect of a Spanish match spurred other plans for increasing the magnificence of the English Court: the redecoration of St James's Palace and Somerset House, the building of a new chapel in St James, and the establishment of a tapestry factory to weave hangings for the royal palaces.[12]

The other influential work of 1619 was the Prince's lodging at Newmarket, a place that James visited frequently out of his love of horses and racing. No trace of the house remains today, but in its time its design was of the first order of importance for English architecture, for it served as the prototype of the Palladian country house that began to make its appearance in the Caroline period and spread throughout the country in the early eighteenth century.[13] From surviving drawings we recognise the familiar components: the symmetrical box-like outline, the rusticated ground floor, the *piano nobile* lit by large, well-spaced windows, the pillared portico in the form of a temple that gives an authoritative centre to the whole façade, a certain garnishing of statuary at the angles. The basic elements of this design were infinitely adaptable to the needs of the prosperous gentry of the next century and a half who wished to affirm their allegiance to the values of classical dignity, order, balance and restraint that this style embodied. It was remarkable that Jones was able to perfect this form so rapidly. With no notable forerunners in the Italianate manner, and working in a country with no tradition of classical design, he was able to create with the aid of the manuals of Palladio, Scamozzi and Serlio, and from the memory of buildings closely observed in Italy, a series of architectural statements that are masterpieces of their kind. His understanding of classical theory of design and ornament was far in advance of his contemporaries', and only his pupil John Webb attained to a comparable fluency before the appearance of Christopher Wren. Even Nicholas Stone, who was the chief mason on the Banqueting House, never mastered the rhythms and harmonies of the big classical design, excellent though he was in small-scale work, such as tombs.[14] The people who fully understood the principles on which Jones was working were, one suspects, relatively few, primarily the connoisseurs of the Arundel and Pembroke circles where he was a respected intimate.

Jones never wrote an architectural treatise himself, the nearest he came to one being the book *Stone-Heng Restored*, which Webb put together from 'some few indigested notes' and published in 1655, two years after the architect's death. The work really belongs to a much earlier date, to the 1620s in fact, when King James, staying at Wilton, asked Jones to provide an account of the origin and purpose of nearby Stonehenge. Since Inigo Jones was the most learned architect in the kingdom, an informed answer might properly be expected of him. The prevailing view of Stonehenge in the early seventeenth century was a mixture of history and legend, largely derived from Geoffrey of Monmouth's *History* written in the middle of the twelfth century. According to Geoffrey, the stones had been erected by the fifth-century Romano-British king Aurelius Ambrosius as a memorial to some British chiefs massacred by Hengist, and had been magically transported from Ireland by Merlin for that purpose. Even Camden had nothing to add to that story, which he repeats in his *Britannia* whilst wishing that more were known about the monument, which he describes as 'a number of monstrous rude stones'. Jones was the first person to offer a reasoned hypothesis on the subject, and he based his views on what he considered was a systematic study of the remains. The emergence of Inigo Jones as an antiquarian was hardly surprising, for a careful study of ancient buildings was part of an architect's training; indeed the fourth book of Palladio's *Quattro Libri dell'Architettura* (1570) deals specifically with the close analysis of Roman antiquities as an essential grounding for an architect. Whilst in Rome in 1613–14, Inigo had made such an analysis, and when he approached the problem of Stonehenge, he did so primarily as a Renaissance architect, concerned with the geometry and proportions of the structure, and with their historical and philosophic significance. He surveyed the ruin, and established the ground plan to his satisfaction, believing that such objective methods were the principal avenues of knowledge to the origins of such an obscure monument. He also excavated around the stones and found ox-heads and Roman pottery. Both his survey and his findings persuaded him that Stonehenge was of Roman origin. According to his measurements, the ground plan formed by an inner hexagon of stones inside a great circle yielded the significant geometry of four equilateral triangles inscribed within a circle, a figure which he declared appeared in Vitruvius as the plan of a temple. Since Vitruvius had written that the form of a temple should reflect the character of the divinity to which it was dedicated, and Palladio had added that the Ancients built temples dedicated to the sun, the moon and the earth in circular form, Jones after much deliberation decided that

> . . . Stoneheng was dedicated, as I conceive, to the God Coelus, by some Authors called Coelum, by others Uranus, from whom the Ancients imagined all things took their beginning. My reasons are, first, in respect of the situation thereof; for it stands in a Plain, remote from any Town or Village, in a free and open air, without any groves or woods about it.
>
> Secondly, in regard of the Aspect; for Stoneheng was never covered, but built without a roof. Which Decorum the Romans ever observed, both in the Situation and Aspect of the Temples dedicated to this their God. . . . To Jove, the Lightner, and to Coelus, and to the Sun, and to the Moon, they erected buildings in the open air and uncovered, saith Vitruvius in the second Chapter of his first Book. . . .
>
> Thirdly, in regard of the Form of Stoneheng, which is circular. This figure was proper to the Temples of Coelus and Tellus, whom the Ancients called Vesta, as Valerianus (in his Hieroglyphicks) affirms. . . . Besides, observe what Philander commenting on Vitruvius tels us. . . . Although (saith he) the Ancients made some Temples square, some of six sides, others of many angles, they were especially delighted with making of them round, as representing thereby the Form or Figure of Coelum, Heaven.[15]

Moreover, Vitruvius helps to confirm Jones's deductions when he states (Book V, vi) that the geometrical figure of 'four equilateral triangles, at equal distances apart and touching the boundary line of a circle' is the same that astrologers draw in a figure of the zodiac 'when they are making computations from the musical harmony of the stars'. Inigo himself notes that 'the Magi adde that a triangle of equal sides is a symbole of Divinitie, or sign of celestiall matters', and then goes on to observe that the figure taken by the inner group of stones at Stonehenge, the hexagon, was also used by astrologers in their studies of the sympathy of the stars. Therefore the geometrical components of the scheme—circle, triangle, and hexagon—all have astrological affinities. Persuaded by the way everything conformed to

Vitruvian models, Inigo was convinced he was dealing with a Roman temple, albeit a rather shattered one. No other nation in antiquity could have raised such a mathematically disciplined structure involving such mastery of mechanics in the elevation, except the Romans. The British before the invasion were barbarian, and totally unskilled in the arts, as Jones proves from Roman authorities; therefore we must look to the source of civilisation in the west: 'It's demonstrable, that betwixt this Island of great Britain, and Rome it self, there's no one structure to be seen, wherein more clearly shines those harmoniacall proportions, of which only the best times could vaunt, then in this of Stoneheng.'[16]

If Stonehenge is Roman, it follows that it must be based on one of the classical orders; 'the plainnesse and solidnesse' of the stone suggests to Jones the Tuscan order, for that is the severest and simplest, befitting the worship of Coelus, the most ancient of gods. We may be astonished at the improbable nature of Jones's claims. He was after all an architect who work-ed in the classical manner, and he had had first-hand acquaintance with Roman buildings in Italy; how then could he believe Stonehenge to be Roman? The answer must lie in the nature of his architectural imagination: he was steeped in Vitruvianism, and thought instinctively in such terms. When confronted with a ruined stone circle displaying some architectural properties, he must have attempted to ascertain the idea of the work that underlay the confusion of stones. Seeing evidence of symmetry, his formalis-ing mind improved on what he saw until an approximation of a pattern be-came an ideal geometry. The evidence of the senses was less persuasive than the ideas that appealed to the intellect. But we should remember that Jones did not publish his opinions in his lifetime, a fact which may suggest that he had certain reservations about them. Not simply might his attribu-tion of Stonehenge to the Romans have raised scholarly doubts, but also some central points in his argument were suspect. Most seriously the basic ground plan that he claimed to have discovered at Stonehenge was not in fact that of a temple as described in Vitruvius, but of a theatre, and Jones concealed this critical point by cutting short the relevant quotation. Then there was the matter of the measurements, for the inner ring of stones does not form a hexagon but a horseshoe shape, and Jones appears to have re-arranged the stones slightly to suit his ideal plan. Finally, the deity that he believed the temple was dedicated to, Coelus, had a rather shadowy existence in the Roman pantheon, for he was more a personification of the heavens than a god who was worshipped in the ancient world, and although he would have been credible as a figure in a Renaissance masque, he was less so as the centre of a Roman cult.

Some eight years after John Webb gave *Stone-Heng Restored* to the world, Walter Charleton replied with his *Chorea Gigantum* which largely demolished Jones's arguments, and exposed their shortcomings, proposing instead a Danish origin for the monument. Webb returned to defend his master in *A Vindication of Stone-Heng Restored*, the drab prose and flaccid arguments of which contrast strongly with the original treatise, and make it seem extremely probable that the first thesis is substantially in Inigo Jones's own hand with very little retouching from his pupil.

Although many of the notions aired in this book now seem curiosities of seventeenth-century antiquarianism, some were perceptive for their time, most notably the idea that Stonehenge was a temple dedicated to the god of heaven and included some astrological functions in its design, a view which has received considerable support in our own day. The book also tells us a good deal about its author, who did so much and said so little. It testifies formally to the power of Vitruvian ideas over his imagination, and to his own sense of his place in the line of humanist architects of the Renaissance. The breadth of Jones's scholarly reading is also made apparent by the regiment of authorities cited in the margins, where the classical historians, the Italian humanists and contemporary English historians constitute the most prominent groups of sources acknowledged. Jones is particularly interested in the state of culture that prevailed among the ancient Britons; before the Romans came, he contends, all arts were unknown, but after the invasion a considerable magnificence developed in these islands: 'our Britans, in ancient time possessed, together with the Roman civility, all good Arts'—including unquestionably Roman architecture. Behind the speculations about Stonehenge lies a clear vision of an orderly classical civilisation flourishing in Britain with 'knowledge of Arts, to build stately Temples, Palaces, publick Buildings, to be eloquent in forrain languages, and by their habits, and attire, attain the qualities of a civil, and well ordered people'.[17] It was this world that Inigo Jones would evoke when designing scenery for masques set in ancient Britain, such as *Oberon* or *Coelum Britannicum*, and that he was helping to re-establish by means of his own architectural practice, for his classical buildings were reviving a rightful heritage which had been forgotten beneath the long centuries of gothic domination.[18]

One would expect Jones to be an accomplished antiquarian, given the degree of historical knowledge that his profession demanded, and his close friendship with Arundel, Pembroke, and King Charles. His travels in Italy had given him an enviable acquaintance with the fountainhead of antiquity, and his own skill as an artist made him a reliable connoisseur in the matter of paintings, drawings and statuary. We know that in 1616, when Arundel was absent from London, Jones was receiving a consignment of pictures in his stead and was recommending which should be purchased for the collection. Twenty years later we catch another glimpse of him gazing eagerly at some newly-arrived paintings in the company of King Charles, whom he often advised in the choice of works of art: he 'threw off his coat, put on his eye-glasses, took a candle and, together with the King, began to examine them very closely'.[19] The intimacy of the scene is very revealing, and well illustrates Inigo's privileged role as artistic counsellor that he played to two generations of Stuart connoisseurs.

Generally speaking, Jones's most significant work was carried out during the term of his surveyorship under James, simply because there was more money available from the Exchequer than was the case under Charles, who had grandiose schemes, but slender means. James, as we have seen, was able to make some progress in providing the monarchy with buildings expressive of a new era with new values, but Charles had largely to make do with the painted architecture of his masques. One of the last commissions that Inigo received from James was for a new chapel in St James's Palace for the use of Prince Charles's bride, Henrietta Maria, who was permitted the full exercise of her Catholic faith by the terms of the marriage contract. Here again, Jones was able to deploy his innovative power to design a building that would serve as a model for generations of English churches: a chaste rectangle inspired by Palladio, with plain, beautifully proportioned windows, surmounted by an assertive pediment. Inside, the space was uninterrupted by columns, and there were few concessions made to the needs of Catholic worship. The sumptuously coffered roof evoked Rome—ancient Rome. Modern Rome was represented by the remarkable machine for exhibiting the sacrament in glory constructed by François Dieussart, who had recently been in Rome; his full-blown baroque installation would have seemed more proper to the Vatican than to St James. It consisted of a baldacchino-like structure some forty feet high over the altar, sheltering the Paraclete raised on seven banks of clouds crowded with celestial and ecclesiastical worshippers shown adoring the Host. Perspective seems to have been cleverly employed to create a sense of depth, while concealed lighting and hidden musicians added to the glamorous effect. The contraption was fronted with curtains, which were swept aside whenever the Queen arrived for a service. Apart from this curiosity, however, the chapel was the prototype of the style of church that Wren was to adapt so variously in his rebuilding of the City, and which we tend to think of as a Restoration form.

Under the new reign, civic projects occupied Jones's time more intensively than hitherto, for Charles's finances were weak. The reconstruction of

St Paul's, which went on for much of the thirties, we have discussed else-where. A scheme of some importance that he began in the early thirties was the laying out of Covent Garden for the Earl of Bedford, who had decided to develop the area speculatively as an estate for gentlemen. Jones was able to carry out the first exercise in town planning that London had seen, creating a large square surrounded by houses built over arcades, essentially an Italianate piazza set down behind the Strand. On the north side he placed a church, the only public church that he ever designed, a simple, austere affair that he came up with after he had promised the Earl 'the handsomest barn in England' for his new square. Puritanism and economy met in the Earl, and there was little he could complain about in this church, except perhaps its essentially pagan form, for it was a porticoed Roman temple of the plainest order, Tuscan. It was hardly surprising that Jones should attempt to translate a classical temple into a Christian church, given the analogies that were operating between Augustan and Stuart times, and so at this first opportunity to design a Protestant church he turned to the severest Roman style.

Of his royal commissions at this time, the most interesting was the scheme for rebuilding the Cockpit Theatre at Whitehall during 1629–31. Previously, this had been a modest arena variously adaptable to cockfighting or plays, but now Jones redesigned it as an elegant indoor theatre, with an octagonal interior set within a square. On stage Jones introduced a permanent architectural proscenium, as in Palladio's Teatro Olimpico at Vicenza, itself based on Roman theatres with their monumental architectural backdrops. Inigo's construction was of much more modest proportions than Palladio's noble screen, which he had viewed on his visit to Vicenza in 1614. The designs that survive at Worcester College, Oxford, in the hand of Jones's assistant Webb, show that it consisted of a concave façade of a two-storied Palladian pavilion, built across a thirty-five-foot stage, with five doorways for entrances and exits, and a large central window above that took the place of the old Elizabethan balcony. According to the Whitehall accounts the proscenium was made of wood and plaster, yet the effect must have been one of dignified refinement, enhanced by the overall décor of light blue and gold. A distinguished addition to the decoration was the display around the auditorium of the twelve heads of emperors by Titian from the Duke of Mantua's collection. The auditorium itself had quite modest dimensions, with a maximum width of fifty-eight feet, and a depth of twenty-nine feet. Only the King, centrally seated at the rear, could see the performance face on, all the other seats being set at an angle to the stage so that spectators should not sit with their backs to the monarch. Of all the grandiose plans that

Charles had for the rebuilding of Whitehall, the Cockpit was the only work accomplished, a testimony to his abiding love of the theatre. It was demolished about 1675.[20]

Henrietta Maria proved to be a more active patron, for her income was more assured than her husband's. Her main London residence at Somerset House was the scene of prolonged activity from 1627 onwards as she set about rebuilding and redecorating; she also employed Jones to complete the royal villa at Greenwich. The scale of the work at Somerset House enabled Jones to deploy the full range of his abilities, designing new galleries, a chapel, whole new suites of rooms, and ultimately solving the problem of a grand palace frontage on the Strand. This palace represented Jones's most complete scheme of interior decoration, for which some exquisite designs survive for fireplaces, mouldings, and a great screen, elegant and light in manner. Many of these fittings derive their inspiration from French models to suit the Queen's taste.[21] As everything was demolished in the 1770s to make way for the present Somerset House, we have lost our best example of a full-scale interior by Inigo Jones, although we can form an excellent impression of its quality from the scheme at Wilton House, long thought to be by Jones, but now ascribed to Webb.

One detail that deserves attention at Somerset is the design for the water stairs. More than anyone else in his age, Inigo understood the psychology of gateways, liminal structures that mark boundaries and new terrain, formal entrances that announce the greatness of those that dwell within, archways that enlarge the stature of those that pass through them. Capable of endless variations in design, relatively inexpensive to erect, they were a speciality that Jones furnished to the aristocracy throughout his career, and they include some of his happiest inventions. They offered opportunities for a model display of the orders, they ranged in character from the antique rusticity of the Vineyard Gate at Oatlands to the imperial magnificence of the triumphal gateway that Jones designed as the entry to the City at Temple Bar. The waterside entrances to the houses of the nobility along the Thames afforded ideal settings for these gateways. Arundel, Buckingham and the Queen all had Jonesian portals. For the Queen he raised twin obelisks topped by spheres, and decorated with ships' prows or rostra, a Roman victory symbol that provided a simple yet exalted approach to her residence.

Some time around 1638 Jones addressed himself to the question of the Strand frontage of Somerset House, 480 feet long. He projected a monumental façade on an unprecedented scale which brings to mind the Louvre with its horizontal strength and alternating sections of plain and pillared work. A comparison with the modest scale of the Banqueting House shows at once how much grander were the architectural aspirations of the second generation of Stuart kings. This sensation is reinforced when one looks at the plans that Inigo Jones submitted for Charles's most ambitious dream, the building of a completely new Whitehall Palace. The elevations of the principal façades appear to be very closely related to those of Somerset House, and in Inigo's mind the two palaces must have been complementary buildings. Whitehall would have consisted of enormous ranges of building grouped around a central square, having an extremely long river frontage and an equally long range facing St James's Park. Classical throughout, and integrating all the functions of the Court with a rational scheme, it would have done away for ever with the rambling undistinguished hodge-podge of buildings that made up medieval Whitehall. The burgeoning megalomania of King Charles is quite evident in this scheme, which he began to entertain in the late 1630s. It must have been clear from the beginning that the money for it would never be found, yet equally clearly Charles desired a palace that would declare the absolute power of the Stuart monarchy: the palace would dwarf the Houses of Parliament and dress Stuart power in the harmonious discipline and dignity of antique architecture. The obvious parallels are with the Louvre and the Escorial, but their monarchs genuinely possessed the power and wealth implicit in their palaces, whereas Charles still had only a sheaf of paper plans when the Civil Wars put an end to his delusions of grandeur.

After he had designed the last masque, *Salmacida Spolia*, in 1640, Jones largely disappeared from the record. He remained faithful to the Royalist cause he had served so long: in 1642 we hear of him lending £500 to the King, and in 1645 he was captured, in company with Thomas Fuller, at the seige of Basing House. Basing, the home of the Marquis of Winchester, and one of the great Royalist bastions, was besieged by Cromwell himself, who pressed the assault with such ferocity that it is remarkable that Jones was not run through on the spot when his identity was discovered, as the principal image-maker of royal authority. His estates were sequestered, and he had to compound heavily to have them restored. He died in 1652, at the age of seventy-nine, and was buried in St Benet's Church in the City. His monument had a thoroughly secular air: twin obelisks guarding his bust on the top of a tomb-chest, which carried at each end bas-reliefs of his two most celebrated works, the Banqueting House and the portico of St Paul's.

The first two generations of Stuarts were extraordinarily fortunate to have such a man at their disposition. Unique in his range of skills and knowledge, he alone in England was capable of proposing an architecture that was the accepted measure of civility throughout Europe; his work was the first to enable English princes and noblemen to look back across the ages to Rome with an equal eye, and he gave the Stuart monarchy a serene dignity that James and Charles could never quite attain in their personal and political lives.

Notes to Chapter Seven

1   The few details we have about Jones's early career are to be found in his book *Stone-Heng Restored* (1655) and in his pupil John Webb's *Vindication of Stone-Heng Restored* (1665). See also *The King's Arcadia: Inigo Jones and the Stuart Court*, a catalogue of the 1973 exhibition, by J. Harris, S. Orgel and R. Strong.

2   See Vitruvius *De Architectura*, Book I (Loeb Library edition) for the education of the architect. R. Wittkower's *Architectural Principles in the Age of Humanism*, London 1949, provides the best account of the application of Vitruvian principles in the Renaissance.

3   We know Jones had read Dee's book, as he quotes from it in his treatise on Stonehenge.

4   *The Complete Works of Samuel Daniel*, ed. Grosart, London 1885, III, pp. 318–19.

5   Ben Jonson, *Works*, VII, pp. 229–30.

6   The Queen's bill from her 'silkman' for the costumes for *Tethys Festivall* came to £1,984. For details of the cost of masques, see Orgel and Strong, *Inigo Jones; the Theatre of the Stuart Court*, Berkeley, Cal. 1973.

7   *Ibid.*, p. 34.

8   Ben Jonson, *Works*, VII, pp. 171–2.

9   *Ibid.*, pp. 216–17.

10   To some extent Jones applied to the Banqueting House plans that he had already drawn up for the reconstruction of the Star Chamber, where the King sat in council and pronounced on state affairs. This design combined elements from Palladio's reconstruction of a Roman basilica and a temple, and included a great judicial niche. See Palme, *Triumph of Peace*, London 1957, pp. 185–9.

11   For an extended argument relating the rebuilding of the Banqueting House to the preparations for the Spanish wedding, see Palme, *op. cit.*, pp. 7–40.

12   Sir Francis Crane was given a twenty year monopoly, and set up the works at Mortlake with Flemish weavers; he proceeded to produce excellent tapestries. For details, see W. G. Thompson, *Tapestry Weaving in England*, London 1914, and Palme, *op. cit.*, pp. 26–8.

13   For example, the following houses designed by Webb show the influence of the Newmarket Lodge: Cobham Hall, Kent (1648), the designs for Belvoir Castle (1654), Gunnersbury, Middlesex (1657), Amesbury Abbey, Wilts. (1661).

14   See, for example, his exquisitely chaste and correct tomb for Lord Dorchester (Sir Dudley Carleton) in Westminster Abbey (1632). As ambassador in Venice and a lover of the Italian arts, Carleton deserved such a monument.

15   Inigo Jones, *Stone-Heng Restored*, 1655, pp. 101–2.

16   *Ibid.*, p. 33.

17   *Ibid.*, p. 13.

18   The masque costumes of Prince Henry and King Charles as Roman emperors belong to a related scenario, in which the Stuart princes are seen as the inheritors and renewers of the classical values of Romano-British times.

19   See *The King's Arcadia*, p. 67.

20   See G. E. Bentley, *The Jacobean and Caroline Stage*, Oxford 1968, vol. VI, pp. 267–84.

21   For details of these designs, see *The King's Arcadia*, pp. 148–58.

[8]

Ben Jonson among the courtiers

If Inigo Jones set the visual tone for the Stuart Court, Ben Jonson expressed the complementary morality. His stance was Roman, ethical and severe; he took it upon himself to become the arbiter of civil virtue in his time, and during James's reign he achieved wide recognition in this role. Horace and Martial were the models he most enduringly admired, for their sharp commentary on men and morals, and it was their instruments of social observation, the epistle and the epigram, that Jonson adapted to his own needs. In both forms Jonson employs a plain, direct style, sinewy and spare, direct and questioning; there is little concern for surface beauty, but a constant interplay of observation and judgement on the quality of contemporary life. By addressing the wide circle of his friends he was able to build up the idea of a society whose nobility was as much a matter of elevation of mind as of birth. No previous English poet had attempted to treat his own immediate society as material for poetry in this way. Jonson for the most part eschewed the standard poetic subjects of his time—matters of love, heroic action, history or romance—but found his inspiration in the behaviour of his friends and patrons, after the fashion of the social poetry of Horace. In taking this approach, Jonson underlined his sense of affinity with the Roman poet, an affinity announced as early as 1601 in *Cynthia's Revels*, where the quarrels of London's literary world were transferred into a classical Roman setting, with Jonson as Horace. He also intended to give his subjects the stature of Roman figures of the Augustan age by associating their lives with Roman literary models. The details of his social poems have a powerful English flavour, but the verbal allusions and aspects of behaviour selected for comment subtly establish that his characters are being measured by a Roman scale, and are not found wanting. The very theme of friendship that Jonson so often celebrates shows in itself a Roman bias, while the intimate relations that Jonson enjoys with great men and women as a result of his privileged status as poet also reflect the circumstances of Horace's own position in Roman society. Naturally, Jonson was patronised by that section of the nobility and gentry that was sensitive to literary merit, and in return for hospitality and support, he undertook to record the virtues of those families in enduring poetry. That verse shall outlast marble or the gilded monuments of princes is an agreeable half-truth which has a certain undeniable validity, for a number of names eminent in the early seventeenth century survive today primarily because they were honoured in Jonson's poetry.

A survey of Jonson's patrons and friends brings us into contact with the principal encouragers of literature in the Court circle. If King James stood as Augustus to Jonson, who could praise his virtues on the great state occasions of the masques, then William Herbert, Earl of Pembroke, occupied the role of Maecenas. William's mother, Mary, Countess of Pembroke, was Sir Philip Sidney's sister, and the closely connected Herbert and Sidney families provided Jonson with his most enlightened patrons. Pembroke himself sustained a remarkable reputation for integrity and intelligence unblemished until his death in 1630. Amidst all the venality and favouritism of James's Court he occupied the controlling position of Lord Chamberlain with firmness and honour; Clarendon, a historian hesitant to praise, regarded him as the most admirable of the principal officers of state: 'the most universally belov'd and esteem'd of any man of that age; and, having a great Office in the Court, he made the Court it self better esteem'd, and more reverenced in the Country'.

He was a great lover of his Country, and of the Religion, and Justice, which he believ'd could only support it; and his Friendships were only with men of those Principles. And as his Conversation was most with men of the most pregnant parts, and understanding, so towards any such, who needed support, or encouragement, though unknown, if fairly recommended to him, he was very liberal. Sure never man was planted in a Court, that was fitter for that Soil, or brought better qualities with him to purify that Air.[1]

His liberality towards Jonson included a substantial annual gift of twenty pounds for the purchase of books, as well as the hospitality and protection that patronage traditionally extended. In return, Jonson dedicated to Pembroke his tragedy *Catiline* (1611), which he considered his best play, his *Epigrams*, 'the ripest fruit of my studies', which he valued far above his plays because of their humanist content, and in 1616 the Folio of his complete works. In 1619, Pembroke's influence as Chancellor of the University of Oxford secured for Jonson the rare award of an M.A. for his achievement in *literae humaniores*, an act which gave Jonson, who had never attended university, the coveted scholarly approval that he had long wished for. In the dedication to the *Epigrams* he speaks of Pembroke's 'honour of leading

forth so many good and great names . . . to their remembrance with pos-
teritie', a reminder of how Pembroke had continued his mother's tradition
of promoting English letters. The value of his approbation may be known
by the number of books dedicated to Pembroke: over ninety, a figure that
far exceeded the dedications to any of his non-royal contemporaries. Himself a poet of modest abilities, he was a generous friend to the artistic fratern-
ity of the day. He had recognised and encouraged the rising genius of
Shakespeare. Samuel Daniel had been his tutor, and John Ford the future
playwright had received help from him in his early years. Sir John Harington's much admired *Epigrams* were dedicated to him in 1613, William
Browne offered his *Britannia's Pastorals* in 1616. John Davies of Hereford,
whom King James esteemed as one of England's finest poets because of the
philosophical nature of his verse, also moved in the Pembroke circle. At the
other end of the scale of respectability, the itinerant water-boatman John
Taylor, the indefatigable composer of doggerel verse who intruded into so
many great men's lives, grappled his way into Pembroke's good will with a
dedication of his works in 1617 and again in 1630. Thomas Tompkins
presented his *Songs* in 1622, and a rising poet of the new generation, Francis
Quarles, found encouragement for his *Sion's Elegies* in 1624. Noble recognition and support were essential to counterbalance the vicissitudes of a
literary career in this period, and Pembroke more than any of his peers
performed these services with magnanimity. In the eyes of posterity his
reward was to receive, jointly with his brother Philip, the dedication of the
Shakespeare Folio in 1623, the most enviable dedication in the history of
English literature.

It may well have been Jonson's authorship of the masques that gave him
his entrée into the interlocking circles of the cultivated aristocracy. The dancers in *The Masque of Blacknesse*, for example, included the Countess of
Bedford, the Countess of Suffolk, Lady Anne Herbert, Lady Susan Herbert,
and Lady Mary Wroth, all of whom became involved in Jonson's life. The
Countess of Suffolk's husband was instrumental in 1605 in freeing Jonson
from prison, where he had been sent for his contributions to the anti-
Scottish satire in *Eastward-Ho*, and at the end of the same year he wrote the
masque *Hymenaei* for the marriage of the Suffolks' daughter Frances
Howard to the Earl of Essex. Of the other ladies, Lady Mary Wroth and
Lucy, Countess of Bedford, developed especially close relations with
Jonson.

Lady Mary was the daughter of Sir Robert Sidney, the niece of Sir
Philip Sidney, and the cousin to William, Earl of Pembroke. She inherited a
fair measure of the literary talent that flowed so abundantly in her family,

writing love poetry and composing a voluminous romance *Urania* (1621) in the style of the *Arcadia* and dedicated to her cousin's wife Susan Herbert, Countess of Montgomery. It is an accomplished work of amoristic chivalry, coloured by neo-platonism—the very title suggests the heavenly love that is the ultimate goal of the many quests. What strikes one about the *Urania* is its masculine vigour: the author takes particular pleasure in the rituals of chivalric encounter, in set combats and in tournaments with their display of devices and *imprese*. The language of the romance also commands respect: the courteous discourse of the gentle characters proclaims a considerable verbal adroitness to be one of Lady Mary's special gifts. To this brilliant, spirited woman Jonson dedicated *The Alchemist* in 1610, and directed several short poems of praise, one of which, Epigram cv, casts an appreciative glance at her intelligent realisation of classical deities in her masquing roles:

> If dancing, all would cry th' Idalian Queene,
>   Were leading forth the Graces on the greene:
> And, armed to the chase, so bare her bow
>   Diana alone, so hit, and hunted so.
> There's none so dull, that for your stile would aske,
>   That saw you put on Pallas plumed caske:
>   . . .
> So are you Natures Index, and restore,
>   I' your selfe, all treasure lost of th' age before.

Lady Mary's husband, Sir Robert Wroth, was the recipient of one of Jonson's finest epistles. Modelled on Horace's Second Epode, in praise of a country life, it mythologises Sir Robert's life on his Middlesex estate into a timeless ideal of rural contentment. For peace of mind, independence of spirit, self-sufficiency and sanity, the congenial routines of the changing year offer a perpetual yet temperate pleasure. Here is no country lethargy, but a full round of rewarding labour and recreation evoked in a mature verse, alive with spirit and judgement. Wroth's rural year moves in a productive cycle of natural wealth:

> The whil'st, the severall seasons thou hast seene
>   Of flowrie fields, of cop'ces greene,
> The mowed meddowes, with the fleeced sheepe,
>   And feasts, that either shearers keepe;
> The ripened eares, yet humble in their height,
>   And furrowes laden with their weight;
> The apple-harvest, that both longer last;
>   The hogs return'd home fat from mast;

The trees cut out in log; and those boughes made
    A fire now, that lent a shade!

(ll. 37–46)

The life Wroth leads is self-contained and innocent, causing no harm or
disruption to his fellow men. Inspired by the noble simplicity of his Horatian
theme, Jonson could turn a moralist's eye on the vanity and extravagance of
Court life, seeing it as the epitome of prodigal waste, the enemy of contentment:

Nor throng'st (when masquing is) to have a sight
    Of the short braverie of the night;
To view the jewells, stuffes, the paines, the wit
    There wasted, some not paid for yet!

(ll. 9–12)

The structure of the poem closely follows that of Horace, although the details have been thoroughly anglicised; the total effect is to make Wroth a
naturalised inhabitant of the antique world, and to make the reader feel
that there is a natural continuity between the moderated, virtuous life of
Horace's country gentleman and that of the Jacobean Wroth. The final
meditation on the good life, on the right relationship between man and
heaven, with its emphasis on *pietas* and its echo of Juvenal, would be as
acceptable to a first-century Roman of philosophic mind as to a reflective
seventeenth-century Christian:

God wisheth, none should wracke on a strange shelfe:
    To him, man's dearer, then t' himselfe.
And, howsoever we may thinke things sweet,
    He alwayes gives what he knowes meet;
Which who can use is happy: Such be thou.
    Thy morning's, and thy evening's vow
Be thankes to him, and earnest prayer, to finde
    A body sound, with sounder minde;
To doe thy countrey service, thy selfe right;
    That neither want doe thee affright,
Nor death; but when thy latest sand is spent,
    Thou maist thinke life, a thing but lent.

(ll. 95–106)

It is the spacious mind of the poet that perceives these shared values and
confirms their enduring importance by means of judicious expression and
example; in the familiar tone of the opening line of the epistle ('How blest
art thou, canst love the country, Wroth'), we hear Jonson claiming equality
with his noble friend on the basis of his special status as a poet, who by his

learning and his moral eminence deserves to hold a privileged place in a cultivated society.

That society may be observed in its most distinguished form in the poem 'To Penshurst'. Its recipient must have been Sir Robert Sidney, brother of Sir Philip and father of Lady Mary Wroth, but the poem essentially commemorates the house of Sidney rather than any individual. Deeply attached to its estates and to the local landscape that has gathered powerful associations through generations of possession, the family maintains the admirable tradition of liberal hospitality in its modest, venerable house, thriving on a mutual interchange of good will and respect with its tenantry. The natural world of flesh, fowl, fruit and fish offers itself up in willing sacrifice to these noble lords of creation. Everywhere there is a sense of proper order, dignity, good husbandry and generosity, all verified by the poet's own experience. The arts have no special place (except by implication, in that a poet chooses to celebrate Penshurst) yet they form an accepted part of the rounded life of the family. An air of *pietas* prevails amongst the family, a reverence for what is honorable and just. Jonson's indebtedness to several of Martial's epigrams for the central sections of this poem has long been recognised, yet so skilfully have the details of the Latin poems been adapted to the English setting that there seems a perfect consonance between the idealised Roman life of the first century A.D. as described by Martial and the quality of life attained by the Sidneys.[2] Their existence moves in a classical pattern. As Inigo Jones was attempting to introduce into early seventeenth-century England an architecture derived from first-century Rome, Jonson was trying to advance the ideal of a full, balanced life based on the precepts of Horace, Juvenal and Martial. Jonson and Jones were complementary figures in areas far beyond their collaboration on the masques.

When Jonson came to celebrate the coming of age of Sir William Sidney, Sir Robert's son, in 1611, he did so by means of an ode, still a novel form in English poetry at this time. Its elaborate stanzaic pattern demonstrates Jonson's command of the form, yet for all its structural complexity the poem has a lightness and buoyancy proper to the occasion:

> Now that the harth is crown'd with smiling fire,
>   And some doe drinke, and some doe dance.
>   Some ring,
>   Some sing,
>   And all doe strive t' advance
> The gladnesse higher:
>   Wherefore should I
>   Stand silent by.

> Who not the least,
> Both love the cause, and authors of the feast?
> Give me my cup, but from the Thespian well,
> That I may tell to Sydney, what
> This day
> Doth say,
> And he may thinke on that
> Which I doe tell:
> When all the noyse
> Of these forc'd joyes,
> Are fled and gone,
> And he, with his best Genius left alone.
>
> (ll. 1–20)

The ode proceeds to encourage in the young Sidney a heroic resolution to pursue honour and renown, adding to his great family's store. Jonson himself confers some of that renown by the tribute of this poem, which classicises its subject, furnishing him out in antique dress, the poetic equivalent of the costume so often adopted in the masques. We notice that Jonson is usually present on the edge of his poems, associating himself with his noble subjects and subtly implying his own stature by his strong, plain language and his informal tone of authority. Jonson knew that the right to adopt this position of judge and moral preceptor depended on his own possession of certain necessary qualities: classical learning, a knowledge of men and manners, a sense of history, and a moral integrity of his own. He explained his belief in the Preface to *Volpone*:

If men will impartially, and not asquint, look toward the offices and function of a poet, they will easily conclude to themselves the impossibility of any man's being the good poet, without first being a good man. He that is said to be able to inform young men to all good disciplines, inflame grown men to all great virtues, keep old men in their best and supreme state, or, as they decline to childhood, recover them to their first strength; that comes forth the interpreter and arbiter of nature, a teacher of things divine no less than human, a master in manners; and can alone, or with a few, effect the business of mankind: this, I take him, is no subject for pride and ignorance to exercise their railing rhetoric upon.

One of Jonson's early poems, addressed to Sir Philip Sidney's daughter, Elizabeth, Countess of Rutland, established the reciprocal need of great spirits for great poets. Reflecting on all the unsung greatness of the world that has sunk into unremembered oblivion, he writes:

> Madame, thinke what store
> The world hath seene, which all these had in trust,
> And now lye lost in their forgotten dust.
> It is the Muse, alone, can raise to heaven,

> And, at her strong armes end, hold up, and even,
> The soules shee loves.

>> (ll. 38–43)

His ambition aspires to immortalise the house of Sidney, so worthy of his Muse:

> Who made a lampe of Berenices hayre?
> Or lifted Cassiopea in her chayre?
> But onely Poets, rapt with rage divine?
> And such, or my hopes faile, shall make you shine.

>> (ll. 61–4)[3]

Jonson seems to have found literary relationships with great ladies easy to sustain. In general, he found friendship a more rewarding emotion than love, and several of his finest epistles are addressed to women from whom he received sympathetic entertainment. One of these was Katherine, Lady Aubigny, married to Jonson's earliest patron Esmé Stuart, younger brother to the Duke of Lennox, cousin and favourite of the King. Her quiet retired life, so different from her husband's involvement in Court affairs, drew from Jonson a poem that made her virtuous career exemplary in an age too avid for vain delights:

> Wherewith, then, Madame, can you better pay
>   This blessing of your starres, then by that way
> Of vertue, which you tread? what if alone?
>   Without companions? 'Tis safe to have none.
> In single paths, dangers with ease are watch'd:
>   Contagion in the prease is soonest catch'd.
> This makes, that wisely you decline your life,
>   Farre from the maze of custome, error, strife,
>   And keepe an even, and unalter'd gaite;
>   Not looking by, or back (like those, that waite
> Times, and occasions, to start forth, and seeme)
>   Which though the turning world may dis-esteeme,
> Because that studies spectacles, and showes,
>   And after varyed, as fresh objects goes,
> Giddie with change, and therefore cannot see
>   Right, the right way: yet must your comfort bee
> Your conscience, and not wonder, if none askes
>   For truthes complexion, where they all weare maskes.

>> (ll. 53–70)

Jonson's serious appraisal of feminine lives represented a new development in English letters: his poems to the great ladies of his time are contributions to a humanist view of society in which men and women move on equal terms, in which character, although conditioned by ancestry and breeding, is essentially a conscious creation of liberal spirit.4 Qualities of mind and morals in women attract Jonson much more than their beauty.

Jonson was inevitably drawn into the orbit of the most remarkable of the Jacobean intellectual ladies, Lucy, Countess of Bedford. Born into a family noted for its literary interests and courtly attainments, the Haringtons of Exton, she had married the Earl of Bedford in 1594. In the new reign she occupied a central position at Court, being the closest companion of Queen Anne and famous for her beauty and wit, as well as the most brilliant participant in the early masques. Her house at Twickenham, which she acquired in 1607, became a resort for the foremost poets of the time. She encouraged the creation of literature in a fashion reminiscent of the Countess of Pembroke, patronising writers in a broad range of subjects both secular and religious, as well as strengthening an English response to continental literature. At her suggestion, John Florio undertook his great translation of Montaigne's Essays, which he dedicated to her in 1603, just as he also offered her the most significant dictionary of Italian and English, his *World of Words*, which did so much to improve an Englishman's access to Italian. Samuel Daniel lived in her household for a while, working on some of his philosophical poems on English history, and also inventing the first Jacobean masque, *The Vision of the Twelve Goddesses*, rather elementary in its action and heavy with learned devices, which was presented at Court in January 1604, the forerunner of the much more elaborate productions of Jonson and Jones. The *Vision* was dedicated to the Countess, who had danced the part of Vesta. Daniel's friend Drayton long enjoyed the Countess's support for his many reconstructions of medieval English history, as a sequence of dedications bears witness. Donne was her most eminent literary friend; their association lasted from the beginning of the century until her death in 1627. Since Chapman belonged to her circle, and then Jonson, it is evident that Lucy Harington was the gravitational centre of an impressive system of literary planets, and poets never tired of extolling the light-giving power of her Christian name. What one would dearly like to possess is some account of the conversation that animated these relationships—an account which would convey some notion of the Countess's brilliance of mind. Clearly, she was an excellent catalyst of ideas, a philosophic 'understander' of the new literary manner that Donne was evolving in his poems and Jonson in his masques. The admiration and affection with which these men viewed her indicate a woman of unusual powers; the paintings and miniatures that survive catch her vivacity and splendour of appearance, but even though we are conscious of an electric feeling in the air when her name is mentioned, the distinctive note of her character has been lost.

Donne caught something of the mood of exalted privilege that her friendship conferred in an epistle to her written about 1607–08:

> Therefore I study you first in your Saints,
> Those friends, whom your election glorifies,
> Then in your deeds, accesses, and restraints,
> And what you reade, and what your selfe devize.
>
> (ll. 9–12)

What we know about those devisings produces the image of an early seventeenth-century virtuoso. The Countess wrote poetry that she exchanged with Donne and Jonson for their scrutiny. She made a translation of Lucretius (still in manuscript in the British Library) which must have been the first translation of this materialist philosopher; the very choice of Lucretius suggests a daring, speculative mind, for his Epicurean views, his denial of Providence and of the immortality of the soul would hardly have been approved in Jacobean times. This translation must belong before 1612–13, when illness and family afflictions induced a pronounced religious cast of thought in her. Music flowed through her house, where John Dowland was an honoured guest. She collected pictures, although we know little about her collection, and she evidently had some expertise in the matter of antique coins and medals. Although not a great builder, she had an advanced interest in garden design, for at Twickenham, and later at her other house at Moor Park, she laid two of the great gardens of the age. Twickenham (celebrated by Donne in *Songs and Sonets*) was an emblematic garden whose central conceit was a series of concentric circles of walks and trees, a horticultural microcosm of the old Ptolemaic universe. Moor Park exhibited the avant-garde techniques of gardening, with terrace, parterres, grotto, classical statuary and fountains.⁵ Such was the ambiance that the Countess provided for her friends.

Jonson had early penetrated into this world. He must have been on good terms with her by 1601 when he affectionately and gallantly inscribed to her a copy of *Cynthia's Revels*, the satirical comedy by which he hoped to gain favour at Elizabeth's Court, and he obviously regarded Lucy Harington as a promoter of his interests there. Various epigrams record moments of their relationship: the lines on his receipt of a fat buck from the Countess (that Drummond noted as one of Jonson's favourite recitation pieces), the verses he sent to her along with a copy of Donne's *Satires* that she had requested, where he pays her the succinct tribute that 'rare poemes aske rare friends', and that fine complimentary piece, Epigram lxxvi, in which he

sketches the essential character of his muse only to realise that in every respect he is describing the qualities of Lucy, Countess of Bedford.

> This morning, timely rapt with holy fire,
>> I thought to forme unto my zealous Muse,
> What kind of creature I could most desire,
>> To honor, serve, and love; as Poets use.
> I meant to make her faire, and free, and wise,
>> Of greatest bloud, and yet more good then great;
> I meant the day-starre should not brighter rise,
>> Nor lend like influence from his lucent seat.
> I meant shee should be curteous, facile, sweet,
>> Hating that solemne vice of greatnesse, pride;
> I meant each softest vertue, there should meet,
>> Fit in that softer bosome to reside.
> Onely a learned, and a manly soule
>> I purpos'd her; that should, with even powers,
> The rock, the spindle, and the sheeres controule
>> Of destinie, and spin her owne free houres.
> Such when I meant to faine, and wish'd to see,
>> My Muse bad, Bedford write, and that was shee.

One final act of patronage by a noble lady merits attention, the commission for the masque *Hymenaei* that resulted from his friendship with the
Countess of Suffolk. That relationship was neither long nor profound, but
its fruit was rich, for it provided Jonson with the opportunity for a peacock
display of learning and poetry at Court, where the marriage between Suffolk's daughter and the young Earl of Essex was celebrated on 5 January
1606. The occasion gave Jonson an ideal chance to present a substantial
work to a Court audience. *The Masque of Blacknesse* of the previous year had
been brief, with the slenderest of fables and small scope for poetic set pieces,
but *Hymenaei* exhibited Jonson at his favourite task of reconstructing
antiquity for the benefit of his contemporaries. As his play *Sejanus* had
dramatised in minute detail the political intrigues of the reign of Tiberius,
Hymenaei recreates a Roman wedding ceremony of the first century in
honour of the Essex marriage. Inigo Jones co-operated, working out the
costumes in exact antiquarian detail. Jonson's notes in the printed text
constitute a treatise on Roman nuptial customs, but they also authenticate
'the endevour of learning, and sharpnesse in these transitorie devices'.
The feast of learning was accompanied by brilliant strains of the poetry of
marriage, culminating in the great formal Epithalamion. These prominent
elements formed the immediately relevant matter of the masque. Its
'remov'd mystery', as Jonson calls it in the Preface, was a revelation of the

power and necessity of union, corporeally, politically and philosophically understood. The marriage exemplifies the principle of union wrought by love that pervades creation: the union of God with man, heaven with earth, the King with his kingdom, man with wife, all achieved by the rule of Reason and the proper exercise of the desires and affections. Jonson's theme was amplified by Inigo Jones's provision of a great 'Microcosm, or Globe, (signifying Man)' from which the masquers emerged, and which universalised the implications of the action, while the discovery of a heaven behind the rack of clouds showed the secret dimension of divinity that participates in and influences the events of the world below. By a fortunate coincidence (that Jonson would not have regarded as a coincidence at all) Juno the goddess of marriage can become by the process of anagram Unio, the principle of Union. This conceit is central to the masque. The union which he wishes to praise before the King is the Union of Great Britain, achieved by James and often described by him in terms of marriage. Nor does Jonson in this festival of love neglect to praise the royal marriage itself:

> O you, whose better blisses
> Haue proou'd the strict embrace
>   Of VNION, with chast kisses,
> And seene it flow so in your happie race;
>
>   That know, how well it binds
> The fighting seedes of things,
>   Winnes natures, sexes, minds,
>   And eu'rie discord in true musique brings.

(ll. 95–102)

By easy unforced association Jonson links the marriage of Essex and Suffolk to the royal marriage of James and Anne, to James's marriage to his kingdom (which is a union effected by the King's divine love for his people), to the union of the wayward elements of human nature under the governance of Reason, and to the union of heaven and earth by the love of God: 'Such was the Golden Chaine let downe from Heaven'. Music naturally expresses the concord that the masque describes in so many ways, just as the measured dance shows men and women caught in an abstract harmony. Much more than *The Masque of Blacknesse*, *Hymenaei* demonstrated the capacity of the masque form for large intellectual statement, revealing in its different levels of activity the complex inter-relationship of the divine, the human and the natural.[6] Jones was able to introduce a gigantic turning globe and a whirling region of fire in the heavens; these memorable images were supplemented by a cloud-borne consort of musicians, and by a more sophisticated mode of aerial movement for his deities, 'who descended upon the stage, not after the stale downright perpendicular fashion, like a bucket into a well, but came gently sloping down'.⁷ Ferrabosco's music and Thomas Giles's dances bound up the whole, and the entertainment was a convincing success.

Jonson was quick to claim the lion's share of that success. From the earliest days of his collaboration with Inigo Jones he inclined to play down the scenic side of the masque, which to his mind supported and elaborated the ideas crystallised in his poetry: Jones exercised a mechanic art that was merely instrumental to the soul of Jonson's genius. In his prefatory remarks to *Hymenaei* Jonson immediately emphasises the primacy of the poet over the designer on the ground that the one speaks to the mind, while the other only binds the senses of the spectators.

It is a noble and iust aduantage, that the things subiected to vnderstanding haue of those which are obiected to sense, that the one sort are but momentarie, and meerely taking; the other impressing, and lasting: Else the glorie of all these solemnities had perish'd like a blaze, and gone out, in the beholders eyes. So short-liu'd are the bodies of all things, in comparison of their soules. And, though bodies oft-times haue the ill luck to be sensually preferr'd, they find afterwards, the good fortune (when soules liue) to be vtterly forgotten.

(ll. 1–10)

This was wantonly provocative of Jonson, to try to monopolise the credit for a new art form which was essentially a co-operative venture, for the magic of presentation was as indispensable as the poetry in the ceremonial of the masque, and Jones must have known that he commanded a greater range of skills than his colleague. Jones after all was unique in England, while Jonson was one of a dozen poets who could turn out a masque. One cannot accuse Jonson of resenting intellectual and creative genius, for his friends included the greatest artists of the age, from Shakespeare and Donne downwards. Incompatibility of temperament may well have been the explanation. Even though King James found both Jonson and Jones 'wondrous necessary men', their collaboration seems always to have been marked by a suspicion and an antagonism that grew worse with the years. Royal favouritism later increased the tension, for under Charles Jones became a welcome companion of the King on account of his connoisseurship of the arts, while Jonson suffered royal neglect, in spite of his occasional pathetic appeals for attention and funds.

Their acrimony endured a long history, of which only Jonson's side was written down. He published several malicious epigrams in 1616 apparently aimed at Jones, notably 'On the Townes Honest Man' and 'On the New Motion', and in 1619 Drummond recorded Jonson's boast that 'he said to Prince Charles of Inigo Jones, that when he wanted words to express the

greatest Villaine in ye World, he would call him an Inigo'.[8] In the unper-
formed masque of *Neptune's Triumph* (1624) Jonson parodied the architect's
claim to universal proficiency in the arts with the figure of the Whitehall
cook, who professes to exercise a similar learned competence with the mater-
ials of his art:

> He designes, he drawes,
> He paints, he carues, he builds, he fortifies,
> Makes Citadels of curious foule, and fish,
> Some he dry-ditches, some motes round with broths;
> Mounts marrow-bones; cuts fifty-angled custards;
> Reares bulwarke pies; and, for his outer workes,
> He raiseth ramparts of immortall crust.

> (ll. 89–95)

> He is an Architect, an Inginer,
> A Souldier, a Physitian, a Philosopher,
> A generall Mathematician!

> (ll. 104–6)

This engaging trivialisation of Jones's skills can hardly have sweetened the
relationship.

The quarrel came to a head in 1631, after Jonson had composed the two
Court masques for that year.[9] The cause of the dispute was essentially the
same issue as the one Jonson had touched on in the preface to *Hymenaei*
twenty-five years previously, his insistence on the primacy of the poet in
the invention of the masque, and Jones took offence at Jonson's printing his
name first on the published title-pages. D. J. Gordon points out that
'Renaissance theories of composition imply that finding the subject and
expressing it are separate mental acts',[10] and that Jonson believed the initial
conceptual act in the poet's mind that was the genesis of the masque should
be regarded as the *primum mobile* of the whole work. He refused to accept
that Inigo Jones's contribution had a comparable controlling idea; indeed,
he never acknowledged the intellectually elevated status attributed to
architects in the Renaissance on the basis of Vitruvius's account of their
attainments, just as he never praised any of Jones's buildings that were
bringing an Augustan distinction to London. Instead, he attempted to hold
Jones up to ridicule as a pretentious charlatan in the satire he circulated at
Court entitled 'An Expostulation with Inigo Jones'. The disdainful fleering
tone of the opening reads uncomfortably now, but there is undeniable
power in the main section which resentfully proclaims the plywood triumphs of the recent masques, where, as he sees it, Jonsonian genius has
been conquered by Jonesian trickery:

> O Showes! Showes! Mighty Showes!
> The Eloquence of Masques! What need of prose,
> Or Verse, or sense, t' express Immortall you?
> You are the Spectacles of State! 'Tis true
> Court Hiero-gly-phicks! & all Artes afford,
> In the mere perspective of an Inch board!
> You aske noe more then certeyne politique Eyes!
> Eyes, that can pierce into the Misteryes
> Of many Coulors! read them! & reveale
> Mythology, there, painted on slit-deale!
> O, to make Boardes to speake! There is a taske!
> Painting, & Carpentry, are the Soule of Masque!
>
> (ll. 39–50)

Then the pent-up irritation of years explodes when he attacks what he sees as Jones's failure as a stage manager and mocks at his affectation of 'Design', a word as sacred to Jones as 'Invention' was to Jonson, both words signifying the conceptual centres of their respective arts.

> To plant the Musique where noe eare can reach!
> Attyre the persons as noe thought can teach
> Sense, what they are! which by a specious, fyne
> Terme of the Architects, is called Designe!
> But, in the practisd truth, Destruction is
> Of any Art, besyde what he calls his!
>
> (ll. 53–8)

There follows a withering reduction of Jones's skills and accomplishments which only served in the end to discredit Jonson himself in the opinion of the Court.

This unwillingness to admit that Jones's genius in any way approached the divinely-inspired gifts of the poet must have irked Jones, for when the masquing season came round again in 1632, he placed on the proscenium arch for *Albion's Triumph* figures of Theoria and Practica as a statement of his dual powers as a theorist and executant, and Theoria's gold compasses pointed firmly heavenwards as proof of the divine origin of his Design. Jonson had not been invited to write the masque that year, presumably as a result of Inigo's influence at Court, nor would he ever regain his footing in Whitehall. He retaliated with a sneer at Jones in his unsuccessful play *A Tale of a Tub* (1633), where In-and-In Medlay, an incompetent joiner, prepares a masque for Squire Tub, which turns out to be a very entertaining spoof of Jones's love of effects of light and motion, consisting of a puppet show in a barrel, lit by a candle, proudly presented as a thing of learning and antiquity. In-and-In prides himself on his powers of design:

Medlay: I have a little knowledge in design,
          Which I can vary, sir, to *infinito*.
Tub: *Ad infinitum*, sir, you mean.
Medlay: I do,
          I stand not on my Latin; I'll invent,
          But I must be alone then, join'd with no man.

(V.iii. 10–14)

He claims the honours of authorship, only to be dismissed as 'The workman, sir, the artificer; I grant you'.

These satires come from the pen of a frustrated and increasingly sick poet. Jonson reserved his last attack on Jones for an occasion when he could address King Charles away from the Court, where Inigo's ascendancy made him *persona non grata*. This occasion was the reception of the King and Queen by the Earl of Newcastle at Bolsover Castle in 1634. The Earl, who was the patron of Jonson's later years, commissioned an entertainment, for which Jonson wrote the miniature masque *Love's Welcome at Bolsover*. As a kind of anti-masque, he introduced Coronell Iniquo Vitruvius and his mechanics in an oration followed by a dance. A clownish fellow, Vitruvius exhorts his men to observe time and measure in their dance which is intended as a parody of the Vitruvian principles of proportion and harmony. It is an Architectural Dance performed by painters, glaziers and other component men of the building trade. 'Well done, my Musicall, Arithmeticall, Geometricall Gamesters! or rather my true Mathematicall Boyes! It is carried, in number, weight, and measure, as if the Aires were all Harmonie, and the Figures a well-tim'd Proportion!' (ll. 67–70). Jonson was presumably taking advantage of the construction work that was still proceeding at Bolsover Castle when the King and Queen visited it to introduce these figures of carvers and plasterers and glaziers, and the jokes about Vitruvian principles. Yet, even though the anti-masque sounds like a genial dismissal of the learned principles of architects, the very fact that Jonson was still exercising his grievance against Inigo Jones three years after the quarrel and so far from London indicates just how much it vexed and unbalanced him. If Jonson set great store by his friendships, he could also nurse a grudge with equal care.

The main movements of *Love's Welcome* made a graceful addition to the conventions of platonic love that almost invariably formed the context for compliment to the King and Queen. On this occasion the Earl's banquet was feigned to be a gesture of love made to honour the ideal love of the royal couple: 'Love will feast Love'. The entertainment opens with a proposition:

If Love be call'd a lifting of the Sense
To knowledge of that pure intelligence,
Wherein the Soule hath rest, and residence

(ll. 1–3)

that is then explained and justified. Perfect love begets love in the souls of those that encounter it, with the result that mutual interchange of affection follows, which is the cause of the banquet and also of the music, which is the harmony of love made audible. The sequel relates the story of Eros and Anteros, the myth of the two children of Venus who flourish under the influence of their mutual love. The relevance of the myth to Charles and Henrietta Maria needs little elaboration. Throughout the entertainment Jonson has played with the imagery of circles as a metaphor for the endless movement of love between the royal pair, between the crown and people, and between heaven and earth. To conclude, he transfers the image to the Court itself, now seen as a sphere of perfection:

The King, and Queenes Court, which is circular,
And perfect. The pure schoole that we live in,
And is of purer Love, the Discipline.

(ll. 136–8)

The Lord of Bolsover, William Cavendish, Earl of Newcastle, became Jonson's chief patron in the last decade of his life. He probably patronised Jonson for the same reason that he befriended Shirley and Davenant, namely that he himself had ambitions as a playwright. He enjoyed close relations with Hobbes also, and cultivated a broad spread of intellectual interests. His most brilliant reputation was gained in the art of horseman-ship, of which he was the leading theorist and practitioner in England. Such a man, soldier, scholar, horseman, would have been transformed by Jonson at an earlier stage into a paragon of liberal nobility; in his declining years, however, the poet was grateful for help but no longer disposed to add to his gallery of English worthies.

Jonson never lacked for noble patrons, nor did he lose the gift of modulat-ing patronage into friendship, but after the early 1620s he largely gave up his habit of characterising his patrons as exponents of antique virtue in Stuart England. There are exceptions, of course, most notably the ode to Sir Lucius Cary and Sir Henry Morison, who stand to posterity as the twin pillars of an immortal friendship, but in general Jonson's later panegyrics tend more to flatter than universalise their subjects. His literary friendships remained numerous and sustaining; these had always been the mainstay of his creative life, and as the friends of the older generation fell away, the rising poets and dramatists, 'the sons of Ben', clustered around him, drawn by his unfailing personal magnetism and by the experience of a lifetime of letters that he convivially offered them. The majority of them, men such as Carew, Suckling, Lovelace, Waller and Davenant, were poets who moved in Court circles and who learnt from him the art to please Court taste. Whether it was the management of a masque or a compliment to a mistress that was required, Jonson somewhere in his works had set the precedent, formulated the convention, given the note. Even in love poetry, where Jonson admitted his limitations, he had achieved some lyrics, such as 'Drinke to me, only' and the Charis sequence, which by their finely turned compliments, their neat and appropriate argument and their metrical poise, offered fertile sources of inspiration to younger poets. In his occasional poetry generally, in his epistles, odes, epigrams and elegies, he made available a variety of styles that encouraged an intelligent, ethical, civilised approach to life. As we have noted, the relative plainness of those styles reflects a certain indifference to the surface beauty of the world, but that should not deflect us from the realisation that at the centre of Jonson's world lies a love of intellectual beauty: beauty of soul, of character, of action. Measure, proportion and harmony of parts were his ideal just as much as they were Inigo Jones's, which perhaps helps to explain their long collaboration in spite of their mutual dislike. Jonson's art, 'so ample, full and round, / In weight, in measure, number, sound', was committed to the depiction of many forms and types of perfection in this imperfect world. His personal *impresa* was a broken compass standing in an incomplete circle, with the motto: *Deest quod duceret orbem*—that which should make up the circle is lacking—an avowal both of his pursuit of perfection and of the impossibility of achieving it.

Notes to Chapter Eight

1   Clarendon, *History of the Rebellion*, 1705, vol. I, pp. 56, 57.

2   See H. A. Mason, *Poetry and Humanism*, London 1959, for an account of the carefully adapted borrowings from Martial.

3   Elizabeth Sidney, like Mary Wroth, wrote poetry herself, so the mythological allusions of the epistle act as an index of a common interest; the main themes of the poem are classical commonplaces that have been adapted to the circumstances of Jonson's praise of the Countess.

4   Donne's verse letters to gentlewomen of his acquaintance also date from the early years of the century, but they are by no means as prominent in his work as are Jonson's addresses to his noble ladies.

5   See Roy Strong, *The Renaissance Garden in England*, London 1979, pp. 120–2, 139–46.

6   For a detailed discussion of *Hymenaei*, see D. J. Gordon, *The Renaissance Imagination*, pp. 157–84.

7   Letter from John Pory to Sir Robert Cotton, 7 Jan. 1606, quoted in Orgel and Strong, *op. cit.*, vol. I, p. 106.

8   Jonson, *Works*, vol. I, p. 145.

9   The fullest account of the quarrel between Jonson and Jones is by D. J. Gordon, *The Renaissance Imagination*, pp. 77–101.

10   *Ibid.*, p. 83.

[9]
The Court of Charles I

The style and iconography of the Caroline Court can be most fully appreciated in the masques of the reign, which differ considerably from their Jacobean predecessors. A significant factor was that both the King and Queen were accomplished dancers, and chose to star in their own masques, which they tended to offer each other as reciprocal state gifts, and in which they celebrated their mutual love as the power that animated the kingdom and gave it a mysterious spiritual strength. All the masques of the reign were performed during the years 1631–40, that is to say the decade of absolute rule by Charles I. In consequence, they act as a vindication of royal autocracy, not by an explicit defence of Charles's political actions, but by an assertion of powers so sublime that their exercise is inevitable, irresistible and benign. Charles and Henrietta Maria, one the son of the pacific James, the other the daughter of the warlike Henri IV, have come together in a perfect union that is indissoluble; it is the perfect union Plato described in Aristophanes's speech in *The Symposium* that the gods feared lest its power should prove greater than their own; it is a manifestation of the love that 'will restore us to our ancient nature and heal us and make us blessed and happy'.[1] The platonic hermaphrodite of the two balanced souls mixed equally has reappeared as the controlling spirit of the blessed islands of Great Britain, and its name is CARLOMARIA. In the various depictions of this power, Charles is generally presented as the embodiment of Heroic Virtue, and Henrietta variously glossed as Divine Beauty or Love, but in either case they are each other's destiny and fulfilment, and their union means not merely that Britain is guided by an ideal combination of virtue and love but also that the purity of this reign makes it exemplary to all nations. The equal status of Henrietta Maria in this scheme was no mere fiction, but reflected a political reality, for after the death of Buckingham, the Queen became effectively the chief adviser to King Charles, and remained his intimate counsel throughout the period of personal rule.

Changes of considerable significance took place in the staging of the masques. The long co-operation between Ben Jonson and Inigo Jones came to an end in 1631 with their quarrel over the rivalry for priority between poetry and spectacle. As a result, a variety of lesser poets was conscripted to provide the poetry, while Jones himself took an increasingly large part in inventing the fable in addition to designing the costumes and sets. In their book on Inigo Jones, Stephen Orgel and Roy Strong suggest that the King himself may have been the chief collaborator with Jones on the masques after 1631, and certainly, given the uniformity of approach, the consistent treatment of the 'Carlomaria' image, and the tendency of the masques to address themselves discreetly to current political issues, there is a strong probability that such was the case.[2] The masques grew longer, involving many more dance entries in the anti-masques, and more changes of scenery. Jones's technical mastery now permitted a fluent sequence of sliding shutters to speed the varied action, while greater use of flying machinery crowded the air with celestial visions. Yet at the same time, Jones's inventive faculty was declining, for the majority of his settings for these masques are derivative, based on French or Italian engravings, and his costume designs lack the imaginative bravura that marked his Jacobean creations.

The first two masques of Charles's reign were the last that Jonson wrote before his final break with Jones, and in them he introduced the themes that would persist for the remainder of peacetime. The King's masque, *Love's Triumph through Callipolis*, was commissioned 'for the honour of his court and the dignity of that heroic love and regal respect borne by him to his unmatchable lady and spouse, the Queen's majesty,' (ll. 11–13). The fable celebrates the purifying presence of Ideal Love in Callipolis, 'the city of beauty or goodness', an obvious image of Charles's Court. The Queen, to whom the masque is presented, reigns under the influence of Love 'who was wont to be respected as a special deity in court, and tutelar god of the place'. She is informed that certain forms of distempered love have broken out in the outskirts of her realm; these debased loves then enter to dance the anti-masque, and are dispelled by the exertion of the Queen's will. A song praises Love in conventional platonic terms: such love transcends physical attractions, it is 'the noble appetite of what is best', a striving to unite itself with the ultimate ideas of the Good and the Beautiful, which are concepts only perceived by 'the mind's eye', although traces of goodness and beauty in the created world may act as an incentive to seek after their higher origin; such love remains chaste towards the physical attractions of human beauty, yet is passionate in its pursuit of ideals. With the dispersal of the sensual lovers, the triumph of Platonic Love may commence. This takes the form of a sea pageant, led in by Amphitrite, the wife of Oceanus; she brings forward the principal masquers, noble lovers who form an ascending scale of understanding of love's mysteries, with at their peak the King, the heroical lover. The identity of the King as heroical lover suggests a particular source for Jonson's masque in Giordano Bruno's neo-platonic dialogue *Degli Eroici Furori*. This work had been dedicated to Sir Philip Sidney, and so must have had some currency in English circles interested in the platonic philosophy of Love. Jonson himself shows signs of having been influenced by Bruno's comedy *Il Candelaio* in the course of his own career as a comic dramatist. In the present case he makes only slender use of a very complicated philosophic treatise, just as in a later masque, *Coelum Britannicum*, Thomas Carew will also borrow superficially from Bruno. The heroic fury of Bruno's title refers to the spiritual rapture of the platonic lover as he struggles to achieve the transcendent vision of the divine love that permeates the created universe, that harmonises all discord in the soul and brings the inexpressible delight and peace of intellectual wisdom to the successful amorous mystic. The dedication of Bruno's dialogue, like the opening of Jonson's masque, contains a warning against base, illiberal forms of love, which are tainted by sensuality and disturbed by jealousy. The tightly argued dialogue then proceeds to describe the life of the lover possessed by heroic frenzy, attempting to detach himself from the attractions of physical beauty to the contemplation of intellectual beauty. 'Love presents a world of chaste desires / Which may produce a harmony of parts' (ll. 52–3). As the lover becomes aware of these intellectual harmonies glimpsed fleetingly behind the beauties of the lower world, he yearns restlessly for yet higher revelations.

> Love is the right affection of the minde,
>> The noble appetite of what is best:
> Desire of union with the thing design'd,
>> But in fruition of it cannot rest.
>
> . . .
> . . . onely by the minds eye, may bee seene
>> Your enter-woven lines of good and fayre!
>
> (ll. 54–7, 68–9)

It is Bruno who introduces Amphitrite as the priestess of the highest mysteries, for as the goddess of the sea she is the mysterious goddess of the infinite, which is yet material and infinitely divisible. 'Look then on Amphitrite, the source of all numbers, of all species and arguments, the monad, the true essence of all being.'[3] She controls 'the waters of wisdom, rivers of water of eternal life. These are found not on our earth, but on the bosom of Ocean, of the goddess Amphitrite, in whose realm is the miraculous stream that flows from Divinity, and those nymphs, those blessed and divine intelligences who minister to her sublime intelligence. . . . Amphitrite alone by her triple virtue openeth every seal, looseth every knot, discovereth every secret.'[4] In Jonson's masque, Amphitrite's supreme revelation is of Queen Henrietta Maria as 'Pure obiect, of Heroique Love, alone! . . . The center of proportion—. . . Sweetnesse—. . . Grace! . . . Daigne to receive all lines of love in one' (ll. 128–36). The King gazes enraptured upon her and then, with the masquers, performs a dance of adoration. The scene reveals a rock in the sea bearing the Muses, and the imagery speaks of the love that moved on the waters at the Creation, creating from those waters a world of beauty 'by virtue of divine intelligence'. The masque concludes with an epiphany of Venus, the idea of 'perfect love and beauty', who pays homage to the Queen as her image among mankind. The platonic quest is achieved in this moment, under the eyes of the King. As idea and image converge, the throne of Venus disappears, 'in place of which, there shooteth up a Palme tree with an imperiall crowne on the top, from the roote whereof, Lillies and Roses, twining together, and imbracing the stem, flourish through the crowne' (ll. 205–8). The presence of perfect love and beauty in the Court becomes politically significant in an emblem of Caroline optimism:

> Beauty and Love, whose story is mysteriall,
> In yonder Palme-tree, and the Crowne imperiall,
> Doe from the Rose, and Lilly so delicious,
> Promise a shade, shall ever be propitious
> To both the Kingdomes.
>
> (ll. 210–14)

The Queen's masque *Chloridia*, played a few weeks later, formed a complement to *Love's Triumph*. As that piece had concluded with the fusion of the earthly with the divine, so *Chloridia* proposes a fable that shows the earth radiant with divinity as the gods decide to make earth co-equal with heaven:

> It is decreed, by all the Gods,
> The Heav'n, of Earth shall have no oddes,
>   But one shall love another:
> Their glories they shall mutuall make,
> Earth looke on Heaven, for Heavens sake;
>   Their honours shall bee even:
> All aemulation cease, and iarres;

Ioue will have Earth to have her starres,
  And lights, no lesse then Heauen.

(ll. 47–55)

'Jupiter . . . would have the Earth to be adorn'd with starres, as well as the Heaven' (ll. 11–12); so Chloris the goddess of the earth is to be transformed into Flora, the goddess of flowers, which represent the stars of the new heaven. The myth is taken from Ovid's *Fasti*, and it shadows the type of the philosophic mortal transfigured by an infusion of divine knowledge, effected by Zephyrus, the intermediary of the gods—Botticelli had employed the myth in his 'Primavera', where it forms the opening sequence of a series of philosophic terms showing the divine spirit descending to earth, kindling a passion for a knowledge of the ideal powers that inform creation, and returning to heaven in the spirit of contemplation.[5]

The anti-masque shows the revolt of Cupid, the inflamer of the passions, on account of his exclusion from the council of the gods in their new age of Wisdom. He releases the passions from hell, and summons up tempests on earth, before being suppressed by Juno, the goddess who presides over marriage. This banishment of unruly love prepares the way for the entry of the Queen, as Chloris, and also suggests the refined atmosphere of the cult of love that prevailed in the Caroline Court. The scene has changed to a glorious springtime landscape, backed by a rainbow that symbolises the unity of heaven and earth. The divinely-approved Chloris has brought colour to the world—the masque's motto is *Unius tellus ante coloris erat*: the earth before this was all one colour—and the richness and variety of these new colours signal that earth now equals heaven in its splendour, all due to the merit of Chloris. Then a vision occurs:

Here, out of the Earth, ariseth a Hill, and on the top of it, a globe, on which Fame is seene standing, with her trumpet in her hand; and on the Hill, are seated four Persons, presenting Poesie, History, Architecture, and Sculpture: who together with the Nymphs, Floods, and Fountaynes, make a full Quire; at which, Fame begins to mount, and mooving her wings, flyeth, singing, up to Heaven.

(ll. 275–81)

These are the agents that will perpetuate the glory of Chloris, and it is evident at this point that Jonson has turned away from the myths to assert the claims of Charles's and Henrietta's Court to everlasting fame: Poesy and History one might expect as advocates for a reign, but the presence of Architecture and Sculpture proclaim a reign that wishes to be famous for its grandeur and for its connoisseurship in the arts. So the Queen offers this satisfying vision to the King, to whom it properly belongs. Fame disappears to heaven, but the gifts that the gods have bestowed on Chloris—the spring, the running waters, and the freshness of colour—remain, as the masquers move forward to offer these perfections to the Court in the great dance. The Queen is hymned as 'the top of Par-amours' as she goes out to partner the King, to remind the Court that it is the co-respondent love of the royal couple that is the true cause of the blessings enjoyed by Britain, that springtime bower in a tempestuous world.

Where did the facile platonism come from that shapes these masques? From the beginning there had been a platonic strain in the English masque tradition, for these shows were revelations of the ideas and primal forces that operated upon human experience and society, and suffused the external world of appearances; the iconography books on which Jonson depended were originally popularised code-books that came into being to appease the curiosity of Italians who were aware of arcane philosophic circles in the intellectually distinguished courts of the later Quattrocento and who wished to attain a proficiency in understanding these exciting developments. The iconography books and emblem books were already simplified paraphrases of a rigorous philosophic discipline, and the masques that exploited the figures of the emblem books were, by the nature of their public performance, simplified still further. The shift to the cult of platonic love that is so marked in the Caroline masques appears to have been effected by Ben Jonson in combination with the King and Queen. Jonson was already attuned to the tradition, and could be counted on to act as a dutiful executant. Henrietta Maria had introduced the cult from the French Court where an affected platonism flourished, providing an elegant convention for relationships within the Court circle. Its gesture, vocabulary and attitudes had been finely expressed in Honoré d'Urfée's romance *Astrée* (1620), which set the tone for the fashionable arcadian tales of the twenties and thirties, and lay behind the pastoral romances in which Queen Henrietta acted at Court, such as Racan's *Artenice* (1626) or the anonymous *Florimène* (1635). Charles seems to have been quick to indulge the Queen's taste, seeing in this cult an admirable means of projecting the royal image in a way that distracted attention from the political aspects of his kingship, offering instead a vision of a beneficent love at the heart of the happy nation.[6] This vision was intensified after 1628, when the death of Buckingham brought Charles and Henrietta Maria together in a much more affectionate way than hitherto, thus softening the image of the monarch as he embarked on personal rule in 1629: divine right was complemented by divine love. In addition, this cult accorded well with his own temperamental disposition towards refined courtly behaviour.

The magical virtue of the royal marriage never ceased to furnish a theme for praise throughout the years of peace. Its success required that all those in the royal circle pay tribute to the refining power of love, to its spiritual value in drawing the soul into a state of philosophic contemplation, so that most courtiers were expected to display an understanding of love's transfigurations. Love was the unofficial religion of the Court, yet it was difficult to take it seriously. At all levels from their majesties down to rhyming courtiers, the subject remained a game with its rituals, conventions and responses. There was no serious philosophic thought behind it to sustain it in the way that fifteenth-century Florentine platonism validated the theories of love that prevailed in Renaissance courts in Italy and France. The Caroline cult of love began in convention and rapidly dwindled into platitude. No one of sufficient intellectual stature addressed himself to the issue. Milton might have supplied that deficiency had he been closer to the Court, and indeed, in *Comus*, his most courtly production, he did use the occasion of the masque to express a neo-platonic philosophy of love, except that he proves so stern a moralist that he insists on strict chastity as the necessary condition of enlightenment. The Court needed a system in which an ideal marriage of qualities lay at the centre, so the various myths invented for the masques of the thirties offer the most satisfactory formulation of a philosophy of love, even though it is intellectually not very complex.

The Twelfth Night revels of 1632 saw Aurelian Townshend replacing Jonson as poet, yet his *Albion's Triumph* derives very largely from *Love's Triumph* of the previous year. Callipolis has now become Albipolis, whose King, Albanactus,[7] is a platonic votary of Queen Alba, 'whose native beauties have a great affinity with all purity and whiteness. The King's devoting himself to this goddess is but the seeking of that happy union which was preordained by the greatest of the gods' (ll. 10–14). The time of Albanactus' triumph is at hand:

> A triumph: mighty as the man designed
> To wear those bays, heroic as his mind,
> Just as his actions, glorious as his reign,
> And like his virtues, infinite in train.

(ll. 88–91)

The King is apparelled as a Roman emperor; his city has an antique grandeur. We see here Charles invested with the imperial dignities that were so often associated with James, but the inclination now is to emphasise the heroic virtue of his mind rather than the power and justice of his rule. An engaging interlude between the patrician Platonicus and the plebian Publius points up the idea that the true triumph they have witnessed was not the external display of greatness but the triumph of the moral virtues that may be apprehended only by the philosophic mind. Platonicus expresses it thus:

Know I have seen this brave Albanactus Caesar, seen him with the eyes of understanding, viewed all his actions, looked into his mind, which I find armed with so many moral virtues that he daily conquers a world of vices, which are wild beasts indeed. For example, ambition is a lion, cruelty a bear, avarice a wolf; yet he subdues them all. To be short, no vice is so small to scape him, nor so great but he overcomes it, and in that fashion he triumphs over all the kings and queens that went before him. All his passions are his true subjects; and knowledge, judgement, merit, bounty, and the like, are fit commanders for such a general; these triumph with him.

(ll. 202–14)

Unqualified direct flattery of such magnitude betrays a mental servility that one encounters not infrequently among the minor Caroline writers. Jonson could lay flattery on with a trowel, but in a robust way that forces one to admire the workmanship; in Townshend one encounters the hired admirer, the grateful, uncritical mind favoured by the atmosphere of Charles's Court.

The King makes his triumphal entry 'attended by fourteen consuls, who stood about him, not set in ranks, but in several gracious postures, attending his commands' (ll. 262–4)—a fine image of an ever-dutiful Court—but the conqueror is then conquered, by Love and Chastity. Powerless before these forces, he is purified by them and offers himself as 'Love's Sacrifice' at the shrine of the Queen' The dances represent a ritual worship of Alba, who accepts the heroic Albanactus as worthy of her beauty and goodness. The King then leaves the masque, to take his seat of state beside the Queen, and together they watch as the scene changes from an ideal world to the reality of the present: 'a prospect of the King's palace of Whitehall and part of the city of London'. But we soon understand that this 'real' world is ideal too, for the heavens open to reveal Innocence, Justice, Religion, Affection to the Country, Concord and Peace exerting their influence over the city, and we learn that they have congregated in Britain because the land is ruled by this perfect combination of Virtue and Goodness, cemented by Love, 'the Mary-Charles'.

The Queen's masque at Shrovetide that returned the King's compliment also showed Townshend looking over his shoulder to Jonson's models. *Tempe Restored* again depicts the realm purged of all lustful appetite by the irresistible conjunction of Divine Beauty and Heroic Virtue in the persons of the royal couple, who radiate 'auspicious light' and move to the sound of the spheres. The real triumph that these masques are celebrating is the establishment of an honourable code of courtly behaviour under Charles and Henrietta Maria that was in powerful contrast to the seamy passions of James's Court. Lust in its many virulent forms that ran like a disease through the veins of the old Court had now been driven out, and the reformation had been brought about, rather in the fashion of Shakespeare's last plays, by the revivifying spirit of a younger generation of princely lovers. The new Court is governed by a ruler whose soul is a compound of the virtues, who aspires to the goal of philosophic enlightenment, the ascent of the soul towards union with the divine mind; in this endeavour he is assisted by his consort, whose chastity, love and beauty enable his spirit, tuned by amorous harmony, to ascend from material associations to an intuition of divinity. The benevolent influences which this quest calls down from a sympathetic heaven fall like sunshine on his kingdom. Essentially these are myths that praise the pre-eminent virtue of the King as the power solely responsible for the well-being of the country; he is a hermetic magus, not a reclusive one like Prospero, but an active heroic figure who stands apart from his noblemen and his fellow monarchs by his dedication to platonic mysteries and by his endeavour to harmonise his own soul with the divine mind, with consequent blessedness to himself and to his nation. The masques emphasise the importance of the arts in this scheme, for poetry, painting, sculpture and architecture ennoble the minds of their admirers, awaken a sense of the ideal, strengthen virtue, and direct ambition to worthy ends. The Tempe of Townshend's masque is the valley of the muses, 'lovers of science and virtue'; part of the function of the fable is to vindicate the pursuit of the arts at Charles's Court as the laudable exercise of 'virtù'.

After the lapse of a year, the masques were resumed with unprecedented magnificence in 1634. The most lavish was *The Triumph of Peace*, mounted by the four Inns of Court in February at the prompting of the King, who desired some demonstration of loyalty from the legal profession after the publication of William Prynne's stinging *Histriomastix* in 1633. Prynne was a barrister of Lincoln's Inn and a Puritan of immoderate zeal; his blanket attack on players and theatrical performances contained the aspersion, 'Women actors notorious whores', which was construed as an insult to the Queen, who enjoyed acting. (One might understand something of Prynne's indignation if one looks back to the costume designs for *Chloridia*, for example, where the Queen and her ladies may have appeared bare-breasted on the stage.) Prynne was imprisoned and later savagely treated by the Star Chamber. In the meantime the Inns of Court invested heavily in their testimony of 'love and duty to their Majesties'. James Shirley was commissioned to write the text, and Inigo Jones was retained to produce *The*

Triumph of Peace. A small army of performers was recruited who marched in procession from Holborn to Whitehall in what was effectively the most splendid pageant of Charles's reign. Given the general absence of ceremonial under Charles, this display was remarkable, clearly a demonstration of the wealth of the legal world as much as a tribute to the King. As it moved along, it offered the citizenry a glimpse of the masque to come, rather in the manner of a circus parade. Preceded by footmen in scarlet and silver, and trumpeters, a hundred gentlemen on the Inns rode in gold and silver, attended by pages and torchbearers; then came a gallimaufry of anti-masquers: cripples and beggars on broken-down horses with a kitchen sink band, birds of every feather with avian music, speculators and projectors with bagpipes, all mumming and playing as they went. Consorts of musicians followed, including forty lutenists, many dressed as antique priests; then came chariots of gods and goddesses, and as the climax of the procession, the triumphal chariots of the Grand Masquers themselves, splendid in torchlight. The masque itself was on the whole unworthy of these great forces. Orgel and Strong believe that these anti-masques dramatised a number of complaints held by the law societies about royal prerogatives and royal disregard of the law in such matters as monopolies.[8] Even if the points were seriously intended, it is difficult to imagine that Charles would have sensed them in that setting of splendour and gaiety, and even more unlikely that he would have believed them when the main masque offered an ode of unrestrained praise to the King and Queen.

> To you great King and Queen, whose smile
> Doth scatter blessings through this isle,
> To make it best
> And wonder of the rest,
> We pay the duty of our birth,
> Proud to wait upon that earth
> Whereon you move,
> Which shall be named,
> And by your chaste embraces famed,
> The paradise of love.

(ll. 608–17)

The central fable tells of the return to earth of Peace, Law and Justice, who recognise in Charles and Henrietta Maria their true parents, whom they honour. Peace and Law speak pointedly when they assert, 'The world shall give prerogative to neither. / We cannot flourish but together' (ll. 561–2). Undoubtedly Charles would have agreed, in principle. Masque is not a successful vehicle for critical opinion, for its very soul is extravagant praise in which all other elements combine. The King was delighted with *The Triumph of Peace*, and ordered it repeated; the Queen and her ladies honoured the gentlemen masquers by joining with them in the dances into which the masque devolved. The real lesson of the evening lay in the contrast between the resources of the four private societies who staged the masque and the permanent penury of the monarch, for the charges of the entertainment came to some £20,000, an immense sum, sufficient indeed to raise and equip a small army at the time. The implications of this exhibition of private wealth were not lost on contemporaries. As a correspondent wrote to Lord Deputy Wentworth, 'They speak that it will cost the Men of Law. Oh that they would once give over these Things, or lay them aside for a Time, and bend all their Endeavours to make the King Rich! For it gives me no Satisfaction, who am but a looker on, to see so rich a Commonwealth, as rich People, and the Crown poor. God direct them to remedy this quickly.'⁹

The artificial exaggerations of the masque attained a new peak of hyperbole in *Coelum Britannicum*, the occasion on which Thomas Carew was invited to try his hand at a masque. He possessed a fertility of invention and a copiousness of language that resulted in one of the most substantial Stuart entertainments. The conceit on which the action turns is that the Olympian gods have determined on a reformation of their lives, converted by the incomparable virtues of Charles and Henrietta Maria, and propose to remodel their heaven on the lines of the Caroline Court.

> Your exemplar life
> Hath not alone transfused a jealous heat
> Of imitation through your virtuous court,
> By whose bright blaze your palace is become
> The envied pattern of this underworld,
> But the aspiring flame hath kindled heaven;
> Th' immortal bosoms burn with emulous fires.
>
> (ll. 60–6)

An unexpected enthusiasm for chastity grips Olympus; the old constellations based on memorable rapes are unsphered, and in their stead images of the Stuart rulers shall be pricked out in the night sky:

> So to the British stars this lower globe
> Shall owe its light, and they alone dispense
> To th' world a pure refinèd influence.
>
> (ll. 98–101)

Carew derived the shaping idea of his action from Giordano Bruno's dialogue *Lo Spaccio della Bestia Trionfante*, which, like the *Eroici Furori* that Jonson had used, had been dedicated to Sir Philip Sidney and was a useful mine of neo-platonic conceits. Carew had spent two years in Italy, and had enough Italian to read Bruno, whose attraction for masque-makers lay in his mythological habits of thought and argument and in his vivid accounts of the neo-platonic progress of the soul towards enlightenment by means of the pursuit of virtue. These accounts could easily be adapted to the cult of the English royal couple. The Triumphant Beast of Bruno's dialogue is the many-headed monster of the vices that obscure higher perceptions; when it is expelled, 'The soul will purify itself from error, will deck itself with virtues through love of the beauty in goodness and natural justice'.[10] Bruno imagines the reformation of the heavens, with a casting out of the old constellations with their histories of sensuality and vice, and their replacement by the stellified virtues—Truth, Wisdom,

> Brave bounteous acts, regal magnificence,
> All-seeing prudence, magnanimity
> That knows no bound, and that heroic virtue
> For which antiquity hath left no name,
> But patterns only.

(ll. 668–72)

Carew's principal interlocutors, Mercury and Momus, are taken from Bruno, but the material generally has been wittily converted to a British setting. We learn that Jupiter has entered into a condition of married chastity, 'who besides to eternise the memory of that great example of matrimonial union which he derives from hence, hath on his bedchamber door and ceiling, fretted with stars, in capital letters engraven the inscription of CARLOMARIA' (ll. 275–9). It is the ancient British heroes who will compose the new heavens, together with the royal couple who are the perfection of Virtue, and the fulfilment of the ancient heroism of this island. Carew attempts, in the shorthand way which a masque uncritically allows, to furnish a brief lineage for Charles, showing first in 'a grave Antimasque' the primitive Britons, the Picts and Scots, followed by a ceremonial introduction of the British Worthies (the masquers proper), dressed in antique costume, led by the King, who represents the culmination of this national line of heroes. The scenery reflects the evolution towards the perfection of the present, changing from a wild and craggy scene to a modern garden prospect of parterres, terraces, fountains and grottoes, centring on a palace, all of which was expressive of Caroline civility and the triumph of order and government over the wildness of nature. The final vision occurred after the revels, for *Coelum Britannicum* was a masque that could not stop, but kept bursting into new glories like the exploding stages of a rocket: we see the heavens new-filled with the stellified heroes, with the King's constellation pre-eminent, while the lower prospect reveals a distant view of Windsor Castle, the seat of the Order of the Garter, which was the mainstay of Caroline chivalry. Over this scene hovers a congregation of powers and deities, chief among whom are Eternity, Religion and Wisdom, who hymn the King and Queen with line after soaring line of praise, foreseeing an endless succession of wise, just, religious Stuarts ruling under the propitious influence of Charles and Henrietta Maria. *Coelum Britannicum* marks the summer solstice of royal confidence.

Rather surprisingly after his virtuoso performance as a masque composer, Carew was not retained the following year: he was replaced by the Queen's servant William Davenant, who was responsible for the remaining masques of the reign. Davenant had little sense of the conventions of the genre, and was initially hampered by a weak inventive faculty and a dispirited muse, which resulted in two limp masques, *The Temple of Love* in 1635 for the Queen, and *Britannia Triumphans* in 1638 for the King. Thereafter, however, he showed a growing competence that approached mastery in the last masque, *Salmacida Spolia* of 1640. With such inexperience at the centre of Court entertainment, an ever greater share of the production fell to Inigo Jones, whose technical adventurousness grew as his scenic inventiveness declined. *The Temple of Love* was an empty exercise in Caroline neo-platonism: the temple of Chaste Love is to be established in Great Britain, as a result of the Queen's example. A gratuitous exoticism accompanied this action, for the Queen was fabled to be of Indian origin, and the proscenium arch was diversified with Indian trophies, a camel, and a tiger 'in an extravagant posture'. The geographical disparities are never resolved, nor would it be profitable for them to be. At the consecration of the temple, the Queen is united with 'the last and living hero' Charles in a heavenly transport, and the perfection of their love raises the couple to a condition of divinity.

One myth of neo-platonic significance that enjoyed considerable popularity in the 1630s was the story of Cupid and Psyche, which had long been glossed as an allegory of the soul's ascent to divine fulfilment. Psyche embodied Beauty, and Cupid Desire; together they expressed the equation that Plato used to define Love in *The Symposium*: 'Love is Desire aroused by Beauty'. But Psyche also represents the earthbound soul, and Cupid divine love. The union of Cupid and Psyche is the mingling of the divine with the earthly; Psyche's presumptuous viewing of her husband shows how too intense a preoccupation with the mundane faculties, too conscious a desire for knowledge, destroys the raptures of the soul. The tasks assigned to Psyche by the gods as penance for her crime of looking on the god represent the striving of the soul to regain the moment of lost bliss and to retain it by steadfast perseverance and selfless pursuit of divine love. The individual tasks such as the descent to hell for the Stygian water and the separation of the confused grains were interpreted as stages of mystical initiation, until finally Psyche is reunited with the god Cupid (or Eros or Amor) in a celestial embrace. The child of this mystical union is Voluptas, Pleasure or Joy, the mysterious joy of the soul in its exalted participation in the divine. We find Milton using the myth at the conclusion to *Comus* (1634), a work steeped in the fashionable neo-platonism of the time, where the figures of Cupid and Psyche are seen in the highest of the platonic abodes that the spirit describes in the epilogue. The myth found especial favour with Henrietta Maria, who wished to use it as the basis for the decorative scheme of her cabinet at Greenwich. In the later thirties she tried to commission paintings from various artists including Rubens, Jordaens and Guido Reni on subjects from the story of Cupid and Psyche, but in the end only Van Dyck delivered a canvas, showing the god approaching the sleeping Psyche, who is as yet unconscious of her higher destiny. Shakerley Marmion, a friend of Suckling, wrote a long poem, *Cupid and Psyche*, described on the title-page as an epic, which was dedicated in 1637 to Elizabeth of Bohemia's son Charles Louis, the dispossessed Elector Palatine. It is an engaging work, full of smooth, elegant fancies showing the gods as a sophisticated crew who would be welcome guests at the Court of Charles I; yet Marmion reminds us in his preface, called 'the Mythology', that his poem conceals an account of the platonic progress of the soul. The Prince Elector had come to Britain to seek aid in retrieving his lost Palatinate. He had been welcomed in February 1636 by a masque given by the Middle Temple, *The Triumphs of the Prince d'Amour*, written by Davenant. The central action of the masque depicts the overcoming of martial spirits by the power of love represented by Cupid: 'now you must resign to love / Your warlike hearts', and the military masquers are transformed by 'a more soft and courtly change' into 'a troop of noble lovers'.[11] Davenant's masque and Marmion's poem provide a striking instance of how an outsider like the Elector Charles could be wound in to the amorist ethos that prevailed at the English Court. The contrast between the Elector's need for urgent military assistance and the soothing blandishments of the courtly love cult emphasise the almost instinctive evasion of political realities that was characteristic of Caroline culture.

The intermission of three years between masques, 1635–8, was caused by the installation of Rubens's paintings in the Banqueting House ceiling, and by Charles's realisation that if he wished to preserve them from smoke, then the masques, which required enormous fire-power for their illumination, would have to be moved into new premises. A new timber hall was accordingly erected close by. When the masques recommenced in 1638, they reflected the tightening pressure on the King, for *Britannia Triumphans* had a clear political motivation, to vindicate Charles's dubious demand for Ship Money. The decoration of the proscenium arch announced the themes: classical images of rostra, palms and garlands spoke of naval victory, matched by a figure representing Right Government. Around the arch ran a riotous sea triumph of tritons and putti on sea horses and fishes. However, this confident margin framed a weakly-conceived action. The masque opens with a series of divertissements, one of which flickers with ominous political suggestion when a rout of 'rebellious leaders in war'—mutinous citizens such as Jack Straw, Cade and Kett—are brought in and then expelled by Heroic Virtue. This same Heroic Virtue in the person of Bellerophon then declares it is time to celebrate the triumph of Britanocles, that modern exemplar of antique virtue. Charles appears from a splendid palace—no doubt a prefiguration of the immense new palace of Whitehall that Charles was beginning to dream up in conjunction with Inigo Jones in this same year 1638. Fame hails him, and the chorus sings to the masquing lords of the perfect concord of King and aristocracy.

> Move then in such a noble order here
> As if you each his governed planet were,
> And he moved first, to move you in each sphere.

> (ll. 558–60)

The scene shows a prosperous view of London lying in the sunlight of Britanocles's rule, then changes to a seascape where a nymph sings of Britain's naval might while a great fleet, the fleet that was being paid for by Ship Money, in fact, veers and tacks about in a remarkable display of technical ingenuity. The large ship at the centre of this pageant has been tentatively identified as 'The Sovereign of the Seas', the recently-commissioned British flagship; this would be in keeping with the strong topicality of the masque, and its defence of the King's policy of taxation to strengthen sea-power. A painful indication of the gap between pretence and performance was provided by the contrast between the effortless command of the seas shown by the pasteboard ships and the spineless inactivity of the real fleet (including 'The Sovereign of the Seas') the very next year, when they floated around helplessly as the Dutch fleet bottled up a Spanish armada just off the British coast and then destroyed it in the Battle of the Downs. The Ship-Money fleet could not even exert command over British territorial waters, let alone challenge foreign aggressors on the open sea.

Davenant concluded *Britannia Triumphans* with a gauche epilogue praising the King's prowess in the royal bed, an extraordinary failure of tone, as if Davenant had quite forgotten the Temple of Chaste Love of his previous masque, or the whole tradition of platonic love that had been built up over the decade. He redeemed himself next month with his masque for the Queen, *Luminalia*, one of the simplest of the masques, and one that corresponds most closely to Inigo Jones's airy comment that 'these shows are nothing else but pictures with light and motion'.[12] In this ethereal work, 'the invention consisting of darkness and light', the action begins with a night-piece, a novel exercise in the aesthetics of darkness by Inigo Jones: he created dim mysterious scenes with half-perceived perspectives that provided an eerie setting for nocturnal music and soft dances. A strange vision appeared, of a great city sustained by a rainbow, representing the City of Sleep; then the light of dawn grew steadily stronger, but instead of the sun the Queen's Majesty effulgent with light broke upon the world. We learn that the sun 'has given up his charge of lightening the hemisphere to a terrestrial beauty, in whom intellectual and corporeal brightness are joined'. The elementary platonic imagery of light as divine energy is stated with powerful directness in *Luminalia*, which dramatises the divine power of majesty at a time when the King needed every assurance of his infallible rule.

The last masque was the cryptically-named *Salmacida Spolia* of January 1640. The obscure allusion of the title is explained in the printed introduction, although the spectators were presumably ignorant of it—no matter, in the event, for the action moved clearly enough. Salmacis was a fountain whose pure delicious waters reduced the fierceness of barbarian natures 'to the sweetness of the Grecian customs'. As such it served as an allegory of the King's power, which 'seeks by all means to reduce tempestuous and turbulent natures into a sweet calm of civil concord'. Another adage in the introduction reminds the audience of a Greek battle in which both victors and vanquished were equally depleted. For all the apparent remoteness of the subject, the masque addresses itself to the immediate problems of popular discontent and incipient rebellion. By now the tide of opposition was rising strongly against the King. His campaign against the Scots had ended in discomfiture, there was nation-wide resistance to his taxation policy of Ship Money, and ahead lay the ominous prospect of a new parliament. Public dislike of Laud's religious policy, of the King's tolerance of Catholicism, and of the indulgent royal attitude towards Spain was beginning to turn into outright hatred. As if in response to these pressures, Charles commissioned—and may well have helped to invent—a masque that would put the royal case for wise, benevolent yet absolute government as strongly and as attractively as possible. Exceptionally, both the King and Queen appeared together as masquers, making *Salmacida Spolia* a concerted appeal for support, for although nominally the principal spectator upon the chair of state was the Queen Mother, Marie de Medici, the real audience that the masque aimed at was the Court, where Charles hoped to rally to his side the men he believed most influential in the nation.

The theme of the masque was the power of the King's secret wisdom, a wisdom unappreciated by the populace, but fit matter to be revealed to noble, understanding minds. Jones packed the border of the stage arch with an unprecedented number of allegorical figures in an excessively rhetorical projection of the King's virtues and attributes, many of them unnatural confections such as Intellectual Light accompanied by Doctrine and Discipline, a conceit in favour of High Anglican religious policy, no doubt, but not easily deciphered. Another complex personification, Forgetfulness of Injuries, sounds as if she had been invented by the King as part of a list of points that he wished to make as a preliminary to the masque. Innocence, too, sounds like the King protesting too much. Charles cast himself as Philogenes, the Lover of his People, whose wisdom would defeat all those malignant spirits that envied his greatness, leading his country to un-rivalled peace and contentment. The curtain rose on a tempest with furies, for once an honest image of the forces ranged against the King, although Davenant presents the furies as envious of England's long continued peace, the calculated result of Stuart policy. There are naturally no internal grounds for discontent. This scene of fomenting rebellion is replaced by a calm prospect of a fertile land, 'as might express a country in peace, rich and fruitful', a superficial image of Britain's prosperity under Stuart rule. From the heavens a silver chariot descends, containing the Good Genius of Great Britain and Concord, who sing a lyrical complaint that must have expressed very intimately King Charles's dismay at his people's ingratitude towards him:

> *Concord*: Why should I hasten hither, since the good
>   I bring to men is slowly understood?
> *Genius*: I know it is the people's vice
>   To lay too mean, too cheap a price
>   On every blessing they possess.
>   Th' enjoying makes them think it less.
> *Concord*: If, then, the need of what is good
>   Doth make it loved or understood,
>   Or 'tis by absence better known,
>   I shall be valued when I'm gone.

Genius: Yet stay, O stay! . . .

. . .

Concord: I will! and much I grieve that, though the best
    Of kingly science harbours in his breast,
    Yet 'tis his fate to rule in adverse times,
    When wisdom must awhile give place to crimes.

. . .

Both: O who but he could thus endure
    To live and govern in a sullen age,
    When it is harder far to cure
    The people's folly than resist their rage?

(ll. 170–99)

There follows a long anti-masque of twenty entries, all of a harmless, sportive nature, suggestive perhaps of the simple recreations that Charles recommended to his subjects in his proclamations on lawful pastimes, amusements that often incensed his Puritan opponents. The next scene dramatises the heroic strivings of the monarch on behalf of his people, showing a remote mountainous landscape 'which represented the difficult way which heroes are to pass ere they come to the Throne of Honour', an image that highlights the King's isolation at this stage of his career. At last the spectators are gratified with a sight of the King on his throne of honour, surrounded by his masquing lords. 'This throne was adorned with palm trees [symbols of victory] between which stood the statues of the ancient heroes. In the under parts on each side, lay captives bound, in several postures, lying on trophies of armours, shields and antique weapons, all his throne being feigned of goldsmith's work' (ll. 346–50). Once more we find the hollow symbolism of pretended victories. The bound captives convey a fiction of conquest which never occurred. The song that greets the King praises his forbearance in not crushing his enemies, for his wisdom knows their disaffection is a sickness that will soon pass; in effect, Charles's weakness is being represented as mercy.

> If it be kingly patience to outlast
> Those storms the people's giddy fury raise
> Till like fantastic winds themselves they waste,
> The wisdom of that patience is thy praise.
>
> Murmur's a sickness epidemical.
> 'Tis catching, and infects weak common ears.
> For through those crooked, narrow alleys, all
> Invaded are and killed by whisperers.
>
> This you discerned, and by your mercy taught
> Would not, like monarchs that severe have been,

Invent imperial arts to question thought,
Nor punish vulgar sickness as a sin.

Nor would your valour, when it might subdue,
Be hindered of the pleasure to forgive.
They're worse than overcome, your wisdom knew,
That needed mercy to have leave to live.

Since strength of virtues gained you Honour's throne,
Accept our wonder and enjoy your praise!
He's fit to govern there and rule alone
Whom inward helps, not outward force, doth raise.

(ll. 360–79)

The heavenly wisdom that guides the King's actions now appears in full radiance: the Queen herself descends. Heroic Virtue unites with Heavenly Wisdom in a dance which echoes the music of the spheres. The superhuman powers that operate through the King and Queen are revealed, the heavens fill with music as deities throng to welcome the royal couple, and the essential divinity of kings is confirmed.

Thus Jones, Davenant and (one suspects) Charles himself pull out all the stops to convince the enclosed world of the Court of the benevolence of Stuart intentions. Ultimately Charles relied on magic: the divine right of kings that James had inculcated in him so thoroughly, the special providence of God that favoured the Stuarts, and which gave the King a supernatural wisdom and virtue. The King's touch would heal the country. The masque was a beautifully adapted vehicle for these beliefs, its fictions like stage clouds concealed divine powers. The annual masques of Charles and Henrietta Maria were periodic renewals of confidence in their roles, so we need not be surprised at the weeks or months of rehearsal that they put into these shows, nor at the expense they were prepared to incur in stringent times.

The final statement of *Salmacida Spolia* proposes that the influence of the King will turn all to sweetness in the realm, just like the fountain of the title.

All that are harsh, all that are rude,
Are by your harmony subdued;
Yet so into obedience wrought,
As if not forced to it, but taught.

(ll. 471–4)

It is noteworthy that the model for the King's action is Greek. *Luminalia* also had a Greek component in that one of the minor themes dealt with the expulsion of the Muses from Greece and their eventual settlement in Britain.

Greece signified culture in contrast to Rome with its associations of military and imperial might. Although Charles had cultivated the persona of a Roman emperor for much of his reign, by the end of the thirties he seems to have recognised that culture might be a more subtle way of disarming criticism than armies he could not afford to raise. The projection of a refined, virtuous, philosophic sovereign as ideal ruler may have gratified the rather isolated royal family and its sympathisers, but it must have seemed a weak line of defence even at the time. Other aspects of the masque hint at the cleverly disguised retreat from conviction and assurance of victory: the stress on the patience and endurance of the King, the inward nature of his strength rather than its triumphal sweep over the world, the mistrust of the 'beloved people' who do not reciprocate their sovereign's love. Time with a glass running out should have been the symbolic figure to close up this masque.

Drama and poetry at Court

King Charles had a genuine enthusiasm for the theatre. His well-marked folio of Shakespeare survives at Windsor to show that he had read the greatest works of the previous generation with attention. He took a close interest in the plays written around him, and Shirley even mentions in the preface to *The Gamester* that his plot had been suggested to him by the King. We catch glimpses of the King reading the manuscripts of plays by Massinger and Davenant before performance, primarily to check on the acceptability of the material, but also because drama was a major source of pleasure to him. Of all his building projects at Whitehall, the only one to be carried through was the new Cockpit Theatre, a sure sign of his priorities. But the royal patronage of drama in this period, evidenced most clearly by the large size and incessant activity of the King's Players and Queen Henrietta's Company, produced the undesirable consequence that too many of the plays written with Court performance in mind strove to please the refined yet artificial and restricted taste of Whitehall, and lost touch with the broad spread of experience that animated so much of Jacobean drama. Romance plots with innumerable permutations of amorous relationships showed that the taste that had responded to Fletcher's work in the old reign now dominated the drama of the new. Plays that found approval concentrated on honour and duty entangled with love, usually expressed in an elegant, slightly affected language that reflected the Queen's fondness for a preciosity of manner that she had acquired in her youth, spent in an atmosphere shimmering with ideals of sophisticated speech and conduct that emanated from the Hôtel de Rambouillet. Massinger, Shirley, Brome and Davenant were the chief purveyors of the new taste, although occasionally they jibed at the excessive improbability of fashionable subject matter, and it is difficult always to be sure how seriously they were arguing in favour of the new sensibility. Jonson tried to regain stage success in the late twenties and early thirties, but the failure of his last plays with their abrasive characters and their detailed satirical representation of a wide social spectrum indicates how he misjudged the new atmosphere of Court theatre. In a study of the Caroline audience, Clifford Leech points out that women had come to exercise a determining influence in the private and Court playhouses, and that their approval was essential to the success of a play.[13] Prologues and epilogues praise their discerning minds and flatter their judgement, as does the prologue to Shirley's *The Coronation* (1635):

> But what have I omitted? Is there not
> A blush upon my cheeks, that I forgot
> The ladies? and a female Prologue too!
> Your pardon, noble gentlewomen, you
> Were first within my thoughts; I know you sit,
> As free, and high commissioners of wit,
> Have clear, and active souls, nay, though the men
> Were lost, in your eyes, they'll be found again;
> You are the bright intelligences move,
> And make a harmony in this sphere of love.[14]

This feminine ascendancy in the audience encouraged fine courtly dialogue, elegant repartee and mannered encounters between the sexes. The purified language of the Caroline stage dispenses with the metaphorical density and allusive richness of the older drama, just as the process of thought and speculation in the characters thins out into a superficial observation and wit. The larger issues of the moral predicament of man in a fallen world and the tragic complexity of life were unwelcome at a Court which sought amusement of a lighter kind.[15] If we look at Shirley's *The Gamester*, the play where Charles suggested the plot and admired the result, we can form an idea of what was really appreciated at Court. We find a clever, fast-moving piece about a profligate husband, whose libertine career is reformed by the 'discovery' that his own wife is also engaging in sexual freedoms. She, of course, only pretends to vice in order to bring her husband back to the paths of virtue. The play offers a fairly conventional tale of cuckoldry and deception, enlivened by some brisk verbal comedy in the gaming world haunted by the husband and his friends; it is essentially an amusing entertainment with a light moral icing.

The fashionable popularity of comedy of manners and amorous tragi-comedy, of plays praising platonic love and altruistic friendship, could provoke a dramatist to the edge of parody, as with Brome, in his play of the mid-thirties entitled *The Love-Sick Court*, which is tuned to the prevailing fashion, although the handling of the action betrays a certain critical attitude towards the ruling conventions. In spite of a Grecian setting, the title seems aimed at the English Court, where an excessive preoccupation with the etiquette of love and stylised adoration of women threatened to turn to morbidity. The preposterous plot centres on twin brothers in love with the same princess, who loves them equally. As the brothers enjoy a perfect friendship, each wishes to renounce his love in favour of the other, and neither will permit such a sacrifice from his brother. Another suitor exists in the person of the scheming politician Stratocles, who has designs on the kingdom (and who brings to mind the Earl of Strafford). He contrives a duel between the brothers, each of whom offers himself defenceless to the other. The dilemma is resolved by the discovery that the twins are not brothers at all, but one is the lost brother of the princess, so a marriage may be arranged and Stratocles outwitted. The play contains a good deal of mild mockery of the precious language of courtiers, and hints that a Court so preoccupied with artificial behaviour may dangerously isolate itself from political realities and popular support, and eventually incur contempt. *The Love-Sick Court* opens on a warning note, with an account of a widening rift between a king and his subjects:

> Th' unquiet Commons fill his head and breast
> With their impertinent discontents and strife.
> The peace that his good care has kept 'hem in
> For many years, still feeding them with plenty,
> Hath, like ore pampered steeds that throw their Masters,
> Set them at war with him. O misery of kings!
> His vertue breeds their vices; and his goodness
> Pulls all their ills upon him. He has been
> Too long too lenetive.
>
> (I.i.9–17)[16]

At the height of the play, the challenge to a duel states how generally damaging the love-sickness has become: 'Brother . . . we are the laughing stock of the Nation; and injurious both to the King, our Countrey, the divine Eudina, and our selves, by our childish love' (III.iii).

The refined cult of love at Court did indeed have damaging consequences

by highlighting the unreal atmosphere that prevailed at the heart of a kingdom that was becoming steadily more agitated about questions of political
and religious authority. It was an exclusive cult, restricted to the inner circle
of courtiers and literary wits. It haunted the plays of the period, and attained
its fullest manifestation in the platonic subject matter of the masques,
where the King and Queen in person expressed their mutual love. It
permeated relationships between men and women at Court, giving to the
love poetry that circulated there a particularly affected tone of elevated
compliment and hyperbolic purity. Waller's poems to Sacharissa or the
Cavalier lyrics that share the mood of Carew's 'Song' might stand as models
of the type:

> Aske me no more where Jove bestowes,
> When June is past, the fading rose:
> For in your beauties orient deepe,
> These flowers as in their causes, sleepe.

Not surprisingly, such refinement provoked a good deal of reaction, often
from those writers who contributed dutifully to the cult of chaste or platonic
love. Carew's extravagantly sensuous poem 'The Rapture' enjoyed a vast
reputation amongst those gentlemen who preferred a more fleshy kind of
love to that ethereal variety that cast a celestial radiance over the Court, and
the Cavalier poets generally produced a vigorous line of erotic verse to re-
fresh the gallant lover. Cleveland's poem 'The Antiplatonick' achieved
temporary fame for its witty rebuke of contemplative love:

> For shame thou everlasting Woer,
> Still saying grace, and never falling to her!
> Love that's in contemplation plac't,
> Is Venus drawn but to the wast.
> Unlesse your flame confesse it's gender,
> And your Parley cause surrender,
> Y'are Salamanders of a cold desire,
> That live untoucht amid the hottest fire.
>
> . . .
>
> Give me a lover bold and free,
> Not Eunucht with formality:
> Like an Embassador that beds a Queen
> With the nice Caution of a sword between.[17]

A more sophisticated sign of dissatisfaction came from Davenant, whose
play *The Platonic Lovers* (1635) can be construed either as a conventional
tragicomedy of lovers overcoming the obstacles to fulfilment or as a critical

burlesque by a man of normal appetites of the essentially foolish nature of platonic relationships. The platonic conventions of rapt adoration of the beauties of the mind were so unnatural that they came close to the ridiculous. Davenant's play tells of two neighbouring dukes, each of whom loves the other's sister; platonic convictions transmitted amongst the lovers thwart the fruition of these marriages until common sense and natural desires effect a satisfactory *dénouement*. Although in the speeches Davenant maintains a balance between platonic love and physical love, the action makes it clear that the former leads men and women into affectation and folly. Yet, in spite of a great variety of detraction and satire, the conventions of platonic love were honoured and reaffirmed in the royal circle until the last masque in 1640.

The Court poetry of the 1630s has a greater claim to distinction than the drama, although even here the most successful figures are of modest stature, and their achievements assured yet unambitious. Suckling, Lovelace, Davenant, Carew, Waller—each sounds his own distinctive minor note, but they all speak with the voice of the Court. To catch the mood and manner of this time, Carew and Waller may serve as our representative men. Both perpetuate the tradition of poetic civility created by Ben Jonson, without extending its range. Carew however also drew some inspiration from Donne, most notably in his elegies (especially the elegy on Donne himself) and also in the intellectual wit of some of his lyrics. To a large extent the work of both Carew and Waller is complimentary and occasional, centring on life, love and death in the Court circle.

Waller originally dedicated his early poems to the Queen in an epistle written during the late thirties but not printed when the poems were published in 1645, for obvious reasons. The dedication evokes the Olympian atmosphere of perfect felicity enjoyed by the fortunate islands of Great Britain under the protection of their demi-god rulers:

If your Ma^ty had lived in those Tymes which sacrifiz'd to the Sun and Moone and of eatch glorious Creatoure made a new Dyety, as the admiration of your sacrad persone had supply'd them with a more excusable Idolatry, So could no incense have been more worthie your Altar then the odore of his Maties Heroyck deeds. And though the court and universities have no other mater of theer song, yet if your Matie please to listen what Echo the country returnes to so loud a praise, Wee shall likwayes teach the woods to sound your royall name, And tell how great a portion of our present hapines is owing to those Divyne Graces, whairin all the private desires of our soueraine beeing accompleished, hee is wholie at Leasoure to confer faelicitie on others.

The love of the royal couple ensures divine favour for their nation in a troubled world:

We looke not on your Ma^tiee as the cause only But as the pledg of our securitie, For as Heaven threatens a Deluge of all calamities uppone a land condemned to be the seat of warr; soe may our Natione well expect the contrary blessings being chosen for the seat of love.[18]

The poems addressed to Henrietta Maria continue this line of hyperbole, as Waller is overcome by the glory of his Mighty Queen

> In whom the extremes of power and beauty move,
> The Queen of Britain, and the Queen of Love!

('To the Queen', ll. 11–12)

Only 'Sacred Charles' could aspire to so celestial a love, for his heroic ardour burns incomparably more bright than the affections of other men:

> Not so divine a flame, since deathless gods
> Forbore to visit the defiled abodes
> Of men, in any mortal breast did burn.

(*idem.*, ll. 59–61)

Another poem to the Queen speaks of the beneficent virtue that she exercises over the land:

> But since the light which now informs our age
> Breaks from the court . . .
> . . .
>   Those sovereign beams which heal the wounded soul,
> And all our cares, but once beheld, control.
> . . .
> All her affections are to one inclined;
> Her bounty and compassion to mankind.

('Of the Queen')

This poem closes on an epical note with a vision of Henrietta Maria as the mother of men of destiny, a Venus to some new Aeneas. A typical feature of Waller's royal poems is the attempt to present the King and Queen as heroic figures engaged in forging their own epic, and in this respect his poems relate to the masques which were themselves brief epics of Stuart destiny. One of his earliest pieces was an epic fragment narrating the escape of Prince Charles from loss at sea on his voyage back from Spain, with all the mythological accoutrements proper to nautical salvation. Waller also chose the occasion of King Charles receiving the news of Buckingham's death while at prayer as a telling moment of heroic fortitude: the comparisons are Homeric, with Patroclus slain, yet Charles himself embodies a more than antique virtue: 'Bold Homer durst not so great virtue feign / In his best pattern.' Charles, 'this mixed Divinity and Love', belongs to a greater race than any the old world knew.

The King's rebuilding of St Paul's is seen as a miracle of his 'magnanimity and art':

> He, like Amphion, makes those quarries leap
> Into fair figures from a confused heap;
> For in his art of regiment is found
> A power like that of harmony in sound.

The achievement exceeds any architectural performance of antiquity, and of course it is carried out with the evident approval of heaven. Charles's concern for his navy calls forth from Waller another exclamation at a divinely chosen King entrusted with immeasurable power, followed by a vision of the Royal Navy sailing victorious over a submerged world. Almost all his early panegyric poetry has a quality of splendid excess matched with a fantastical inventiveness that succeeds because behind all these inflated conceits lies a conviction that Charles and Henrietta Maria are indeed demi-gods, monarchs by divine right, and therefore fit subjects for a poetry of miracle and vision.

In his love poetry, Waller's manner is largely controlled by Ben Jonson. Although he never knew Jonson, his poetic debt is acknowledged in an elegy, and in his two Penshurst poems he deliberately invites comparison with Jonson's own tribute to the Sidneys. The comparison reveals the narrowing of imaginative scope and the diminished seriousness that afflicted Caroline courtly poetry; in compensation comes a new clarity, evenness of tone and aptness of wit—the refinement for which Waller was noted amongst his contemporaries and Restoration successors. Jonson's 'Penshurst' was a celebration of a family, a house, a way of life that he judged admirable and exemplary, a pattern for an age; Waller's 'Penshurst' has become the decorative setting for his beloved Sacharissa, Lady Dorothy Sidney, where nature has learnt civility and imitates the emotions of a lover.

> When to the beeches I report my flame,
> They bow their heads, as if they felt the same.

Nature in Jonson's poem was at the service of a liberal philosophy of hospitality, obedient to a worthy master and to a noble ideal of lordship; Waller's nature has become a compliant courtier. The poems that record Waller's unrequited infatuation with Sacharissa have a gallant tone which subordinates emotion to the smooth operation of his wit, an unruffled politeness which announces the style of the cavalier in love. His lyrics, which include 'Go lovely Rose', a song perfect of its kind, move under the spell of a marvellous metrical control, beautiful impersonal pieces that appeal to a connoisseur's ear attuned to the finely turned phrase.

Waller was least happy as an elegist. In his funeral poems on great courtiers he employs a witty, conceited style that can create remarkable images, yet the verse lacks moral gravity or intelligent judgement. He can show us the Countess of Carlisle in mourning for her husband, a sable image of grief:

> A spark of virtue by the deepest shade
> Of sad adversity is fairer made;
> Nor less advantage doth thy beauty get;
> A Venus rising from a sea of Jet!

Yet the poet is too pleased with his own wit and never attempts to confront the challenging questions of death. Waller lacks seriousness of enquiry, just as he seems to lack religious conviction. These are secular elegies, decorative forms of mourning, complimentary epistles to the dead. 'Upon the Death of my Lady Rich' blandly consoles the survivors:

> So all we know of what they do above
> Is that they happy are, and that they love.

The Countess of Northumberland is also smoothly disposed of in a consolatory elegy addressed to her husband. Such mild responses to the mystery of death anticipate the cool, secularised mourning of Restoration society, where well-dressed marble figures either stand confidently on tombs which proclaim their public merits and private virtues, or tastefully recline upon their deathbeds as if they expect the visit of some noble friend rather than the Angel of the Resurrection. Waller lived on long into the Restoration period, when the correctness of his taste and its early development came to be fully appreciated, but the fact that his verse already found favour at Court in the 1630s indicates a disposition there to welcome fine surfaces and a congratulatory optimism as a confirmation of the prosperous times that Charles's reign assured.

Thomas Carew's verse contributed greatly to these false feelings of security and peace. The death of the Protestant leader Gustavus Adolphus in battle in 1632 gave him fit occasion to praise the royally maintained felicity of England:

> But let us that in myrtle bowers sit
> Under secure shades, use the benefit
> Of peace and plenty, which the blessed hand
> Of our good King gives this obdurate Land,
> Let us of Revels sing . . .
>
>   . . .

> Tourneyes, Masques, Theaters, better become
> Our Halcyon dayes; what though the German Drum
> Bellow for freedome and revenge, the noyse
> Concernes not us, nor should divert our joyes;
> Nor ought the thunder of their Carabins
> Drowne the sweet Ayres of our tun'd Violins.
>
> ('In answer of an Elegiacall Letter . . .', ll. 45–9, 95–100)[19]

For Carew in this poem, the perfect image of England's happiness is provided by the ideal visions of the masque, probably *Tempe Restored*, by his
friend Aurelian Townshend, with a pastoral setting where all grossness has
been expunged and where the Queen of Beauty moves amongst 'th' Angellike
formes' of her adoring subjects. Carew's poems to the King and Queen
sustain the fictions current in the masques. The Queen incarnates celestial
love, by her very nature winning all souls to worship her, transforming all
amorous response into an aspiring chaste desire for union with the high
ideal she makes apparent to men:

> Thou great Commandresse, that doest move
> Thy Scepter o're the Crowne of Love,
> And through his Empire with the Awe
> Of Thy chaste beames, doest give the Law,
> From his prophaner Altars, we
> Turne to adore Thy Deitie:
> He, only can wilde lust provoke,
> Thou, those impurer flames canst choke;
> And where he scatters looser fires,
> Thou turn'st them into chast desires.
>
> ('To the Queene', ll. 1–10)

Her presence and example inspire men to recreate the lost perfection of love;
she 'Doth either sex to each unite, / And forme loves pure Hermophradite'
(ll. 17–18). The King too appears in his masquing guise of Heroic Virtue:

> Let his strong vertues overcome,
> And bring him bloodlesse Trophies home.
>
> ('A New-yeares gift. To the King', ll. 29–30)

His reign is 'one great continued festivall'. One would expect Carew, as the
author of the most dazzling masque of the reign, *Coelum Britannicum*, to be
a reliable royal encomiast, yet his poems are not the mechanical tributes of a
Court servant but fresh vigorous acts of worship, for Carew like Jonson
responded to the mysterious divinity of kingship as other men did to the
reality of religious power in their lives: it was an irresistible, incontrovert-
ible, impalpable fact that demanded recognition and praise. As long as the

divine right of kings remained credible, the cult of the King's supernatural powers would always find believers, but once those powers lost their credibility, as they did after the Restoration, then extravagant praise of the King would sound hollow and sycophantic. Sincerity in poetry is notoriously hard to judge, as is conviction: it is primarily a matter of tone, but the scale, ingenuity and intensity of complimentary rhetoric before the Civil War may be partly explained by the existence of a vital belief in the immeasurable and fateful influence of royal power.

Carew's art was moulded by Jonson and Donne. From Jonson he learnt the management of the public poem with its mixture of judgement, compliment and praise administered in an authoritative tone of voice that causes one to respect the poet as much as his subject. Sometimes he modelled himself closely on Jonson, as in 'To Saxham', a country house poem based on 'To Penshurst', an assured performance which has however a much more limited scope than Jonson's poem, restricting itself to the abundant hospitality of the house, for which nature willingly sacrifices itself. Carew's other country house poem, 'From Wrest', written in the late 1630s, still looks back to 'Penshurst' with its praise of the modesty of the house, its liberal board, and the civility of its lord, yet the strong colouring and sensuous detail of Carew's imagination establish the individual character of his verse within the Jonson tradition, and he displays a distinctively elaborate wit in his descriptions, as when he gives this fanciful account of the waters surrounding the house:

> . . . where the neighbour sourse
> Powers forth her waters she directs their course,
> And entertaines the flowing streames in deepe
> And spacious channells, where they slowly creepe
> In snakie windings, as the shelving ground
> Leades them in circles, till they twice surround
> This Island Mansion, which i' th' center plac'd,
> Is with a double Crystall heaven embrac'd,
> In which our watery constellations floate,
> Our Fishes, Swans, our Water-man and Boate,
> Envy'd by those above, which wish to slake
> Their starre-burnt limbes, in our refreshing lake,
> But they stick fast nayl'd to the barren Spheare,
> Whilst our encrease in fertile waters here
> Disport, and wander freely where they please
> Within the circuit of our narrow Seas.

(ll. 73–88)

This is essentially decorative compliment, albeit of a high order. Its expressiveness and ingenuity may remind one of Donne, the other master who conditioned Carew's manner. Donne's influence most evidently permeates his elegies, most notably and appropriately the elegy on Donne himself, where the succession of conceits and the sombrely articulated accents of the poetry form a tribute to Donne's own style and indicate Carew's discipleship; the critical intelligence at work in the poem is also worthy of its subject. The language with which Carew opens his elegy on the Lady Anne Hay recalls Donne of the satires in its immediacy and its ability to evoke compact social vignettes:

> I heard the Virgins sigh, I saw the sleeke
> And polisht Courtier, channell his fresh cheeke
> With reall teares; the new-betrothed Maid
> Smild not that day; the Graver Senate layd
> Their businesse by; of all the Courtly throng,
> Griefe seald the heart, and silence bound the tongue.
>
> (ll. 1–6)

The spirit of Donne gleams in Carew's love poetry, from the erotic 'Rapture' that emulates Donne's Elegy XIX 'On his Mistress Going to Bed' with less wit and more sensuousness, to the exquisitely neat song 'Ask me no more' that owes some of its character to the metaphysical lyrics of *Songs and Sonets*. Curiously, much of Carew's most memorable poetry is composed under the tutelage of Donne and Jonson: he writes most assuredly when in the shadow of their models. His career provides a testimony to the fertilising power of the two older poets in the Caroline period, just as it suggests that between them Jonson and Donne had developed techniques of expression and had provided conventions for treating a sufficiently broad range of subject matter that lesser poets could work comfortably within their limits, without any apparent sense of being too confined. Verbal colour and a stylish polish could be added, but as long as the familiar established pattern of Court society persisted, up to the outbreak of the Civil War, the idiom of Donne and Jonson remained valid.

King Charles and painting

The long Stuart peace, and the freer relations with continental countries that it promoted, enabled the arts to be cultivated in England on an unprecedented scale. The creation of great collections, for which open frontiers were a prerequisite, became possible, and in this period three collections of international significance were assembled: those of Charles I, the Earl of Arundel and the Duke of Buckingham. At its height, the royal collection of paintings had an incomparable reputation, outshining the palace galleries of Paris, Madrid, Vienna, Prague and Brussels, a tribute to King Charles's taste, knowledge and persistence in the pursuit of great works of art. A study of its formation reveals a pattern of accident and good fortune improved by patronage and diplomacy. Death and the misfortunes of others inevitably play some part in the growth of great collections; they may be said to have formed the nucleus of Charles's, for he inherited the considerable treasures of his elder brother Prince Henry in 1612, and then these were augmented by his mother's excellent collection, mainly of portraits, upon her death in 1617. Prince Henry must have provided the example, and Queen Anne the encouragement for his love of the fine arts, while in all probability the Earl of Arundel guided him in connoisseurship; nor should one discount the ubiquitous influence of Inigo Jones, who worked closely with all members of the royal family. From the early 1620s Charles began to share a passion for Venetian paintings with the Duke of Buckingham, who seems to have started collecting paintings as an appendage to his glory, but rapidly developed a competent expertise. The visit to Madrid in 1623 gave Prince Charles his first sight of a truly magnificent state collection, built up by Charles V and Philip II, and from this date the serious enlargement of his own collection began. Even though Charles left Spain without a bride, he must have felt his adventure adequately rewarded by the paintings that state etiquette bestowed upon him. From the Prado rich in Titians he brought away the 'Venus del Pardo', now in the Louvre, the full-length portrait of Charles V with a white dog, now back in Madrid, and a portrait of a girl in a fur cloak. He also received a John the Baptist attributed to Correggio, and a statue of Cain and Abel by Gianbologna, and he entered into negotiation, unsuccessfully, to purchase two volumes of Leonardo's drawings. While in Madrid, he was sketched by Velasquez for a painting that never materialised.

In 1623 he managed to purchase the Raphael cartoons of the Acts of the Apostles (now in the Victoria and Albert) which his agents secured for him in Genoa. The cartoons had originally been designed as models for a great series of tapestries for the Vatican, and now Charles desired them not merely for their importance as works of art, but also for use by the royal tapestry factory that had been established at Mortlake in 1619. King James was the nominal patron of this venture, which was founded to produce the acres of wall hangings required for the royal palaces, in emulation of the workshops of Paris and Brussels, but Prince Charles seems to have been the directing power, for his secretary Sir Francis Crane was appointed Controller, and most of the output went to Charles's use, not James's. Several sets of tapestry were woven from the Raphael cartoons, all evidence of the maturity of taste at the Stuart Court, and its alignment with the central tradition of Italian art.

By the time of his accession in 1625, Charles had established a network of agents across Europe whose task was to lure art treasures and artists to England. The most active of these men were Balthazar Gerbier (a roving, polylingual Huguenot of varied talents, an able miniature painter and architect, who began his career in Buckingham's service); Nicholas Lanier (another master of different arts, for he was both a musician and painter who had been in the service of Prince Henry, composing music for masques under James, and eventually becoming Master of the King's Music in 1625), and Daniel Nys (an enigmatic figure who seems to have been a Venetian merchant and who certainly had a sharp scent for pictures in Italy). Charles also exploited his diplomatic representatives for cultural ends: Sir Dudley Carleton at the Hague, Sir Henry Wotton at Venice, and Sir Thomas Roe at Constantinople were all engaged in the search for works of art. At Antwerp the King's interests were looked after by Lionel Wake, an English merchant.

The usefulness of this network was demonstrated by the greatest coup of Charles's career as a collector, the purchase of the Mantua collection in 1627. Two successive spendthrift Dukes of Mantua had caused a financial crisis in the state that Duke Vincenzio decided to alleviate by selling his art treasures. He first contacted the Countess of Arundel in 1623 about the possibility of a sale, but the Arundels discreetly held back, recognising that Charles should have the prior opportunity to buy. Daniel Nys was introduced into the negotiations, and after much covert dealing he was able to strike a bargain of some £15,000. It was an extraordinary collection. In their days of power the Gonzaga family had patronised many great painters including Mantegna, Leonardo, Perugino, Caravaggio and Giulio Romano, and to what was rightfully theirs had been added the illustrious loot of Urbino after its sack in 1502.[20] Nys was ecstatic at his success, although in the letter to his friend Endymion Porter in which he described his achievement he was careful to acknowledge the hand of providence in the deal. After telling of the Raphael Madonna, 'for which the Duke of Mantua gave a Marquisate', he lists the wealth of the collection:

The twelve Emperors of Titian, a large picture of Andrea del Sarto, a picture of Michelangelo di Caravaggio; other pictures of Titian, Correggio, Giulio Romano, Tintoretto and Guido Reni, all of the greatest beauty. In short, so wonderful and glorious a collection that the like will never again be met with; they are truly worthy of so great a King as his Majesty of Great Britain. In this negotiation I have been aided by divine assistance, without which success would have been impossible; to Him then be the glory.[21]

Giorgione's 'Concert Champêtre' was one of the prizes Nys omitted to mention. But this was not all. The Duke had not included in the sale the paintings he most cherished, Mantegna's nine great canvases of 'The Triumph of Julius Caesar', nor had he offered his collection of statuary. Nys now pressed him to part with all of these in a second round of bargaining. Lanier assisted in the negotiations and helped with the problems of transport. Getting a twelve-foot canvas from Mantua to London was no easy business then: some articles were taken to Venice and shipped, suffering trial by tempest before they finally reached London; others went over the Alps by mule to Lyon, then to Paris. The King's gratification at their arrival must have been intensified when he learnt that he had outmanoeuvred the Emperor, the Grand Duke of Tuscany and Cardinal Richelieu in the contest for possession. The acquisition of the Mantegna sequence in particular was an immensely desirable prize, and the reputation of these paintings was internationally so great that they were amongst the very few works (the Raphael cartoons were others) that the parliamentary commissioners decided to retain for the state when they began to auction the royal collection in 1649. More than any other single transaction in the world of art at this time, this event demonstrated to all the courts of Europe the strength and vitality of the new artistic culture in Britain, sustained by a young King (for Charles was only twenty-seven in 1627) who was only just settling into his reign. The Mantua episode also gave substance to the claims in the masques that the Muses, drawn out of their ancient haunts, were finding a new home in the North. Here were the treasures of one of the great Renaissance city-states brought in triumph to the King-Emperor of Great Britain, a conclusive example of the *translatio studii*, the unending process of cultural movement that began with the fall of Greece. One should not forget the other side of the coin, however. As Trevor-Roper points out, the bills for the Mantua collection came in at the same time as Charles was pressed to find money for Buckingham's expedition to relieve the Huguenots who were resisting the French King at La Rochelle. Buckingham got bogged down on the Ile de Rhé, then withdrew with large losses, a humiliation which might never have occurred if Charles had not embarrassed his treasury by excessive spending on art. As it was, he was obliged to sue for peace through the diplomacy of Rubens.[22]

Paintings formed part of the currency of international diplomacy in this period, with the result that Charles benefited extensively from this custom.

Rubens presented him with the large baroque allegory 'Peace and War' at the conclusion of the peace negotiations in 1630. This work, now in the National Gallery, is a rather heavy exercise in baroque rhetoric, perhaps more interesting to the modern spectator for its studies of the naked Mrs Balthazar Gerbier and her children, who sat for Peace and her offspring, than as a commentary on the virtues of diplomacy, symbolised by Minerva, who keeps war at bay in a stormy landscape. In 1636 the Pope tried to persuade Charles to liberalise the position of the Catholics in England by backing his nuncio's appeal with a consignment of paintings including works by Leonardo, Andrea del Sarto and Giulio Romano. In the same year the Dutch States sent five paintings to help resolve a dispute over the herring fisheries in the North Sea. The city of Nuremberg gave him two Dürers as a token of esteem. The catalogue of the Royal Collection made by its keeper Abraham Vanderdoort in the late 1630s records many gifts from courtiers and visitors who wished to obtain or retain the King's favour. The names of Carleton, Wotton, Roe, Cottington, Porter, Killigrew, and Lords Arundel, Buckingham, Newcastle and Pembroke recur in particular. A visiting Frenchman, the Duc de Liancourt, gave Charles Leonardo's 'John the Baptist' (now in the Louvre) and a 'Holy Family' by Titian, and received Holbein's 'Erasmus' in exchange. With the Earl of Pembroke, his Majesty made a deal which gave him enduring pleasure: the acquisition of Raphael's small 'St George' in exchange for a volume of Holbein drawings. This 'St George' (now in Washington) was commissioned from Raphael by the Duke of Urbino as a gift to Henry VII in order to mark the award of the Garter to the Italian Prince. It had been brought to England by Baldassare Castiglione on the one occasion that this arbiter of Renaissance courtesy ventured into the gothic North. Since King Charles was a fervent champion of the Order of the Garter, revising its statutes, increasing the splendour of its costume and ceremonies and regarding it as the most illustrious support of his kingship, one can appreciate how much he must have coveted this painting in which Raphael depicted the patron saint of the Order wearing its insignia.

Direct patronage of artists formed the richest source of contemporary paintings. Charles seized on the presence of Rubens in London in 1629–30 as the representative of the Spanish Netherlands and Spain to commission the ceiling decorations for the Banqueting House. Until this moment Buckingham had had much more profitable relations with Rubens than any other Englishman, although Charles had managed to commission a self-portrait of the artist in 1623 which still remains in the Royal Collection. (The King hung this together with the self-portraits of Mytens and Van

Rubens, 'Charles and Henrietta Maria in a Landscape'

Dyck in a little closet at Whitehall as a memento of the artists who furnished the most memorable paintings of his reign.) During this visit Rubens sketched out the painting that best captures the mood of chivalric romance that Charles was from time to time disposed to affect. It shows King Charles as St George delivering an elegant idealised Henrietta Maria from the dragon, in a superb sweeping landscape, very English in character, over which storm clouds are giving way to sunshine. The subject characterises two of the roles that Charles played out in the masques: the heroic lover who serves the beauty and virtue of his nonpareil queen (as in the finale to *Albion's Triumph*, or *Coelum Britannicum*, where the allusion is specific: 'We bring Prince Arthur, or the brave / St. George himself, great Queen, to you') and also Charles the lover of his people, Philogenes, for all around Rubens's Knight we see the 'beloved people' in an evident state of gratitude at their deliverance. The romance landscape reflects the Queen's own fondness for that kind of fiction. Charles found the chivalric ethic an apt channel for expressing his heroic energy and royal indomitable will. The adventurous ride to Spain to woo the Infanta was on one level an exercise in knight errantry. In his youth he grew adept at tilting, riding at the ring and other knightly sports. After his accession, his special concern for the Order of the Garter which we have already noted gave it a new prominence in the ceremonials of state: his reform of its religious rituals and his scrupulous discrimination over its award made it a centre of moral excellence in his reign. We may recall that at the climax of *Coelum Britannicum*, when the British heroes have occupied their places in the heavens, the prospect that opened beneath them, revealing as it were the seedbed of their virtues, showed Windsor Castle, 'the famous seat' of the Order. Rubens's painting is a central document of Caroline mythology.

The name of Van Dyck is inalienably linked with that of Charles I. Van Dyck conditions the way we envisage the Caroline Court, just as Holbein had imposed a distinctive character on the Court of Henry VIII, or Titian on the Venetian society of the sixteenth century. More than any other artist, Van Dyck mythologised the English Court of the 1630s, peopling it with a race of elegant heroes and their serene silken goddesses. Pose, landscape and the rich textures of silk are important ingredients in the formula that Van Dyck applied. He taught the English how to relax graciously against a pillar: the pillar authenticates the firmness, resolution, dignity of the man, and suggests the harmonious proportions of his soul; the man himself is then free to display his cultivated self in a pose of assured ease. The lustrous silken garments that glow with a Venetian splendour enhance the nobility of Van Dyck's subjects, velvet and lace show the discrimination of their fashionable taste, rich draperies tumble profusely behind them to tell discreetly of their state. The landscapes act as an extension to the character of the subject. Often a tranquil scene touched with a soft melancholic light will suggest a tone of philosophic distinction in the sitter, while a more rugged setting will emphasise a military spirit. Changeable skies reflect complex personalities and one rarely meets with open sunshine. Intelligence brims in the eyes of Van Dyck's people, and above all their sensitivity is expressed by his masterly treatment of hands. Long and slender, sometimes lightly clasped to the sitter's breast in a gesture that one meets so often in portraits and funeral effigies in this and the next age, as if the subject wishes to commend himself to the beholder; at other times appreciatively resting on an antique bust, or familiarly holding a staff of office, they are one of the most subtle and effective means Van Dyck has for conveying refinement. Even the steel-clad Earl of Northumberland, Admiral of the Fleet, rests his hand on an anchor as if it were a Cellini bronze. In group paintings the eloquent interplay of hands holds a family together in sympathetic community. Then again, the fleshly tints of Van Dyck, learnt from Rubens, give an animation to the features that hints at an infinite range of potential expressions. Gone are the firm outline and static pose of Jacobean painting, of which even Daniel Mytens, the most advanced of the painters working in England in the 1620s retained traces; with Van Dyck a style has been created that will remain current as the ideal of portraiture until the death of Sir Thomas Lawrence in 1832.

When it came to painting the King and Queen, Van Dyck understood the requirements of a royal iconography in a way which quite surpassed the conventional trimmings of the earlier portraits of the reign. Mytens's restrained style coupled with his aversion to grandeur resulted at times in a somewhat bourgeois portrayal of the King. His failure to exploit backgrounds deprived him of a significant aid to majestic effect. A useful comparison is afforded by two paintings on the same theme painted about the same year, 1632, one attributed to Mytens, the other a Van Dyck. Each painting shows the King and Queen half-length, exchanging tokens: she offers him a laurel wreath of victory and receives in return an olive sprig of peace. The informing idea of these works is the reconciliation of opposites, the *discordia concors* of the royal marriage, for Henrietta Maria was the daughter of the martial Henri IV, Charles the son of James the Peacemaker. From the resolution of these opposing qualities in marriage (a reflection of the Carlo-Maria theme common in the masques) springs the higher power of triumphant peace that guides the destiny of the nation. The equilibrium in love of the royal couple, conveyed by their mutual gaze and by the balance of the picture, is the essential condition of the mysterious strength symbolised by the interchange of emblems. Presumably it was the significance of the theme that caused Charles to commission the second version. In the version attributed to Mytens the couple face each other with a certain stiff formalism against a blank background of painted cloth. The symbolic plants stand out pointedly, the costumes are dignified, lit by an even light. Under Van Dyck's brush the scene develops into a marvelously animated dialogue: the eyes light up, the interplay of hands creates a beautiful rhythmic relationship between the King and Queen, and chiaroscuro effects play over the rich textures and colouring of the costumes, so that one feels that this is a vital marriage of minds, not simply a formal equation expressed in human terms. The billowing curtains behind Van Dyck's couple have parted to reveal a deep landscape swept by great clouds which add to the freshness of the scene. The royal lovers exchange tokens with an easy naturalness that blends the symbolism into an unaffected gesture of mutual affection. The gleaming regalia on a table behind Charles seem almost superfluous, such is the feeling of majesty and grace that pervades the whole painting.

Further to establish the radical change of manner that Van Dyck introduced, one might consider another royal portrait using the same accoutrements executed by the Dutchman Hendrik Pot in this same year 1632, the first year of Van Dyck's residence in England. Pot's picture is as unfortunate as his name. The Queen sits at one end of a long table, holding the infant Prince of Wales perched on the tabletop, and the King stands stiffly at the other end. On the table the symbols are laid out for inspection: the laurel sprig, crown and sceptre. But the crown is diminished by being set against Charles's hat, which is also on the table, while the olive twig that should complement the laurel has to be sought for, and is eventually found in the Queen's hand. An enormous curtain falls behind the table, overpowering all the characters and producing a great central area of spatial inertia. Yet Charles evidently thought that Pot was worth patronising, for at least two royal portraits survive from his hand. The truth is that Van Dyck's style and technique immediately made all the painters working at the English Court look old-fashioned.

One quality of Van Dyck's style that must have appealed strongly to Charles I was the tendency to dramatise the subject, and this tendency reached its height in the three giant equestrian portraits of the King, one now in the National Gallery, another in the Royal Collection, the third in the Louvre. In these productions Van Dyck's stagecraft is impeccable. The earliest, at Buckingham Palace, dating from about 1633, depicts Charles in armour riding through a triumphal arch preceded by his riding master. By means of this scenario Van Dyck fixed in paint the role of Charles as imperial monarch, a role that Charles affected on many occasions in the triumph-masques of the 1630s. The imperial association of the King on horseback stretched right back to the equestrian statue of Marcus Aurelius at Rome; during the Renaissance the image had been vigorously revived both in sculpture and in painting, achieving its finest statement in Titian's portrait of the Emperor Charles V, finally reaching England in the 1630s.[23] The French sculptor Hubert le Sueur introduced the motif with his bronze statue of Charles, which he cast in 1630 and which now divides the traffic at the top of Whitehall. Inigo Jones wished to set a similar statue on top of the triumphal arch that he designed as a formal entry to the City of London in 1636, in a scheme which recombined the elements of Van Dyck's painting of 1633. As we have seen, the imperial theme had been an important aspect of Stuart kingship under James, but he had surrounded himself with the symbols of imperialism—the twin pillars, the Virgilian allusions, a revived Roman architecture—whereas Charles enacted the role in person, appearing on the Whitehall stage as a Romano-British emperor, as Albanactus or Britanocles, and posing for his portraits on horseback in an image that was traditionally imperial. In the case of the painting in question, its associations were intensified by its setting: it hung at the end of a gallery at St James at the centre of a display of portraits of Roman emperors. The culmination of these claims to imperial state should have been the building of the new palace at Whitehall, but in actuality there was little substance to Charles's ambitions, only assertions made in masques about British domination of the seas that were meaningless in practice. Charles's imperial pose concealed a lamentable weakness: unable to help his humiliated sister Elizabeth and the deposed Elector, incapable of lending any aid to the Protestant cause in Europe, in danger of seeing the American colonies turn hostile to the crown because of their religious disaffection, and unable at home to impose his will upon Scotland or even to hold his own kingdom together. Against such a variety of failure, actual or incipient, the mask of confidence had to be maintained.

The Louvre painting presents Charles in a totally different light, as a country gentleman in a fresh, peaceful landscape. He has just dismounted from his horse, and turns on the viewer with a pleasant, intelligent look as he stands elegant yet relaxed in his plain costume. Such a picture relates to the idea of the King as patron of peace; certainly there were few other European monarchs in the 1630s who could have been painted in this guise. With the great 'Charles I on Horseback' (in the National Gallery), painted around 1638, we move forward to a time when men were beginning to 'oyl th' unused armour's rust', for here the King rides under virtually the same tree that previously shaded his peaceful reflections, now clad in complete steel, with his squire about to hand him his helmet. This painting has been the subject of a book by Roy Strong, who has explored the tradition in which it stands and the implications of its details. He very plausibly argues that the mournful expression that Van Dyck has given Charles in this work, which has often been interpreted as a premonition of doom, should more properly be read as a mood of 'shadowed melancholy', a fashionable pose which to contemporaries would have indicated a noble mind disposed towards contemplation and philosophic elevation.[24] This psychological tone would seem compatible with the mood of heroic stoicism that characterises the King as Philogenes in *Salmacida Spolia* of 1640.

Van Dyck, however, had bestowed this expression of philosophic melancholy on the King before: it was part of his formula for maximising the nobility of the King, just as his paintings always succeed in disguising Charles's diminutive stature. One can see the expression beginning to form as early as the Triumphal Arch painting, and by the time of the triple portrait of 1635 it is fully evolved. This last piece was commissioned by Henrietta Maria for despatch to Bernini in Rome as the working model for a portrait bust. Van Dyck's superb rendering of the royal features has a plasticity calculated to aid the translation of the portrait into marble; indeed, in this close-up study, the contours of the face have an almost palpable fleshliness. The bust was carved, safely delivered, and so much admired that the Queen sent Bernini a diamond of great price in gratitude. She determined to have a companion bust of herself sculpted, so Van Dyck painted her in three positions as a preliminary to the work; but the project lapsed.[25]

While posterity may admire the artistic judgement that caused Charles and his Queen to commission work from the greatest sculptor of the time, many contemporaries in England regarded these moves critically, for Bernini was effectively sculptor to the Papacy, so such dealings added to the resentment felt by keen Protestants against their ruler who seemed so willing to tolerate Catholicism in the Court and city, and to seek favours of the Vatican itself for such vanities as pictures and busts. William Prynne protested in his usual noisy manner, claiming that works of art were being

Van Dyck, triple portrait of Charles I

used as a lure by the Vatican to bring Charles closer to the faith, and Prynne was essentially correct in his intuition, for the consignment of paintings presented by Rome in 1635, the granting of permission to Bernini to accept the English commission, the efforts of Cardinal Barberini to secure Guido Reni's services for Henrietta Maria about the same time, were all part of a papal strategy to bring Charles into a sympathetic relationship with Catholicism.[26] Charles never seemed to realise how much his love of art exposed him to popular censure.

Art was inevitably intermingled with politics in this period, for the images proposed by art invariably carried some religious or political significance, and although continental artists were no longer prevented from travelling to England or accepting English commissions, as was the case in Elizabethan times, the Catholic faith of the great majority of European artists made their work unpleasing to the eyes of many insular Protestants, who had their revenge when the Royal Collection was righteously sold off under the Commonwealth. Rubens and Van Dyck were both Catholic, but Rubens was also an international diplomat and therefore never flaunted his religion provocatively, while Van Dyck remained an unobtrusive Catholic compliant to the desires of his patrons. Nothing shows his willingness to serve the State so well as his scheme for the decoration of the Banqueting House walls with a long processional sequence of the Order of the Garter. The designs would have been worked up into tapestries at the Mortlake factory, but the whole enterprise proved too costly for the King. The surviving designs, dating from about 1638, present a grand panorama in the Venetian manner showing the sumptuously robed knights in procession before a range of classical buildings that evoke once again Charles's dream of an Imperial Whitehall.[27]

During the nine years that he worked in England, Van Dyck virtually monopolised portraiture in Court circles. He extinguished an artist like Daniel Mytens, whom Charles retained as principal painter from his father's reign, for Mytens was quite unable to compete with the grand flowing style of the new man. Just before Van Dyck settled in England, Mytens painted a picture of the King and Queen departing for the hunt, which has great charm but betrays his limitations only too well. All the elements of the subject are accommodated in the same foreground plane, which is awkwardly integrated with the landscape behind. The nature of the subject demands motion here, but everything is static—even the dog jumping off the terrace seems suspended in mid-air. The beautifully decorative horse could have come straight out of Clouet, and would not have been out of place in Uccello. From a cloud over the royal couple protrudes an utterly improbable

Mytens, 'Charles and Henrietta Maria depart for the Chase'

cupid scattering flowers; the difficulty that Mytens experiences in giving this figure a mythological naturalness in the composition reveals how uncomfortable he was with baroque accessories: they were quite alien to his imagination. When Mytens was brought over by Arundel in 1618, he represented in English eyes the avant-garde of Dutch portraiture, yet within fourteen years he was superseded effortlessly by the fluent mastery of Van Dyck, skilled in baroque mythology and capable of transforming a whole generation of English patrons into citizens of an elegant world of valour and romance.

Various other artists were invited to England early in the reign to broaden the range of expression available to the King, who was beginning to develop an interest in mythological and allegorical painting, a genre virtually non-existent in the time of James, though current everywhere on the continent. One might complain that Charles's preference for mythological versions of his political and cultural relationships, seen most fully in the masques, lay at the centre of his state problems, and were symptomatic of the divorce between himself and the political, religious and social discontents of his reign. Mythological painting has a tendency to glorify a central group of figures, and, by a facile typing of forces and powers as desirable or undesirable, encourages a powerful, dramatic yet simplistic view of events

Honthorst, 'Buckingham presents the Liberal Arts to Charles and Henrietta'

which artist and patron agree to see as an ideal representation of powers at work. A characteristic example is provided by the Dutch painter Honthorst. He passed into Charles's service in 1628 from the Court in exile of Elizabeth of Bohemia at the Hague, where he had developed a style indebted to Caravaggio, but one in which Flemish realism struggles with an aspiration to the heroic, and ultimately predominates. He exerted himself most fully on the huge canvas, now at Hampton Court, of 'Apollo and Diana' or Buckingham presenting the Liberal Arts to Charles and Henrietta Maria, a scene conceived entirely in terms of masque, and one which celebrates Buckingham's intimate relationship with the King. Whether Buckingham was a fit person to introduce the Liberal Arts to his sovereign is beside the question, for part of the function of this painting was to assert Buckingham's position as patron and master of arts and sciences. Enthroned on a cloud, the King and Queen as Apollo and Diana, the sun and moon of the English heavens, welcome Buckingham as Mercury, who enacts the appropriate ambassadorial role as go-between, bringing the Liberal Arts into the royal presence. Among the many subjects traditionally under the tutelage of Mercury–Hermes were music, astronomy, mathematics and architecture, all aspects of the science of measurement of which he was master. In

Honthorst's painting he leads on the train of allegorical figures with their globes, armillary sphere, compasses, navigational devices and musical instruments, the first figure holding a book with the alphabet, which Mercury helped to compose. A riot of cupids in the darkened air greets their arrival; other figures rout the forces of satire (in the form of a goat) and detraction. The entire scene could be the action of a masque compressed into a single movement: the anti-masque of base figures, the main masque with Buckingham as the presenter leading up to the glorification of the royal couple as the encouragers of the arts, which in turn give distinction to the reign, the King and Queen together as celestial powers of light, the centre of intellectual light in the kingdom, individually as heroic lover and the ideally chaste beloved. The Queen is surrounded by her ladies, the air filled with quiring spirits. These details could all be referred one way or another to the themes of most of the masques of the 1630s, a fact that indicates how stable the elements of Caroline mythology remained. In the preliminary sketch for this work, the Liberal Arts emerge from a cave, drawn towards the 'sciental light' of the King and Queen, a device which prefigures the theme of Davenant's *Luminalia*:

The muses being long since drawn out of Greece by the fierce Thracians . . . wandered here and there . . . being constrained either to live in disguises or hide their heads in caves; . . . till by the divine minds of these incomparable pair, the muses . . . were received into protection and established in this monarchy . . . making this happy island a pattern to all nations, as Greece was amongst the ancients.[28]

A less effective treatment of the subject of the Liberal Arts was provided in the late 1620s by Orazio Gentileschi, another artist invited to England whose style owed something to Caravaggio. Gentileschi received a lavish welcome from the Crown as the first significant Italian master to be drawn to Whitehall, but the general level of his productions here was unremarkable. His composition for the central ceiling of the Queen's house at Greenwich resulted in a large circular grouping of allegorical figures of the arts and sciences, a vapid and cold design. He adorned other ceilings at Greenwich with the Muses, all intended to proclaim the renaissance of the arts under the Stuarts. Rather better, one imagines, must have been the ceilings painted by the French master Simon Vouet at Oatlands. Henrietta Maria developed more ambitious schemes for the decoration of Greenwich in the 1630s, attempting to commission works from Rubens, Jordaens and Guido Reni, but in vain.

During Charles's reign, England entered the mainstream of European art from which she has never since separated. This development was largely due to the active exercise of the King's own taste, and to the taste and encouragement of the Earl of Arundel. In the space of some twenty years, 1620–40, the growing body of Englishmen responsive to the arts became naturalised citizens of a baroque world filled with mythological personages and heroic activity. They entered into it with *gusto*.

Notes to Chapter Nine

Quotations from Jonson's masques in this chapter are taken from volume VII of Herford and Simpson's edition of Jonson's *Works*. Quotations from masques by all other writers are taken from Stephen Orgel and Roy Strong's *Inigo Jones: the Theatre of the Stuart Court*, volume II.

1   The Symposium, in *Great Dialogues of Plato*, trans. W. H. D. Rouse, New York 1956, p. 89.

2   See Orgel and Strong, vol. I, p. 52. The discussion of the Caroline masque in this book is central to a modern understanding of the subject.

3   Giordano Bruno, *De gli Eroici Furori*, Part II, Dial. II, in *Opere Italiane*, ed. G. Gentile, Bari 1908, vol. II, p. 471. Trans. by Dorothy W. Singer, in *Giordano Bruno, His Life and Thought*, New York 1950, pp. 129–30.

4   Singer, p. 131.

5   See Edgar Wind's discussion of the painting in *Pagan Mysteries in the Renaissance*, London 1958, pp. 100–10.

6   See G. F. Sensabaugh, 'Love Ethics in Platonic Court Drama, 1625–42', in *Huntington Library Quarterly*, I, 1938.

7   The name Albanactus is taken from Geoffrey of Monmouth's *History of the Kings of Britain*, where he is named as the son of the founder of Britain, Brutus, and the first king of Scotland. The name, therefore, is a tribute to Charles's Scottish birth and ancestry.

8   See Orgel and Strong, vol. I, pp. 63–6.

9   Letter from George Garrard in *Strafforde's Letters and Dispatches*, 1739, vol. I, p. 177.

10   Dedicatory Epistle, trans. Singer, *op. cit.*, p. 118.

11   W. Davenant, *The Triumphs of the Prince d'Amour*, in *Trois Masques à la Cour de Charles Ier d'Angleterre*, ed. M. Lefkowitz, Paris 1970, p. 133.

12   The phrase comes from the Introduction to *Tempe Restored*, where Jones wished to play down the contributions made by poetry to the masque at the time of his quarrel with Jonson.

13   In *Shakespeare's Tragedies and Other Studies in 17th Century Drama*, London 1950, pp. 159–81.

14   Quoted in Leech, *op. cit.*, p. 164.

15   From these strictures the figure of John Ford should be exempted. His extant plays, dating mainly from the 1630s, depict an aristocratic code of conduct, and his characters know and endure the joys and distress of love in a fate-driven world. The fortitude and passionate nobility of these characters enforce respect, just as their doomed condition

compels us to believe that they are the inhabitants of a tragic world and not merely elegant victims of misfortune. Ford's plays still occasionally appear upon today's stage, whereas Shirley, Brome and Davenant have incurred a prolonged neglect because their commentary on human nature is so shallow and insubstantial.

16   R. Brome, *Works*, London 1873, vol. II.

17   John Cleveland, *Poems*, 1653, pp. 71–3.

18   *The Poems of Edmund Waller*, ed. G. Thorn Drury, London 1893, pp. ix–x. Quotations from Waller's poems hereafter are taken from this edition.

19   *The Poems of Thomas Carew*, ed. Rhodes Dunlap, Oxford 1957, p. 75. Quotations from Carew's poems hereafter are taken from this edition.

20   See H. Trevor-Roper, *The Plunder of the Arts in the Seventeenth Century*, London 1970, p. 28.

21   Gervas Huxley, *Endymion Porter*, London 1959, p. 150.

22   H. Trevor-Roper, *op. cit.*, p. 36.

23   See Roy Strong, *Charles I on Horseback*, London 1972, for a detailed discussion of this line of iconography.

24   *Ibid.*, pp. 95–6.

25   The bust of Charles was destroyed in the Whitehall fire of 1697, but we are fortunate to have one surviving bust of an Englishman by Bernini, the marvellously zestful head of Thomas Baker, now in the Victoria and Albert Museum. Baker seems to have acted as an intermediary in the dealings over the King's marble, and his success in persuading Bernini to sculpt him has not only guaranteed him a high place in the history of portrait sculpture, but has also preserved that elusive quality, 'the Cavalier spirit', in an intensely memorable image.

26   See Oliver Millar, *The Age of Charles I*, London 1972, p. 60.

27   For an extended discussion of these designs, see O. Millar, 'Charles I, Honthorst and Van Dyck', in *Burlington Magazine* XCVI, 1954, pp. 39–42.

28   *Luminalia*, 15–38, in Orgel and Strong, *op. cit.*, vol. II, p. 706.

[10]
The religious arts under James and Charles

One of the familiar Court sights of James's reign was the King at dinner, engaged in theological conversation with one or two divines who stood behind him. Such argument afforded James a pleasure comparable only to the chase, for James was a mighty hunter before the Lord: divinity and hunting formed his chief intellectual and physical recreations.[1] When he came to the throne he was already an accomplished theologian with a considerable body of writings to his name. His accession was welcomed alike by middle-of-the-road churchmen and by those of a puritan persuasion within the Church, the former because they knew that here was a King who would cherish the Church, the latter because they believed that such a King would appreciate their doctrinal scruples. The puritan party was rapidly disillusioned when James, recognising their anti-episcopal drift, brusquely swept aside their arguments at the Hampton Court Conference of 1604. But, for the Church of England generally, the period from 1603 to 1640 was a time when divines were amongst the most favoured of men, and when the arts of the sermon and of sacred verse reached their finest expression, before the whole edifice of the Church was shattered in the 1640s.

In an age when the sermon rivalled the plays of the public theatres in eloquence and power to move (and at times matched them in length), the Court was able to call upon the most celebrated practitioners for its edification: Lancelot Andrewes, George Abbot, Joseph Hall, John Williams, John Donne, James Ussher and William Laud were the men most in request. James was an exacting auditor, and preaching before him—offering spiritual counsel to a theologian-king—must have been a formidable trial, but the Church was amply supplied with talent. It was rare for a preacher to criticise the King to his face for his policies or behaviour, most preferring to engage in a modest flattery through biblical allusion, flattery that the King regarded as his proper due, for, as we have seen, he knew himself to have been chosen by the divine will, and he ruled as an instrument of God's providence. Allusions to the kings and patriarchs of the Old Testament were perfectly apt; James was if anything more blessed than they, living in the era of grace, and free from the excesses that marred the rule of David or Solomon.

It was as a new David that James was welcomed to the throne in 1604 by the London preacher Andrew Willet, in a sermon entitled *Ecclesia Triumphans*, which may serve as a convenient introduction to the main religious themes of the reign. Willet established twenty heads under which James could be compared to David. The chief grounds of comparison were these: David ended the strife between himself and the house of Saul, and brought all Israel under one government (alluding to James's achievement of unity); under David, the true religion was continued; 'David was a learned Prince, an inditer of heavenly songs and sonnets' (and James's divine writings gave him a pre-eminence over all his predecessors in England); David brought the Ark to Jerusalem, and in guaranteeing a secure Protestant succession, James and his children ensured that the ark of the true religion was now firmly settled in England. This emphasis on James's succession is important, for after all the childless children of Henry VIII, James and his quiverful of offspring were the surest promise for a Protestant future, leading the chosen people of Britain in the paths of righteousness until the Second Coming should mark the end of time. The heirs of James 'shall be continued to the end of the world, we trust', says Willet, uttering a hope that was widely shared, and which was expressed, for example, in *Macbeth*, through the vision of the heirs of Banquo (of whom James was one), when Macbeth sees 'the line stretch out to the crack of doom' (IV.i.117). The long race of kings of the Stuart line was a theme often sounded in Court entertainments, usually in association with praise of the fertility of Anne and Henrietta Maria, for James was ambitiously dynastic, and liked to imagine the house of Stuart enduring to the last days of historical time. Other significant parallels between the reigns of David and James include the expulsion from Israel of the Jebusites, here glossed as the Jesuits. The people of David were thereby freed from fear of the enemy, for 'David procureth the peace of Hierusalem'. The main body of *Ecclesia Triumphans* is a meditation upon Psalm 122, which sings of the peace, wealth and piety of Jerusalem, 'shewing so many blessings upon the Church and Commonwealth, answerable to those which Israel enjoyed under David'. Naturally, any reference to David as the warrior king has been avoided.

Identification with David was helped by the fact that James had written sacred poetry, and had also undertaken a translation of the Psalms, an enterprise that continued intermittently throughout his life. Although much of the credit for this translation should go to Sir William Alexander, who had a large share in the work, it was the King's reputation that was enhanced.[2] The harp that figured as the emblem of Ireland in the royal standard could now be interpreted as the British David's harp, and the concord of the united kingdoms was the music of that harp. This image appeared, for example, in Peacham's emblem book of 1612, to illustrate a country 'from discord drawne, to sweetest unitie' and a panegyrist of 1610 spoke fulsomely of the order and harmony of James's rule: 'Such are the accents of this misticall simphony, and the lofty tunes of . . . our royal harp.'[3] A classical variant on this theme was Orpheus, also a harper, whose music soothed the savage world, and brought a creative harmony to nature. Conceits of an orphic kind, along with related allusions to Arion, who charmed the dolphins, or Amphion, who raised a city to music, are common in the masques and Court poetry of James's reign, often serving as metaphors for the King's peace.[4]

Willet's discourse also abounds with predictable allusions to Solomon, and associated images such as James as the cedar tree sheltering the country, his children being the branches and green shoots. More significantly, Willet opens on a note of rejoicing that the Church of England is enjoying 'a golden time: such as the like (as his Maiestie saith) hath not been read nor heard of since the daies of the Romane Emperor Augustus'.[5] As we have seen, the title of Augustus had been bestowed on the new King by Jonson in the London Entry of the same year; now it comes from a religious source, carrying with it this time the associations of peace and the full revelation of Christian grace and truth in the world.

But there was another emperor whose establishment and defence of the true faith made him a more appropriate analogue for James, and that was Constantine. As he had been born in Britain of a British mother, the link was strong. Moreover, he had moved the seat of empire from Rome, and by his laws and succession had planted the Christian religion in primitive purity, just as James hoped to make London a seat of Christian empire. Constantine had presided over the early councils of the Church to achieve a uniformity of doctrine, a precedent for James to call the Hampton Court Conference of 1604. Constantine had defended the Church by arms; James's militant writings against Catholic opponents justified his title of Defender of the Faith. Perhaps the fullest elaboration of these themes occurs in an important sermon by Joseph Hall, preached on the tenth anniversary of James's accession in 1613, entitled *An Holy Panegyrick*. Hall had been one of Prince Henry's favoured chaplains, and continued to enjoy the approval of both James and Charles, rising to be Bishop of Exeter and finally of Norwich. His sermon provides a spiritual assessment of the first decade of Stuart rule.

He began by reminding his congregation that 'the example of those ancient Romane Christians' teaches us 'that the tenth compleat year of our Constantine deserves to be solemne and Iubilar'. England has much cause for thanksgiving, as the scene of so many of God's mercies. 'This Kingdome (though divided from the world) was one of the first that received the Gospell. That it yielded the first Christian Emperor that gave peace and honour to the Church, the first and greatest lights that shone forth in the darkest of poperie, and that it was the first Kingdome that shooke Antichrist fully out of the saddle.'[6] The mention of the Gospel refers to the legend that Britain was first christianised by Joseph of Arimathea, a legend that was of great service to the apologists of the Anglican Church, for it gave them a claim to apostolic descent and primitive purity. The claim was often coupled with the story of the foundation of Britain by the Trojan Brutus, for both legends by-passed the need for dependency on Rome; Britain could thereby assert an equal antiquity with Rome, thus giving both Elizabethan and Stuart propagandists a basis from which to defend the authenticity of the Anglican Church and to justify the legitimate renewal of empire in these islands. These last ideas are ingeniously repeated in Hall's observations that 'This Day [24 March] was both Queen Elizabeth's *Initium Gloriae* and King James his *initium regni*. To her *Natalitum salutis*, as the passion dayes of the martyrs were called of old; and *natalis imperii* to him.' Elizabeth is envisaged here as a saint of the primitive Church who has steadfastly kept the faith alive in difficult times; now under James, as under Constantine, the full confident sway of a pure Christianity is assured, and with it the prospect of a Christian empire.[7] The duration of the new age is guaranteed by the fertility of the Stuart line: 'Surely a new and golden world began this day to us and (which it could not have done of her loynes) promises continuance to our posterities.'

Hall is a good specimen of the committed Anglican whose sense of recent history is shaped by Foxe's profoundly influential *Book of Martyrs*, which recorded the rebirth of the primitive faith of the early Church in the purified doctrine of the Reformers, a faith fertilised by the blood of the martyrs of the Marian persecutions. God's special providence has been active in the English nation, which is the latter-day Israel where He has chosen to plant the true Church under the guidance of divinely ordained monarchs. English history is providential history, wherein the interpreter will find revealed God's special graces to this nation. 'And if any nation under heaven could either parallel or second Jerusalem in the favours of God, this poore little Island of ours is it. The cloud of his protection has covered us. The blood-red sea of persecution has given way to us, and we are passed it dry-shod. . . .

The water of life gusheth out plenteously to us.' The role of the Stuart line in this scheme of history was the consolidation of the reformed religion and the maintenance of prosperity in the new Israel. Nothing about James's life had been accidental, all had been controlled by God's will: his preservation from the many plots and hazards of his youth in Scotland, his adventurous courtship of Queen Anne, his exaltation from the lowly Scottish throne to be 'The Emperor of Great Britain', his signal escape from the Gunpowder Plot. In the eyes of his contemporaries this last mercy was an unmistakeable sign of God's protection, and it was celebrated as such in the annual ceremony of thanksgiving that was immediately instituted. Moreover, the advance warning of the plot had been delivered in a riddling fashion which the divine rays of the royal mind had instantly found out: 'If there had not been a divination in the lips of the King, wee had all been in the jawes of death', reflected Hall. It was no accident that God had caused Great Britain's King to be a theologian, one who knew God's laws in their finest degree. The visible signs of God's special favour to Britain were the peace and prosperity that were endlessly remarked upon, because, after all, they were undeniable proofs of a special fate: 'Looke about you: All your neighbours have seen and tasted . . . calamities. All the rest of the world have been whirled about in these woeful tumults; onely this island like the centre hath stood unmoveable. . . . Whither should we ascribe it, but next under God, to his Anointed, as a King, as a King of Peace?' This last note causes Hall to modulate into the Augustan key of praise: 'He alone, like Noah's Dove, brought an Olive of Peace to the tossed Arke of Christendom:[8] Hee like another Augustus, before the second coming of *Christ* hath becalmed the world, and shut the iron gates of warre; and is the bond of that peace he hath made.'

Hall closes his discourse with a reassuring assessment of the health of the Anglican Church: under James it is now a church triumphant. The comparison with the emperor Constantine returns with greater force, for James

hath trod in the steps of that blessed Constantine, in all his religious proceedings. . . . Constantine caused fifty volumes of the scriptures to be faire written out on parchment, for the use of the Church. King James hath caused the Book of the Scriptures to be translated and published by thousands. Constantine made a zealous edict against Novatians. . . . King James besides his powerful proclamations and sovereign lawes hath effectually written against Poperie. Constantine took away the libertie of the meetings of Heretickes: King James hath by wholesome lawes inhibited the assemblies of Papists and Schismatickes. Constantine sate in the middest of Bishops, as if he had been one of them, King James besides his solemne conferences, vouchsafes (not seldome) to spend his meales in discourse with his Bishops and other worthy Divines. Constantine charged his sonnes . . . that they should be Christians in earnest. King James hath done the like in learned and divine precepts, which shall live till time be no more. Yea, in their very coynes is a resemblance: Constantine had his picture stampt upon his metals praying, King James hath his picture with a prayer about it; O Lord, protect the Kingdomes which thou hast united.9

In this last section of the *Panegyrick* we may sense an intemperate zeal for Holy Church, admitting no shadow of variant opinion to dim its purity. Puritan views are dismissed as schismatic, and James's church triumphant is already seen approvingly as an intolerant church. From Hall's secure position, it was easy to affirm the establishment line. It was almost inevitable in the seventeenth century that literature, sacred or secular, addressed to the King and Court should be adulatory and uncritical, praising the real or imagined achievements of the monarch, and helping to create a glorious atmosphere in which sour disaffection went unacknowledged. In a sense, the literature and acclamation that pervaded the Court helped increase the isolation of the monarch from the critical and discontented world beyond Whitehall. Royal misfortunes are tactfully ignored in Hall's summary of the reign: the death of Prince Henry is not touched on, and indeed he is rarely ever mentioned in the King's presence again. (Similarly, Queen Anne's death in 1619 is scarcely ever referred to.) Silence or suppression was the best way of dealing with disconcerting facts or unacceptable views. Outside Court circles, however, criticism of royal policy surfaced in sermons. By 1620 James began to warn preachers against discussing state topics and in 1622 he was obliged to issue 'Directions for Preachers' prohibiting ministers from raising questions which touched on doctrinal matters that differed from orthodox Anglicanism or on matters concerning the King's authority.10

There was much that was praiseworthy in James's religious actions. The sense of kinship with the primitive Church which was so strong amongst the sixteenth-century reformers received new force from the general council of the Church which the King called in 1604 in order to regulate its affairs and determine doctrine. The comparison with the Emperor Constantine was inescapable, as were the implications for the Church of England's role in the world. The defensive phase of the Tudor period was over, and now under the Stuarts a new era was beginning, the era of the Church triumphant (Willet's *Ecclesia Triumphans*), and (until James began to develop a policy of rapprochement with the Catholic powers in his marriage strategy of 1611–12) a time of the Church militant, engaged in fierce doctrinal disputes with Catholic apologists abroad. James valiantly led his Church in these attacks; spiritual warfare was the one area of combat in which he excelled. His controversial writings against the Papacy had little effect on Catholic opinion abroad, where they were coolly, sometimes derisively, received, but they were naturally acclaimed by Church circles in England as devastating shots, and undoubtedly they were good for Anglican morale. The principal titles were *An Apologie for the Oath of Allegiance* (1608) (attacking papal denunciation of the oath that James required English Catholics to take, acknowledging loyalty to him as lawful King), *A Premonition to All Most Mightie Monarchs* (1609) (warning the rulers of Europe of the threats to their thrones and persons posed by a temporally ambitious Papacy), and *A Remonstrance for the Rights of Kings* (1615) (addressed to the French Catholic clergy in defence once more of the oath of allegiance to lawful monarchs). James relied very heavily on the opinions and talents of his scholarly favourites in these polemics, in particular Lancelot Andrewes, James Montague, Isaac Casaubon, John Barclay and Pierre du Moulin, although their help went unrecorded, for James liked to appear as sole champion, and as he once remarked, he valued more the title of Defender of the Faith than that of King.[11]

The most enduring religious achievement associated with James was the Authorised Version of the Bible published in 1611. The new translation grew out of a proposal made at the Hampton Court Conference of 1604 by Dr John Rainolds, Professor of Divinity at Oxford and a firm Puritan. The adoption of this proposal was one of the few points gained by the Puritan side at the Conference, and it succeeded because James himself had already entertained the idea. When James became head of the Church, there were two bibles in widespread circulation: the Bishops' Bible was the official bible of the Church of England, whereas the Geneva Bible was the one most widely used by the people. James disliked the Geneva Bible for the anti-monarchist tone of many of its marginal notes, and he had already proposed the need for a new translation before the General Assembly of the Kirk of Scotland in 1601. Now, as he sought to impose more conformity on the Church of England, he recognised how valuable it would be to have one bible in uniform use, and he assiduously promoted the work of translation. Fifty-four translators working in six groups and consulting intensively amongst themselves completed the Authorised Version in just over six years. The King kept in close touch with the work as it progressed, providing instructions as to the general principles to be observed: the Bishops' Bible should serve as a model as far as possible, the established ecclesiastical words should be kept, the proper names that were familiar to the people should be retained. Above all, the language of the translation should be simple, clear, memorable and direct, avoiding ambiguity and consequent doctrinal confusion.[12] The instructions were admirably carried out, the royal approval secured, and the new bible was published with a fulsome dedication to King James as 'the principall moover and Author of the Worke', praise which for once was fully deserved, in view of the magnitude of the project and the keenness of his support. The Epistle Dedicatory reflects on God's providence in bestowing so wise and religious a monarch on Great Britain for the care and preservation of the Reformed Church. James's zeal in 'writing in defence of the truth, which hath given such a blow unto the Man of Sin' (i.e. the Pope as Anti-Christ) is applauded, as is his avoidance of the 'self-conceited Brethren' or Puritans.

In the translators' address to the reader, they explain the need for a new translation to make available the treasures of the spirit to a religious people, and in doing so they introduce the figure of the patriarch Jacob as the provider of the waters of life. The shepherd-king Jacob was an antetype of James (Jacobus), and the image therefore acts as a witty tribute to the British King's care for the well-being of his flock:

Translation it is that openeth the window, to let in light; that breaketh the shell, that we may eat the kernel; that pulleth aside the curtaine, that we may looke into the most Holy place; that remooveth the cover of the well, that we may come by the water, even as Jacob rolled away the stone from the mouth of the well, by which meanes the flockes of Laban were watered. Indeed, without translation into the vulgar tongue, the unlearned are but like children at Jacob's Well (which was deepe) without a bucket or something to draw with: or as that person mentioned in Esay, to whom when a sealed book was delivered, with this motion, Reade this, I pray thee, he was faine to make answere, I cannot, for it is sealed.[13]

The circle of Anglican divines around James formed a highly intelligent group of men who drove a middle path between Rome and the Puritans. The most prominent of the old guard from Elizabeth's reign was Lancelot Andrewes, whose learning and temper accorded well with James, who promoted him steadily through the sees of Chichester and Ely to Winchester. He was the most eminent scholar on the committee for translating the bible, and his qualities were well described by Fuller in the *Church History*:

The world wanted learning to know how learned this Man was, so skil'd in all (especially oriental) Languages, that some conceive he might (if then living) almost have served as an Interpreter Generall at the Confusion of Tongues. Nor are the Fathers more faithfully cited in his books, than lively copied out in his countenance and carriage, his gravity in a manner awing King James, who refrained from that mirth and liberty, in the presence of this Prelate, which otherwise he assumed to himself.[14]

Andrewes's terse, agile, intellectually demanding sermons helped more than any others to establish the fashion for witty preaching that prevailed at Court under both James and Charles. His genius lay in a spectroscopic analysis of biblical texts, identifying the minutest atoms of meaning that lay hidden in the sacred words, and from those atoms creating new worlds of words that were intellectually habitable by his avid readers. He exploited his philological talents to the full in the pulpit, and above all his contemporaries demonstrated that the language of the Bible could yield inexhaustible significance: time after time he circles back to a word, a phrase, a syllable in the text to press out yet more spiritual wine for his congregation. His sermons are so tightly argued and so tautly phrased that they demand the utmost concentration for their understanding, yet Andrewes remained one of the most valued preachers at Court throughout his life, a measure of the intellectuality of the Court in religious matters. In part his multi-lingual virtuosity, his cryptic allusions and his ability to produce meaty kernels out of tought nuts must have appealed to a Court audience adept at paradoxes, epigrams, anagrams, and other such dense verbal structures. But his armoury of rhetorical devices exercised in the service of religion must also have won much admiration, and above all his evident godliness subdued the vanity of the Court into compliance with his own spirit. His sermons do not lend themselves to representative quotation, for their web is not easily cut, but in reading them one's intellect is kept constantly surprised, each surprise being followed by a gratifying sense of the aptness of Andrewes's pious wit. At Christmas, Easter and Lent he was in request at Court, and he was also the preferred preacher of the Gunpowder Plot sermons at the annual service of thanksgiving which dwelt on God's special preservation of James from his enemies and the assurance of his favour towards the Stuarts. When James was on his deathbed, Lancelot Andrewes was the Bishop he most desired should attend him, but by then Andrewes himself was in a fatal decline.

Andrewes's only intellectual equal was John Donne, whom James encouraged into holy orders with the promise of rapid advancement. The King probably felt that Donne would prove an eloquent supporter of royal prerogative and policy, on the basis of his book *Pseudo-Martyr* (1610), which was dedicated to James, and which was calculated to win James's approval by arguing that Catholic recusants in England should take the Oath of Allegiance to the King and thus establish their loyalty as his subjects. But in the case of Donne, James was not simply moved by flattery of his policies: his prime concern was to attract into the Church a man of exceptional learning and spiritual integrity, one who was also likely to prove a powerful preacher and comforter of souls. James was eager to build up a learned clergy and encourage a strong preaching ministry in order to assure the Church's strength in the land, and to equip it intellectually for debate in an age of religious controversy. His foundation of Chelsea College for divinity, although it came to nothing, was one aspect of this strategy, the encouragement and promotion of able divines was another, and Donne's recruitment into the Church is a fine example of James's discernment. The fact that Donne had been raised a Catholic, and yet had found the arguments for the Anglican Church irresistible undoubtedly helped to make him an exemplary figure in James's eye. Ordained in 1615, he was immediately made one of the King's chaplains. His first recorded sermon before the Court was on 21 April 1616. Though a notable recipient of royal favour, Donne did not flatter. He confined himself to the unfolding of his text and the extracting of spiritual profit from it. Strenuous intellectual exploration of themes raised by the text, striking applications of the sense, meditative power, learning and rhetorical splendour came together to form the unmistakable style of Donne's sermons, a style that was well adapted to the vogue for witty preaching that prevailed at Court. The Court liked its piety salted with a bright intelligence, and Donne was instantly to their taste. Izaac Walton provides a picture of him preaching his first sermon at Whitehall—a contrived and indulgent picture one assumes, given Walton's tendency to sanctify his subject.

Though much were expected from him, both by his Majesty and others, yet he was so happy —which few are—as to satisfy and exceed their expectations: preaching the Word so, as showed his own heart was possessed with those very thoughts and joys that he laboured to distil into others; a preacher in earnest; weeping sometimes for his auditory, sometimes with them; always preaching to himself, like an angel from a cloud, but in none; carrying some, as St. Paul was, to heaven in holy raptures, and enticing others by a sacred art and courtship to amend their lives; here picturing a vice so as to make it ugly to those that practised it, and a virtue so as to make it beloved even by those that loved it not; and all this with a most particular grace and an unexpressible addition of comeliness.[15]

Preaching to the King posed a special difficulty, for, as James often stated in his own writings, the King was two persons: as sovereign he reigned with divine power upon earth, as a man he was subject to mortality, a creature with a conscience and a soul. 'For in that same Psalme where God saith to Kings, Vos Dii estis, he immediately thereafter concludes, But ye shall die like men.'[16] Although the King sat upon an elevated seat in the Chapel Royal, effectively the real presence of divinity in the hall, it was Donne, pre-eminently amongst the Stuart divines, who addressed the King both as the image of God and as sinful man, capable of salvation, sure of salvation in fact, as long as his conscience was kept active and clear by prayer, meditation and constant dwelling on the Christian mysteries. When, for example, Donne was summoned to preach before the King and Court on Accession

Day 1617, a joyful occasion that invited flattery, he uttered a few brief phrases of compliment on the King's peace, and made a passing reference to Constantine, but there were no other signs of sycophancy: he gave a characteristic display of brilliant exegesis for the spiritual good of the auditors. As James lay sick on Easter Day 1619, Donne preached on the preparations requisite for death, a necessary topic, but completely distasteful to a King who was terrified of death. When Donne preached, the priorities of the spirit were upheld in the Chapel Royal.

The death of King James in fact occasioned one of Donne's finest sermons, based on the text 'Behold King Solomon Crowned'. In the climactic passage, Donne anatomises the dead sovereign in a sequence of clauses in which each attribute is extinguished by the force of one leaden word:

And when you shall find that hand that has signed to one of you a Patent for Title, to another for Pension, to another for Pardon, to another for Dispensation, Dead: That hand that settled Possessions by his Seale, in the Keeper, and rectified Honours by the sword, in his Marshall, and distributed relief to the Poore, in his Almoner, and Health to the Diseased, by his immediate Touch, Dead: That Hand that ballanced his own three Kingdomes so equally, as that none of them complained of one another, nor of him; and carried the Keyes of all the Christian world, and locked up, and let out Armies in their due season, Dead; how poore, how faint, how pale, how momenta[r]y, how transitory, how empty, how frivolous, how Dead things, must you necessarily thinke Titles, and Possessions, and Favours, and all, when you see that Hand, which was the hand of Destinie, of Christian Destinie, of the Almighty God, lie dead![17]

From these overwhelming concepts, the sermon retreats along a line of personal memories in which all the listening courtiers could share, and which move the affections towards a composed resignation in God's will. But mourning was also a fine art, and the skills of virtuoso rhetoric, playing brilliantly with synecdoche and incremental repetition, accompany James to the grave:

It was not so hard a hand when we touched it last, nor so cold a hand when we kissed it last: That hand which was wont to wipe all teares from all our eyes, doth now but presse and squeaze us as so many spunges, filled one with one, another with another cause of teares. Teares that can have no other banke to bound them, but the declared and manifested will of God.[18]

Donne's style and person were equally acceptable to King Charles. A week after James's death, Donne was preaching before the new King, on the text from the Psalms, 'If the foundations be destroyed, what can the righteous do?' a sermon that sought to offer the King guidance for the success of the new reign, now that James, the 'foundation' of the Stuart age, was dead. What strange instinct was it that moved Donne to his prophetic choice of topics in this sermon? Within minutes of his opening he was inviting Charles to consider the blessed fate of martyrs, and was telling him that his text was chosen from the psalm traditionally used to celebrate the martyrs of the Church!

The Church of God ever delighted herselfe in a holy officiousnesse in the Commemoration of Martyrs: Almost all their solemne, and extraordinarie Meetings, and Congregations, in the Primitive Church, were for that, for the honorable Commemoration of Martyrs. . . . And in the Office and Service of a Martyr, the Church did use this Psalme.[19]

A strange psalm with which to usher in the new reign. But Donne's prescient sense of foreboding extended further, for as he counselled the King that the four foundations of the state lay in the honouring of religion, the law, the family and the soul, he concluded with an appeal: 'Dispute not the Lawes, but obey them when they are made. . . . Let the Law bee sacred to thee, and the Dispensers of the Lawe, reverend. Keepe the Lawe, and the Lawe shall keepe thee.' We are told that the King listened to this sermon attentively and devoutly.[20]

In his office as preacher, Donne acknowledged that he was occasionally visited by a prophetic power which impelled his mind to burn through the opacity of events, causing in him mingled exaltation and dejection. 'Shall I shed upon you *lumen visionis*', he asked the King in his Lenten sermon of 1627, 'the light of that vision, which God hath afforded me in this Prophecie, the light of his countenance, and his gracious blessings, and not lay upon you *Onus Visionis*, as the Prophets speak often, the burthen of that Vision which I have seen in this Text too?'[21]

A presentiment of his own death suffused Donne's last sermon before King Charles and his Court in February, 1631. Visibly dying, himself his own exhausted hourglass, he delivered on that occasion the most sustained meditation upon death in an age that was funereally eloquent, on the text 'And unto God the Lord belong the issues of death', and with his own body an illustration of that text.

When, to the amazement of some of the beholders, he appeared in the pulpit, many of them thought he presented himself not to preach mortification by a living voice, but mortality by a decayed body and a dying face. And doubtless many did secretly ask that question in Ezekiel,—'Do these bones live? . . .'[22]

After Donne's death, King Charles himself was moved to compose an epitaph, 'To the Memory of my ever Desired Friend, Dr Donne'.

> At common graves we have poetic eyes
> Can melt themselves in easy elegies,
> But at thine, poem or inscription,

(Rich soul of wit and language) we have none.
Indeed a silence doth that tomb befit,
When is no herald left to blazon it.

Indifferent verse perhaps, but if these were indeed the King's own lines, an extraordinary tribute from a sovereign to a subject.[23]

King Charles did not attract the biblical parallels that distinguished his father, and no consistent religious imagery seems to have evolved around him until after his death. His characteristic imagery was Roman Imperial, with an admixture of the cult of *pater patriae*, father of the country, omnipotent but kind. Charles was the successor to the Stuart throne, not its inaugurator, the inheritor of the precepts of *Basilikon Doron*, not their creator, and consequently the great surge of propaganda both religious and secular that launched the Stuart line lost some of its impetus when he settled into his reign. Not being a theologian, he was not treated to banquets of biblical learning as often as his father had been, sermons before his Court naturally tending to vindicate the royal policy of conformity in religion and the divine right of Stuart authority. The witty style of preaching still prevailed in the first decade of Charles's reign, fortified until 1631 by the practice of Donne, whose brilliant earnest sermons tended to stay clear of political issues, concentrating instead on the permanent battleground of the soul. The conscious artistry that typified a good deal of Court preaching must however have seemed superfluous luxury in the minds of Puritans who sought salvation through a more urgent and direct kind of sermon. The men who preached at Whitehall were inevitably upholders of the Establishment, believers in the divine right of kings and the truth of the Anglican Church. Laud, the mainstay of the Caroline Church during the thirities, had a relatively uninteresting preaching style, but his sermons were full of comforting matter for the King. Joseph Hall continued to preach his learned sermons counselling moderation and recommending obedience to royal decisions in religious questions. His book *Episcopacy by Divine Right* (1640), dedicated to King Charles, provided a firm vindication of the Caroline dispensation at the time when it had received its first serious check with the Scottish rejection of the new prayer book. In many ways, the sermons delivered in the Chapel Royal were as misleadingly reassuring as the masques of the 1620s and 1630s were about the power and popularity of the Crown.

King Charles encouraged a ceremonious Anglicanism in the services of his Chapel, and he approved of formal ritual and ordered beauty as both proper to the Court of a King and consonant with the practice of the early

Church which the English Church professed to take as its model. Charles had been brought up entirely within the Church of England, and had never doubted that it was a living branch of the True Church, or that episcopalianism was the right method of Church government. His sensitivity to the arts, particularly to the painting of sixteenth-century Italy, naturally disposed him towards visual beauty in the services of his Church as a way of directing the senses to a religious end, and surrounding devotion with harmonious symbolism. Such an attitude presupposed a gracious God, a God of mercy, whose worship was properly celebrated with an ordered beauty, a gentler God than the strict deity honoured by the intense and forthright Puritans.

The most sensitive and decorous expression of Caroline piety may be found in the works of George Herbert, whose poems display 'the beauty of holiness' more subtly and more persuasively than any of his contemporaries', recording the history of a soul that derives profound comfort from the liturgy, rituals and symbolism of the Anglican Church. His responsiveness to the formal beauties of worship can probably be traced back to his days at Westminster School, where Lancelot Andrewes had instituted a particularly high form of service, and Herbert later came to know and love Andrewes as a man whose Christian temper was very close to his own. Andrewes was one of several patrons—they included Bacon, the Duke of Lennox and the Marquis of Hamilton—who Herbert hoped would draw him from the academic prominence of his Oratorship at Cambridge to a position of state significance, but their untimely deaths and his own growing distaste for Court life and politics moved him to take orders in 1630 and accept a life of rural ministry. Izaac Walton reports that Herbert confided to a friend on the evening of his induction to his parish at Bemerton that

I now look back upon my aspiring thoughts, and think myself more happy than if I had attained what then I so ambitiously thirsted for. And I now can behold the court with an impartial eye, and see plainly that it is made up of fraud and titles, and flattery, and many other such empty, imaginary, painted pleasures; pleasures that are so empty as not to satisfy when they are enjoyed. But in God, and his service, is a fulness of all joy and pleasure, and no satiety.[24]

In contrast to the earthly Court that had been so unresponsive to his pleas, in the poems that form the record of his spiritual life Herbert was to envisage an ideal Court, whose lord was the King of Kings; here true courtesy is found, here are Grace and Justice and Mercy, here is generosity beyond measure, here the quintessence of Majesty. In the service of the Lord there is always satisfaction and reward, and the Lord of the heavenly Court is always attentive.

Of what an easie quick accesse,
My blessed Lord, art thou! how suddenly
    May our requests thine eare invade!
To shew that state dislikes not easinesse,
If I but lift mine eyes, my suit is made:
Thou canst no more not heare, than thou canst die.

                                        ('Prayer')

The courteous tone of *The Temple*, the polite and restrained manner that characterises the surface of so many of the poems, testifies to the beauty and order of the heavenly Court where Herbert now kept a perpetual attendance. The sorrows and sufferings of earthly life are dispelled by the love and care of a Lord who could never disappoint his servants. The poem 'Love', which closes the volume, expresses most finely the candid courtesy of the Anglican heaven, where the unworthy guest is with infinite kindness bidden to sit at the Lord's table:

Love bade me welcome: yet my soul drew back,
    Guiltie of dust and sinne.
But quick-ey'd Love, observing me grow slack
    From my first entrance in,
Drew nearer to me, sweetly questioning,
    If I lack'd any thing.

A guest, I answer'd, worthy to be here:
    Love said, you shall be he.
I the unkinde, ungratefull? Ah my deare,
    I cannot look on thee.
Love took my hand, and smiling did reply,
    Who made the eyes but I?

Truth Lord, but I have marr'd them: let my shame
    Go where it doth deserve.
And know you not, sayes Love, who bore the blame?
    My deare, then I will serve.
You must sit down, sayes Love, and taste my meat:
    So I did sit and eat.

                                        ('Love')

One might feel that Herbert's poetry reflects the ceremonious Anglicanism that Laud fostered in the 1630s, but Herbert's sense of the formal harmonies of the Anglican Church is evident as early as 1620 in *Musae Responsoriae*, poems in defence of the discipline of the Church, and most of the poems that from *The Temple* were written later in the same decade, before Laud began to assert his influence. In a poem addressed to King James in *Musae Responsoriae*, Herbert breaks into these words of praise:

Cernite, quàm formosa suas Ecclesia pennas
Explicat, & radijs ipsum pertingit Olympum!
Vicini populi passim mirantur, & aequos
Mentibus attonitis cupiunt addiscere ritus:
Angelicae turmae nostris se coetibus addunt:
Ipse etiam Christus coelo speculatus ab alto,
Intuitúque uno stringens habitacula mundi,
Sola mihi plenos, ait, exhibet Anglia cultus.

    See how
The lovely Church outspreads its wings and sheds
Its radiance as far as heaven. Far and wide
The neighbour nations wonder, and, their minds adazzle,
Want to learn a ritual in harmony with yours.
Angelic hosts increase our company;
And Christ himself, watching from the skies,
Taking in the houses of the world at a glance,
Says that only England offers him a finished worship.[25]

The richness of that worship is everywhere apparent in *The Temple*, with its emphasis on the beauty and significance of the rituals and on the mystery of the sacraments. Many physical aspects of the Church that were anathema to the Puritans are praised by Herbert for the additional wealth of spiritual symbolism they bring to the receptive Christian: the church windows which show 'Doctrine and life, colours and light, in one / When they combine and mingle, bring / A strong regard and aw' and serve as types of the preacher; the church music, which makes the church 'a house of pleasure' and shows 'the way to heaven's doore' also transports Herbert in a trance of spiritual delight in which he scorns to change his state with kings:

Now I in you without a bodie move,
    Rising and falling with your wings:
We both together sweetly live and love,
    Yet say sometimes, God help poore Kings.

                ('Church Musick')

Music resounds through *The Temple*, from 'Mattins' and 'Even-Song' to the 'Church-Bels beyond the stars heard'. Praise, though not worship, is accorded to the angels, saints, and the Virgin Mary. The priest of *The Temple* is a mysterious figure of hieratic solemnity:

    Holinesse on the head
  Light and perfections on the breast,
Harmonious bells below raising the dead
    To leade them unto life and rest.
      Thus are true Aarons drest.

                ('Aaron')

The very title of *The Temple*, with its allusion to Solomon's Temple which was the shrine of the living God and the place where the Ark of the Covenant reposed, the building ordained by God as the perpetual place of his praise, carried with it associations of splendour and perfection which had passed to the Church of England. Herbert's delight in Anglicanism is simply expressed in his poem to 'The British Church':

> I joy, deare Mother, when I view,
> Thy perfect lineaments, and hue
>   Both sweet and bright:
>
> Beautie in thee takes up her place,
> And dates her letters from thy face,
>   When she doth write.
>
> A fine aspect in fit aray,
> Neither too mean, nor yet too gay,
>   Shows who is best:
>
> . . .
>
> Blessed be God, whose love it was
> To double-moat thee with his grace,
>   And none but thee.

('The British Church')

Herbert's poetry remains the finest expression of seventeenth-century high Anglicanism. Although the sensibility that informs these poems is uniquely Herbert's, the ordered religious beauty in which they move was not entirely of Herbert's making: it belonged to a tradition of decorous worship that was shaped by Hooker and refined by Lancelot Andrewes; William Laud would attempt to make it the dominant character of the Anglican Church, and it was certainly the mode of worship approved by King Charles. The Anglican community at Little Gidding, founded by George Herbert's close friend Nicholas Ferrar, extended this tradition of worship in response to a need for a full devotional life that was not adequately met by the ordinary services of the Church of England. The emphasis at Little Gidding lay on the meditative life, and on the constant practice of piety. The feasts, fasts and vigils of the Church were kept, and the pattern of daily life was shaped by the requirements of religious observance. Herbert was profoundedly in sympathy with Ferrar's holy way of life, and he made Ferrar his spiritual executor, bequeathing to him the manuscript of *The Temple* in 1633. Both men had turned away, disillusioned, from Court life at the end of James's reign to seek fulfilment in the ways of religion, and neither found cause to reconsider that decision. Herbert in his prose work

The Priest to the Temple, which details his ideal of the life of the Christian pastor, and is full of advice about the right behaviour of a Christian gentleman, carefully recommends that a gentleman of good family should avoid the Court, as it was a snare for souls. King Charles himself must have felt the truth of that observation, as he endeavoured to uphold the purity of his religious life in the increasingly dangerous swirl of politics in the 1630s, and his three visits to Little Gidding seem to have represented a sincere desire for devotion and peace. He sought refuge there in 1646, while in flight from his enemies, and later, in captivity, he chose Herbert's poems as one of his books of consolation.

An important project which enabled Charles to express his care for the Church was the rebuilding of St Paul's Cathedral, the metropolitan centre of Anglicanism. James had already occupied himself with this matter, and over the years it acquired considerable significance as a sign of Stuart concern for the state of the Church of England. The decayed condition of St Paul's was a notorious sign of public indifference to the national Church; reconstruction was a Christian duty as well as a practical necessity. Although great crowds attended the sermons at Paul's Cross, the outdoor pulpit in the north-east angle, the church proper was not reverently treated, and much of it had fallen to secular use as a public loitering place. As early as 1608 James had formed a commission to repair the cathedral, but it was not until 1620 that he made a determined effort to initiate the work, going in person to hear a sermon by the Bishop of London, John King, urging an immediate start to the restoration. Royal visits to the City were very rare, for the King usually confined himself to Westminster when in London; indeed, the Bishop remarked that 'such comings are not often, but like *ludi saeculares* in Rome, once in an age'.[26] Bishop King's sermon was directed to the City merchants in the hope that they would provide the finance, but he reminded them that it was the King's will which had moved this project forward. All actions of the King tended to be recast in mythological terms, and this was no exception. The Bishop chose the image of Amphion, the music of whose lyre miraculously caused the city of Thebes to be built; here, the lyre has given way to the harp, the familiar emblem of James's concord. The equally familiar theme of imperial renewal is also employed:

The tongue of a King, like the harpe of Amphion, [will] drawe Stones to the building. It hath ever been the care of religious princes to build and beautify Churches. Great Constantine, the Noah and father of the new Christian world after the floud of bloody persecution, in founding the Lateran, bare twelve baskets of earth upon his own shoulders. . . . I received it in a message . . . from our own religious Constantine, that he would be contented to do a penance, and to fast with bread and water, so this church might be built.[27]

Excited by the prospect of St Paul's restored as a promise of the triumphant times of the Church of England now beginning, Bishop King gasps out at the glory of the vision: 'I am full as the Moone, and must speak and take breath. . . . I think I see a cluster and bunch of grapes of Canaan, the very first and best of the fruits, throughout the whole Kingdom.'[28]

Other clergymen preaching in support of the restoration turned to the parallel with Solomon once again: as Solomon had built the Temple in Jerusalem, so the British Solomon was intent on re-edifying the Temple in his new Jerusalem.[29] Contributions to the repair of St Paul's were clearly understood to be a vote of confidence for James's rule, for the new building would be both a restored Temple and a monument to the glory of the Stuarts. It has been suggested by Per Palme that James turned his attention to the rebuilding of St Paul's just after Inigo Jones had begun to erect the new Banqueting House, because both projects were part of a scheme to give his capital some marks of grandeur at a time when the prospect of a Spanish marriage for Prince Charles involving a dynastic alliance with the Hapsburgs encouraged James to assert his own magnificence as he played a more important role on the international stage.[30] The anticipated reception of the Spanish Infanta justified not only the rapid rebuilding of the Banqueting Hall, but also the restoration of St Paul's to demonstrate the splendour and strength of the Anglican Church. Inigo Jones's designs for St Paul's involved recasing the gothic church with a Roman exterior, a style appropriate to the reign of the new Constantine, and perhaps also relevant to the conceit of the British Solomon rebuilding his Temple, for there was a widely-held belief in this period that Solomon's Temple was the true origin of the classical orders of architecture, expressing the fundamental harmonies of the universe, which had been revealed by God himself when he charged Solomon to build in his praise.[31]

Funds for St Paul's were slow in accumulating, the Spanish match was called off in 1623, and the stone intended for the cathedral was appropriated by Buckingham for York House. Nothing was achieved until some years into the new reign, when William Laud, made Bishop of London in 1629, took up the cause again, and succeeded in carrying it through. Knowing Laud's desire to honour the Church of England, to beautify its buildings and dignify its ceremonies, one can well understand his determination to make his own church a model. King Charles was more eager than his father to promote the work, offering £500 a year for ten years, and finally bearing the whole expense for the repair of the West End. Jones's classical designs were re-adopted in a modified form; work started in 1633 and continued throughout the decade. Of course, the existing gothic masonry of the cathedral could have been renewed, and Jones did in fact repair the old work eastwards of the crossing; but the classical recasing of the transepts and the nave, although it could not disguise the fundamental gothic structure, served as a visual demonstration of the church's return to the pristine strength of Roman times. The *coup de génie* that won all men's admiration was the superb portico that Jones raised against the West End and which was the personal gift of King Charles. Here, where Jones was free to invent and to commemorate the royal bounty, he exploited the full celebratory power of the Corinthian order to produce a luxuriant portico, fifty-six feet high, which gave a totally new splendour to St Paul's.[32] Along the architrave ran an inscription honouring Charles's munificence, and on the balustrade of the portico statues of James and Charles were set, as if to emphasise how much the restored dignity of the church was the result of Stuart policy.[33]

While the portico was going up, the City Council sought Inigo Jones's advice over the rebuilding of Temple Bar, the traditional point of entry into the City. Jones, ever alive to the enhancement of royal power by architectural means, proposed a triumphal arch based on the Arch of Constantine at Rome, topped by an equestrian statue of King Charles. The allusions are discernible: the Christian emperor would be able to ride from his Roman hall of state at Whitehall to his restored Temple at St Paul's, meeting his citizens at an arch that proclaimed the felicity of Stuart rule by means of emblems of public contentment on the entablature. By these monuments the Stuart ascendancy in Church and State would be confirmed.[34]

That ascendancy was most vigorously sustained through the 1630s by William Laud. He rose slowly into power during the 1620s under the patronage of Buckingham, whose soul he had preserved for the Church of England in a famous disputation with the Jesuit Fisher in the presence of King James and Prince Charles. Buckingham was wavering between the two faiths, but was convinced of the superior truth of Anglicanism by the force of Laud's arguments. As a result of this success he became Buckingham's chaplain and effectively his confessor, gaining at the same time the confidence of King and Prince. Even then, James had been reluctant to promote him, fearing that his uncompromising spirit would encourage division within the Church, but Charles favoured the man and his policies, and gave him the most prominent role in his coronation ceremonies, even though Laud was only Bishop of St David's at the time. When he became Bishop of London in 1629, his authority began to eclipse that of all the other English bishops, even that of George Abbot, Archbishop of Canterbury, whose moderate puritanism was in any event uncongenial to King Charles, and whose reputation and influence declined after the untoward accident in 1621 in which he killed a keeper while hunting. The restoration of St Paul's that Laud set about so energetically enabled the King and his most vigorous prelate to show their concern for the Church of England in an ostentatious way: for Charles, his lavish subsidies to the work helped create a monument of triumphant Stuart Anglicanism; for Laud, the work was also a pledge of the material renewal and beautification of the Church throughout England, done in conjunction with the King's will. When Laud was promoted to Canterbury in 1633, he was in a position to effect his desires nationally. Although not a man of aesthetic sensibility as King Charles was, Laud was a cause of much beauty in the kingdom. Beauty was a form of Church discipline, a sign of conformity to regulations imposed by a central authority, obedience to a uniform mode of worship. Laud's policy of restoring dilapidated churches and tidying up the interiors, his insistence on placing the communion table as an altar at the east end of the church, railed off as a holy place, on the use of the Prayer Book, on the wearing of ceremonial vestments and on the proper consecration of churches, all was intended to bring order, dignity and holiness to a Church that should be uniform in its practice and beliefs.

Today it is almost impossible for us to imagine the filth and irreverence that prevailed in many churches at this time: pigs, chickens, horses were kept there, parts of churches were used as ale-houses or bowling alleys, widespread desecration and abuse were reported by Laud's commissioners as they roamed the land.[35] However interested James might have been in the doctrine of the Church, he had made no exertion to combat the dereliction of the average parish church. Laud did as much as he could to change all that. The Anglo-Catholic doctrines that he sought to impose, with the approval of the King, prompted the re-emergence, in schemes of decoration or in new building, of images that had vanished since the Reformation: angels, cherubs, saints, sunbursts round the holy name, even statues of the Virgin Mary. Protagonists of the Laudian style would doubtless have agreed with Hooker that 'the house of prayer is a Court beautified with the presence of celestial powers; that there we stand, we pray, we sound forth hymns unto God, having his Angels intermingled as our associates'.[36] Opponents saw the effrontery of Jesuitism. Under the Laud-inspired revival, a modest English baroque architecture appeared, with scrolls and swags, broken pediments and twisted pillars, small-scale northern essays in a barely understood manner. Mostly it occurred in the private confines of Oxford and Cambridge colleges, where it was paid for by private benefactions (Peterhouse Chapel, built 1628–32 under the mastership of Matthew Wren, is a prime example) but it broke out publicly in the new south porch of St Mary's, Oxford, where the florid composition by Nicholas Stone was erected at the expense of Morgan Owen, Laud's chaplain, in 1637. Laud's own major architectural undertaking was the quadrangle he built for his old college, St John's, Oxford between 1631 and 1636 in an odd mixture of styles: a cloister range of Tuscan columns carries the late gothic upper stories. Baroque modernism asserts itself in the great frontispieces of the east and west ranges, which are sumptuously pillared and carved, heavy with armorial cartouches, and which frame bronze statues of the King and Queen by Le Sueur, who by this time had the virtual monopoly of royal images.[37] It is typical of Laud's sense of himself as a servant of royal policy that the dominant figures in his own quadrangle should be Charles and Henrietta Maria.

Laud was also a generous benefactor to the university in the field of Oriental Studies, founding a chair of Arabic in 1636, and making many donations of Oriental and Greek books to the Bodleian Library, as well as being instrumental in prompting similar donations from others.[38] Although Laud himself had no knowledge of Arabic, Persian or the ancient languages of the Near East, he believed these subjects should be represented at Oxford, and should be an important adjunct to patristic studies. So anxious was he to promote Oriental languages at Oxford that he obtained a royal letter addressed to the Turkey Company stipulating that every one of their ships that returned from the Levant should bring back one Persian or Arabic manuscript.[39] Throughout the 1630s Laud's concern for education was intense, yet the chief purpose of his benefactions was that the Church should be strengthened in her foundations by an increased flow of learned clergy from the universities into the parishes.

The visual beauty that Laud brought to the places of worship, and the uniformity that he tried to impose on the services of the Church contributed heavily to his downfall, for to the majority of Protestant Englishmen these practices seemed eloquent of Rome and tyranny. On the scaffold on Tower Hill in January 1645, he acknowledged the intense strains he had suffered in the enforcement of his policies: 'What Clamors and Slanders I have endured for labouring to keep a Uniformity in the external service of God according to the Doctrine and Discipline of this Church all men knowe and I have abundantly felt.' Yet he insisted on their necessity to the end. In his valedictory sermon he summed up his condition with that grave wit which was a hallmark of the Court style of preaching, and though in his career his sermons had not been characterised by the witty manner, his use of conceits on this fatal occasion amounted to a final defiant demonstration of his commitment to the High Anglican style of the Court:

I am going apace, as you see, towards the Red-sea, and my feet are upon the very brinks of it, an Argument, I hope, that God is bringing me to the Land of Promise, for that was the way by which of old he led his people; But before they came to the Sea, he instituted a Passeover for them, a Lamb it was, but it was to bee eaten with very soure Herbs, as in the Twelfth of *Exodus*.

I shall obey, and labour to digest the sowre Herbs, as well as the Lamb, and I shall remember that it is the Lords Passeover; I shall not think of the Herbs, nor be angry with the hands which gathered them, but look up onely to him who instituted the one, and governeth the other: For men can have no more power over me, then that which is given them from above; I am not in love with this passage through the red Sea, for I have the weaknesse and infirmity of flesh and blood in me, and I have prayed as my Saviour taught me, and exampled me, *Ut transiret calix ista*,

That this Cup of red Wine might passe away from me, but since it is not that my will may, his will be done; and I shall most willingly drink of this Cup as deep as he pleases, and enter into this Sea, ay and passe through it, in the way that he shall be pleased to leade me.[40]

The King himself was executed in January 1649, regarded by many as a martyr dying in defence of the Holy Anglican Church. Scores of spectators dipped their handkerchiefs in his blood, and his clothes were torn up and carried away as relics. Locks of the royal hair multiplied like fragments of the true cross. Within a few days was published *Eikon Basilike*, 'The Portrait of the King', purporting to be a work from the King's hand vindicating his policy during the last years of his reign, and professing the total sincerity of his affection for the Church of England. The book is now recognised to be a compilation based on the King's own notes by the minor cleric John Gauden but, apart from Milton, no one questioned its authorship at the time; it went through thirty-six editions in one year, and was a powerful agent in the process that turned the defeated King into a royal martyr. The Greek title is a poignant allusion to *Basilikon Doron*, for it recounts the tragic fate of a King who carried out his duties to God, Church and his people as James had enjoined. Instead of the gratitude of a nation, he had been persecuted to death just as his Saviour had been, thus fulfilling the prophetic destiny hidden in an imperfect anagram of the royal name which had circulated throughout the reign: 'CHAROLVS STVARTVS = CHRISTVS SALVATOR'. The Christ-like sufferings of His Majesty are frequently alluded to in the text of *Eikon Basilike*, and are made explicit in the powerful frontispiece to the book which shows Charles kneeling in a pose reminiscent of the Agony in the Garden, taking up a crown of thorns.

Frontispiece to the *Eikon Basilike*

His earthly crown is cast aside as he sees a heavenly crown of glory shining through the window of his Church, which is still the Church of Tudor Anglicanism, as the roses and crosses woven into the altar-cloth indicate. Emblems of his virtue and constancy lie behind him. The picture is based on the passage:

In what concerns Truth, Justice, the Rights of the Church, and my Crown, together with the general good of my Kingdoms (which I am bound to preserve as much as morally lies in me) here I am, and ever shall be fixt and resolute . . . nor will I be brought to affirm that to men, which in my conscience I deny before God. I will rather chuse to wear a Crown of Thorns with my Saviour, then to exchange that of God, (which is due to me) for one of Lead.[41]

The prayers which conclude the different sections of the book often present Charles as the Man of Sorrows, and as a man who has undergone trials 'which often raise the greatest sufferers to be the most glorious Saints'. At the Restoration King Charles was proclaimed a saint and martyr of the Church of England, the most unsought of all the titles of honour that the Stuart Kings accumulated.

In a chapter dealing with the Court and the religious arts, royal burials make a fitting conclusion. One would have expected that the myth-making proclivities of the early Stuarts, coupled with their piety, would have resulted in an outstanding group of funeral monuments, especially as this was a remarkable age of monumental sculpture in England, when the mighty dead were 'splendid in ashes, and pompous in the grave'. Artists of the quality of Maximilian Colt, Gerard Christmas, Cornelius Cure, Nicholas Stone and Hubert le Sueur designed some of the boldest tombs in English Church history, confident alabaster memorials of dignity or pathos, decorated with sombre images and funereal conceits. Under Elizabeth and James the exequies of great men were enacted with prodigious expenditure. The vast processions formed by the bereaved household, the kindred nobility and the troops of hired mourners announced to the world the importance of the deceased; the cost of these solemn pageants to the family was immense, given the need for acres of black cloth, distributions of alms, funeral banquets and heralds' fees. Yet most households accepted these expenses as a necessary part of a display of greatness and influence that funerals had traditionally encouraged, for the reaction to a death was to assert the living strength of the family. The culmination of these exercises was the erection of a substantial monument which would declare to all posterity the wealth, lineage and piety of the deceased, and also, as sculptural styles became more varied in James's reign, the taste of the family as well.

Ironically, amidst these generations obsessed with posthumous renown, the Stuarts were buried virtually without trace, only the most insignificant of their offspring receiving the tribute of a modest tomb. James began his reign well, from the necrological point of view. He commissioned a distinguished tomb for his predecessor, Queen Elizabeth, from Maximilian Colt, a Huguenot from Arras who was the outstanding sculptor of the turn of the century in England. Stylistically, Elizabeth's tomb was conventional, not altogether dissimilar to the tomb of Lord Burleigh at Stamford. The Queen's sensitively-sculpted marble effigy lies beneath a coffered stone canopy, arched in the centre, which is supported by ten jet columns. The tomb was raised in the north aisle of Henry VII's Chapel in Westminster Abbey, an expected act of homage to the old Queen. What was not expected, and gave a sign of dynastic ambition in the new line, was that James also proceeded to raise a tomb in the corresponding position in the south aisle to his mother, Mary, Queen of Scots, whose body he had exhumed from her ignominious grave in Peterborough and brought for honourable interment at Westminster. Mary's new tomb, by Cornelius Cure, was almost identical to Elizabeth's, but slightly larger and more expensive, a discreet vindication of his mother's merits. James also caused to be carved on the stone tablets at the ends of the canopy the Latin verses from the First Epistle of Peter: 'Christus pro nobis passus est, reliquem exemplum ut sequamini vestigia ejus. Qui cum malediceretur, non maledicebat; cum pateretur, non comminabatur; tradebat antem judicanti juste.' These verses the Authorised Version translates as, 'Christ also suffered for us, leaving us an example, that ye should follow his steps: . . . who, when he was reviled, reviled not again, when he suffered, he threatened not; but committed himself to him that judgeth righteously' (1 Peter 2.21–3). So Mary was justified by her son, and ranked with Elizabeth in death.

While these tombs were building, two of James's infant daughters perished in quick succession, Sophia in 1606, and Mary in 1607. Maximilian Colt, now made Master Carver to the Crown, executed the first tombs of the new dynasty, miniature masterpieces. Princess Sophia lies in her stone cradle, her puckered little face peering over the alabaster sheets, facing eastwards, awaiting a glorious resurrection. The cradle stands on a pedestal of black marble, with a black band round the hood, with finely carved lacework over all. The work is a visual conceit which achieves considerable pathos in its setting adjacent to the majestic pomp of Elizabeth's tomb. Sophia's sister Princess Mary, who died at the age of two, reclines sadly on her arm on top of an alabaster altar tomb; she is dressed in the tiny adult clothes that children wore as soon as they could walk, and her feet are incongruously supported by the royal lion while weeping cherubs mourn at the angles of the tomb.

The total cost of these four monuments was some £3,500, a very considerable amount indeed, clear evidence that James in his early years intended to commemorate his line splendidly. *Dis aliter visum*, however: the gods saw otherwise. When Prince Henry died universally lamented in 1612, his funeral procession was one of the grandest ever seen in England, and his body lay in state in the Abbey under a magnificent catafalque, but he sank into an anonymous grave in Henry VII's Chapel, covered by a mere stone slab.[42] The reason for this astonishing neglect was the wedding of his sister Elizabeth, which cost the Crown over £13,000, an expense which crippled the royal finances for years afterwards. The death of Queen Anne in 1619 also coincided with a financial crisis. She died of dropsy at Hampton

Court on 2 March, but her funeral was delayed for over two months because of the shortage of money. The catafalque for the lying in state was designed on this occasion by Inigo Jones. The usual form for this structure was a recumbent effigy lying on a raised tomb beneath an elaborate canopy, the whole surrounded by emblems of state. As a temporary construction, it was usually made out of wood and plaster, with the effigy itself made of wood or wax, the latter being particularly suitable for the face, which was modelled on a death mask of the deceased. In Queen Anne's case, Jones represented the Queen seated on her throne with orb and sceptre within a rectangular tabernacle upheld by caryatid pilasters. On the canopy Jones placed the golden tree laden with fruit, the dynastic tree of fertility, the emblem that the Queen had carried in her first masque, and which now accompanied her ultimate Masque of Blackness. Queen Anne also disappeared underground into the vaults of Henry VII's Chapel without a trace. With his fear of death, the King had moved far away from his wife in her last days, and did not attend her funeral—he had behaved identically at the death of Prince Henry—but he did write some verses on her death which reflected on the divine immortality of kings:

> Thee to invite the great God sent His star,
> Whose friends and nearest kin good princes are,
> Who, though they run the race of men and die,
> Death serves but to refine their majesty.
> So did my Queen from hence her court remove,
> And left off earth to be enthroned above.
> She's changed, not dead, for sure no good prince dies,
> But as the sun, sets, only for to rise.[43]

Although James could scarcely pay for the funeral, and made no move to erect a tomb, he was able to raise the money for the rebuilding of the Banqueting House, which was the urgent undertaking of the moment, showing that as in the case of Princess Elizabeth's wedding, the active and ostentatious measures of state policy, wherein James's majesty was diplomatically vaunted, received priority over the commemoration of inconvenient deaths.

King James himself died in March 1625, at Theobalds, within a ring of bishops. His embalmed body was transported to Denmark House in London, where it lay in state; once again Maximilian Colt went through the melancholy duty of carving a royal effigy to lie upon the coffin, but this time he made a figure with movable joints so that it could be posed with greater verisimilitude.

Inigo Jones, drawing for the hearse of James I

The great funeral was on the 7th of [May], the greatest indeed that ever was known in England, there being blacks distributed for above 9000 persons, the hearse likewise being the fairest and best-fashioned that hath been seen, wherein Inigo Jones, the surveyor, did his part. . . . All was performed with great magnificence, but the order was very confused and disorderly. The whole charge is said to arise to above £50,000.[44]

Jones's design for the hearse or catafalque under which the body lay in Westminster Abbey was in the form of a domed temple, an image perhaps inspired by the James–Solomon motif that provided the ground plan for Bishop William's funeral sermon. This circular temple was constructed of

Inigo Jones, design for a supposed Stuart Mausoleum

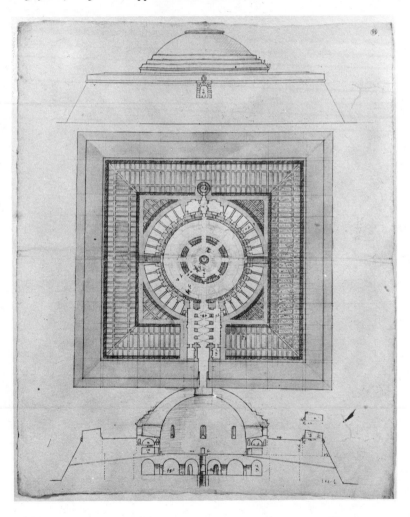

wood and plaster, painted, and festooned with the flags, pennants and coats of arms of the royal titles, a final piece of ceremonial architecture for the King. Mourning figures of the virtues were seated around the drum of the dome, and four statues of the cardinal virtues stood at the corners of the surrounding enclosure. When one remembers the fantastic and variegated architecture that welcomed James to London in 1604, and then considers the noble and serene dignity of this Italianate funerary temple, the refinement of taste that occurred during the reign can be tellingly observed.

James was buried with Henry VII beneath Torregiano's great brass tomb and Anne was placed with him. Thus he sealed his kinship with the first of the Tudors to whom he had always looked as the guarantor of his legitimate kingship, and the presiding genius of his line. No monument was ever raised to James, for King Charles inherited the perennial Stuart problem of inadequate funds, and although he could afford entertainments for the living, he could spare nothing for the dead. But plans do seem to have been made to glorify the Stuarts perpetually: in the library at Worcester College, Oxford, there is a drawing by Inigo Jones for what appears to be a great mausoleum, a large, low, domed building lit from above surrounded by massive walls.[45] A unique and enigmatic design, it is by no means certain that it represents a mausoleum, but one would certainly have expected that the Stuarts, James especially, would have projected an enduring monument to a dynasty that they hoped would rule to the last age of the world. Jones's building has an indestructible air, the Stuart challenge to the pyramids.

King Charles raised no monuments to his house. A king who could not afford a coronation procession for himself was hardly likely to spend money on a tomb for his dead father. His great grief over Buckingham's death in 1628 did move him to propose a sumptuous funeral and a half-acre tomb at royal expense, but his counsellors persuaded him that such generosity was impossible.

Given the circumstances of his own death, Charles was fortunate to find the shelter of any grave at all. After his execution, his body was removed by night to Windsor, for the regicides were determined that his grave should not become a martyr's shrine in the capital. The next day, in the presence of a few friends and servants, he was buried beside the remains of Henry VIII, whose vault had been fortuitously located in the morning.[46] There was no ceremony or prayer. Not even an inscribed stone marked the site.

Notes to Chapter Ten

1   James's tendency to let hunting encroach upon theology led to some unseemly moments, as when George Abbot, Archbishop of Canterbury, had the misfortune to kill a keeper while out hunting in 1621, and James was able to dismiss such manslaughter with the observation: 'Why, an angel might have miscarried in such sort'. Such a phrase also reveals James's understanding of the pleasures of heaven more clearly than any remark in his writings. In his work *Meditations upon the Lord's Prayer* (1619), under the guise of illustrating holy matters, he indulged in several extensive digressions that are essentialy reminiscences of his most successful days in the field.

2   James's translation of the Psalms was not published in his lifetime, but it was widely known at Court that he was engaged on this work.

3   H. Peacham, *Minerva Britanna* (1612), p. 45; G. Marcelline, *The Triumphs of King James the First* (1610), p. 35.

4   See P. Palme, *The Triumph of Peace*, London 1957, p. 70.

5   The reference is to the preface to the 1603 edition of *Basilikon Doron*, where James speaks of the reign of Elizabeth as a new Augustan age.

6   Joseph Hall, *An Holy Panegyrick*, in *Works* (1627), p. 479.

7   One would expect here some reference to the American plantations as the territory of this future empire, but there is none. The imperial concept is essentially limited to the micro-empire of the islands of Britain; hence the common use of the phrases from Virgil and Claudian that these isles are a world divided from the world, a microcosm that can be ruled by a micro-emperor.

8   A reference, no doubt, to the peace that James signed with Spain in 1604.

9   Hall, *op. cit.*, pp. 482–3. On James's coinage, the title 'King of Great Britain' was added in October 1604. Some coins were inscribed with the legend 'Henricus Rosas Regna Jacobus'—Henry united the Roses, James the Kingdoms—and to celebrate the union a new coin called the *unite* was issued.

10   Ministers below the rank of Bishop or Dean were not to 'presume to teach in any popular auditory the deep points of Predestination, Election, Reprobation, or universality of efficacy or irresistibility of God's grace'; nor should any preacher touch on the 'Power, Prerogative, Jurisdiction, Authority or Duty of the Sovereign Princes'.

11   For a concise account of James's religious writings, see Willson, *James VI & I*, chapter xiii.

12   See Willson, *op. cit.*, pp. 213–14, and D. Daiches, *The King James Version of the English Bible*, Chicago 1941.

13   *The Holy Bible* (1611), folio B1.

14   T. Fuller, *Church History* (1655), XI, 126.

15   I. Walton, 'The Life of Dr. Donne', in *Walton's Lives*, ed. C. H. Dick, 1899, pp. 32–3.

16   'A Speech to the Lords and Commons of the Parliament at Whitehall, 1609', in *The Political Works of James I*, ed. C. H. McIlwain, Cambridge, Mass. 1918, p. 309. See also P. Palme, *op. cit.*, pp. 173–5.

17   'Sermon preached at Denmark House, April 26th, 1625', in E. Simpson and G. Potter, eds., *The Sermons of John Donne*, Berkeley, Cal. 1953, vol. VI, p. 290.

18   *Ibid.*

19   'The First Sermon preached to King Charles, 3 April, 1625', in Simpson and Potter, *Sermons*, vol. VI, pp. 241–2.

20   *Ibid.*, Introduction, p. 23.

21   'Sermon preached to the King, February 11th, 1626/7', in *Sermons*, vol. VII, p. 350.

22   Walton, *op. cit.*, p. 54.

23   Recorded as verses by King Charles in G. Keynes, *A Bibliography of Dr. John Donne*, Oxford 1973, p. 286. These lines, in a fuller version, also appear in Henry King's elegy for Donne.

24   I. Walton, 'The Life of Mr. George Herbert', in *Lives*, p. 223.

25   *The Latin Poetry of George Herbert*, trans. M. McCloskey and P. Murphy, Athens, Ohio 1965, pp. 56–7.

26   There had been the celebrated occasion in 1604 when James had visited the Royal Exchange incognito, an incident which may have provided Shakespeare with his motif of 'The Duke of dark corners' in *Measure for Measure*. In fact, James may have provided the originating germ of this play in the following passage from *Basilikon Doron*: 'Remember that among the differences that I put betwixt the formes of the gouernment of a good King, and an vsurping Tyran; I shew how a Tyran would enter like a Saint while he found himselfe fast vnder-foot, and then would suffer his vnrulie affections to burst foorth . . .; feare no vproares for doing of iustice, since ye may assure your selfe, the most part of your people will euer naturally fauour Iustice: prouiding alwaies, that ye doe it onely for loue to Iustice, and not for satisfying any particular passions of yours, vnder colour thereof: otherwise, how iustly that euer the offender deserue it, ye are guiltie of murther before God: For ye must consider, that God euer looketh to your inward intention in all your actions.

       'And when yee haue by the seueritie of Iustice once setled your countries, and made them know that ye can strike, then may ye thereafter all the daies of your life mixe Iustice with Mercie, punishing or sparing, as ye shall finde the crime to haue bene wilfully or rashly committed, and according to the by-past behauiour of the committer. For if otherwise ye kyth your clemencie at the first, the offences would soone come to such heapes, and the contempt of you grow so great, that when ye would fall to punish, the number of them to be punished, would exceed the innocent; and yee would be troubled to resolue whom-at to begin' (*Political Works*, ed. McIlwain, p. 20). *Basilikon Doron* was reprinted in London in 1603; *Measure for Measure* was first performed in 1604.

27   John King, 'A Sermon at Paules Crosse, on behalfe of Paules Church', (1620), pp. 53–4.

28   *Ibid.*, p. 56.

29   E.g., W. Laud in 'Pray for the Peace of Jerusalem', in *Seven Sermons* (1651), and John Donne in his sermon preached in March 1620 in *Sermons*, vol. III.

30   See P. Palme, *Triumph of Peace*, pp. 17–24.

31   The Catholic theologian G. B. Villalpando's commentary on Ezechiel, *In Ezechielem Explanationes* (1594–1604), contained a very elaborate account of the architecture of Solomon's Temple, in which he saw the platonic musical harmonies registered in architectural terms and in the classical orders. The work was widely known in the early seventeenth century, and was cited several times by Bishop Williams in his funeral sermon on King James, *Great Britain's Salomon*.

32   Jones based his design on Palladio's reconstruction of the Temple of Antoninus and Faustina in Rome. Even a generation later, the widely travelled John Evelyn thought that the Portico and the Banqueting House were the only completely satisfying build-

ings in London. See Evelyn's *A Character of England* (1659).

33   Waller's poem on the repairing of St Paul's sees the act as symbolic of Charles's
relations with the Church of England:

'an earnest of his grand design,
To frame no new church, but the old refine;
Which, spouse-like, may with comely grace command,
More than by force of argument or hand.'

Statues of the two Stuart kings also appeared on the new screen for Winchester
Cathedral which Charles commissioned from Jones in 1638. In this burial place of the
old Saxon kings, the Stuarts also asserted themselves as the revivers and guardians of
the Church of England. The fine bronze statues by Hubert le Sueur still remain in
the cathedral, but the screen was removed in 1845.

34   The arch was never built. See *The King's Arcadia*, pp. 143–4, for details.

35   For some heartfelt accounts of the squalor common in churches at this time, see
John Weever's *Ancient Funerall Monuments* (1631) (dedicated to King Charles), in
which he frequently complains of this 'Atheisticall uncleannesse' in 'polluted and
stinking churches'. The working conditions of the church antiquary in the early
seventeenth century were extremely unwholesome.

36   *Of the Laws of Ecclesiastical Polity*, V.25.2 (Everyman ed., vol. II, p. 109).

37   For the latest views on who was the architect of the Canterbury Quadrangle, see
Pevsner's *Oxfordshire*, Harmondsworth 1975, pp. 199–200.

38   The most important of these donations were the Barocci Collection of Greek manuscripts which Laud persuaded the Earl of Pembroke to give to the Bodleian in 1628,
and the two gifts of Oriental books from Sir Kenelm Digby.

39   See H. Trevor-Roper, *Archbishop Laud*, London 1940, p. 274.

40   'The Last Words of the Archbishop of Canterbury', in *In God's Name*, ed. J.
Chandos, London 1971, pp. 415–16.

41   *Eikon Basilike* (1648), section 6, p. 38.

42   Prince Henry is buried in Henry VII's Chapel at Westminster. 'The leaden case
wherein his Corps is contained is shaped closely to the Figure of his Body; and in the
midst of the Vault is an Inscription in Brass, intimating that his Bowels are buried
thereabouts at the Head of the Princess Royal Elizabeth, Princess of Orange.' *The
Antiquities of . . . the Abbey Church of Westminster*, 1722, p. 129.

43   The star refers to a comet which was troubling men and the heavens at this time.
James was thrown into a violent disorder by Anne's death. His doctor Mayerne reports
that he suffered 'a shrewd fit of the stone', gout and 'a scouring vomit'. 'After the
Queen's death, pain in the joints and nephritis, with a thick sand, continued fever,
bilious diarrhoea, hiccoughs for several days, bitter humours boiling from his mouth
so as to cause ulcers on his lips and chin, fainting, sighing, dread, incredible sadness,
intermittent pulse. The force of this, the most dangerous illness the King ever had,
lasted for eight days.' Quoted in Willson, *op. cit.*, p. 404.

44   *The Letters of John Chamberlain*, ed. N. E. McClure, Philadelphia, Pa. 1939, vol. II,
p. 607.

45   Illustrated in *The King's Arcadia*, p. 136.

46   T. Fuller, *Church History* (1655), XI, pp. 237–8. See also C. V. Wedgwood, *The
Trial of Charles I*, London 1966, pp. 202–5.

[11]
Conclusion

The Courts of the first two Stuart Kings bore strongly contrasting characters: the common verdict inclines to take the more favourable view of Charles's Court, as a place of culture and discrimination controlled by a King whose taste was impeccable, while James's Court is often felt to be somewhat provincial and its lustre diminished by the crude character of the King himself. Yet, in terms of achievements in the arts, the first two decades of the earlier reign saw the most remarkable upsurge of creativity. However questionable the moral tone of James's Court may have been, there can be no doubting its intellectual vigour. The Court was central to the energies of the nation. Nowhere is this more true than in drama: Shakespeare was a member of The King's Men, and that company of actors performed the most outstanding repertory of plays in English stage history. The unbounded range of experience and speculation that powered the Jacobean drama provided the Court with regular and appreciated entertainment. Besides Shakespeare, the playwrights writing for The King's Men included Jonson, Beaumont and Fletcher. Under Charles, the royal company maintained its superiority over the other London groups, but although many of the old plays were revived from time to time, the great generation of actors had passed, and the playwrights who now furnished new drama to suit the taste of the twenties and thirties were men of slenderer imagination: Massinger, Shirley, Brome and Davenant. Jonson towered over the Court poets of James's day, ritually exalting the King on state occasions, grafting moral poetry on to the lives of courtiers, satirically commenting on the hypocrisy, pretence and gross folly of the times, and acting as a tireless intermediary between Bankside, Whitehall and the City. Bacon commanded the high offices of state from 1613 onwards, when he was advanced to Attorney General; although James was sceptical about the worth of his scientific speculations, the presence at Court of such an exceptional philosopher, historian and moralist must have been intellectually animating in the highest degree. The King's interest in theology filled the Court with divines who were generally of a more distinguished cast of mind than those whom Charles encouraged. Andrewes and Donne preached periodically in the Chapel Royal. Andrewes, who had been born in 1555, possessed some of the intellectual toughness and knottiness that characterised the theologians of the English Reformation; Donne's splendour of utterance matched with his wit gave an urgent gravity to his sermons that renders them powerful even today. Against these two Jacobean divines one might set William Laud and Jeremy Taylor as representatives of the Caroline Court: Laud a brilliant and conscientious administrator and a gifted disputant, Taylor (who became a royal chaplain in 1636) a golden-tongued pietist whose smooth, elegant rhetoric moves easily and comfortingly over a rather conventional religious content. Their sermons lack a certain vital drive, which could be found then outside the Court, and often directed against the Court, in the sermons of the alienated Puritan preachers. At James's Court, the poetry of Donne and Jonson found appreciative understanders; it spoke to them in hard language of the complexities of their experience in love, religion and social intercourse. In Charles's generation these poets were still admired, but the poetry that responded best to the tone and attitudes of the Court now came from Carew, Waller, Davenant, Suckling and Lovelace—a poetry that was more refined and more uncritically flattering than the earlier mode, yet more artificial, more superficial and more literary. The Caroline Court poets all developed in the shadow of Donne and Jonson: they have more polish, but less dynamism.

The career of Inigo Jones was threaded through the length of both reigns, and yet even he, who must have found King Charles a much more compatible and sympathetic figure than James, produced his freshest and most vigorous works in the areas of both masque and architecture in the earlier reign when his imagination had a vivacity that faded a little as his practice and mastery increased. Taste in architecture, as in poetry and drama, settled into a certain uniformity during the thirties, and with that uniformity much of the speculative and experimental energy disappeared. Only in painting was a new impetus felt, and that was imparted largely by artists imported from the continent.

When one considers the broad spectrum of intellectual and literary activities that were going forward in the ambit of James's Court, one is conscious of an exhilarating sense of innovation; under Charles, this innovation has largely been replaced by cultivation. Charles's Court achieved its refined tone to a large extent by sealing itself off from the central currents of thought and enquiry of the time, and the result was a certain preciousness of manner, and an etiolated sensibility. The gap between

Court fiction and social actuality may be most instructively gauged in the masques of Charles's reign, which are sublimely inward-looking and dangerously preoccupied with the virtues of the King and Queen, which light up the charmed circle of the Court. James had many crude aspects to his character, but there had been an intellectual openness about his Court that ensured that it remained a forum of national activity. Certainly the poets and dramatists frequently expressed their misgivings about the political chicanery and the degenerate behaviour around Court, and occasionally a dramatist got into trouble through impertinent criticism that struck the King too hard (as Middleton did over *A Game of Chess*, or Jonson, Marston and Chapman over *Eastward Ho*), yet in general the Jacobean establishment accommodated a great diversity of opinion, and absorbed a good deal of criticism without being particularly threatened. After 1625 one has the sense that the formative energies of the period begin to flow in channels that by-pass the Court. This is obviously the case with religious developments. In addition, the emerging scientific movement, growing from the scattered seeds of Bacon's proposals, hardly came into contact with the Court at all. Political criticism was kept at arm's length after the Parliament of 1629 was dissolved. Literature written for the Court tended increasingly to be tailored to suit the prevailing taste, with the result that a contrived, artificial, repetitive note is too often struck in the writing of the thirties. Language grows less vigorous and more affected as it breathes an over-courtly air. Almost predictably, the rising genius of the age, John Milton, matures outside the Court, and ultimately stands in opposition to it.

Many of the differences between the culture of the two reigns may be traced back to the contrasting temperaments of the sovereigns, and to their education. James was tutored by the humanist scholar George Buchanan, a man who enjoyed a European reputation for his Latin poetry, and who mixed his Protestantism with stoic philosophy. His rigorous instruction was abetted by the amiable Peter Young, who enlarged James's interests in the Renaissance curriculum. Together they formed a broad, omnivorous mind in the young King, who would always enjoy the rough and tumble of debate, and who always assumed he would win in an argument. An instructive glimpse of King James establishing intellectual relations with one of his courtiers occurs in a letter from Sir John Harington in 1606. Harington had pursued a successful career as a Court wit under Elizabeth, and had a literary reputation, based on his translation of Ariosto. So far he had not made much headway at James's Court, in spite of having sent him an ingenious New Year present in 1603 when the Queen's health was failing, a lantern of gold and silver, with the words of the good thief engraved upon it: 'Lord, remember me when thou comest into thy kingdom'. Eventually James invited Harington into a private closet, and subjected him to what was in effect a qualifying examination for royal favour:

He enquyrede muche of lernynge, and showede me his owne in suche sorte, as made me remember my examiner at Cambridge aforetyme. He soughte muche to knowe my advances in philosophie, and utterede profounde sentences of Aristotle, and suche lyke wryters, whiche I had never reade, and which some are bolde enoughe to saye, others do not understand: but this I must passe by. The Prince did nowe presse my readinge to him parte of a canto in 'Ariosto;' praysede my utterance, and said he had been informede of manie, as to my lernynge, in the tyme of the Queene. He asked me 'what I thoughte pure witte was made of; and whom it did best become? Whether a Kynge shoulde not be the beste clerke in his owne countrie; and, if this lande did not entertayne goode opinion of his lernynge and good wisdome?' His Majestie did much presse for my opinion touchinge the power of Satane in matter of witchcraft; and askede me, with muche gravitie,—'If I did trulie understande, why the devil did worke more with anciente women than others?' I did not refraine from a scurvey jeste, and even saide (notwithstandinge to whom it was saide) that— 'we were taught hereof in scripture, where it is tolde, that the devil walketh in dry places.' His Majestie, moreover, was pleasede to saie much, and favouredlye, of my good report for merth and good conceite: to which I did covertlie answer; as not willinge a subjecte shoude be wiser than his Prince, nor even appeare so.

· More serious discourse did next ensue, wherein I wanted roome to continue, and sometime roome to escape; for the Queene his mother was not forgotten. . . . His Highnesse tolde me her deathe was visible in Scotlande before it did really happen, being, as he said, 'spoken of in secrete by those whose power of sighte presentede to them a bloodie heade dancinge in the aire.' He then did remarke muche on this gifte, and saide he had soughte out of certaine bookes a sure waie to attaine knowledge of future chances. Hereat, he namede many bookes, which I did not knowe, nor by whom written; but advisede me not to consult some authors which woulde leade me to evile consultations. I tolde his Majestie, 'the power of Satan had, I muche fearede, damagede my bodilie frame; but I had not farther will to cowrte his friendshipe, for my soules hurte.'—We nexte discoursede somewhat on religion, when at lengthe he saide: 'Now, Sir, you have seen my wisdome in some sorte, and I have pried into yours. I praye you, do me justice in your reporte, and in good season, I will not fail to add to your understandinge, in suche pointes as I maye find you lacke amendmente.' I made courtesie hereat, and withdrewe downe the passage, and out at the gate, amidst the manie varlets and lordlie servantes who stoode arounde.

. . . His Majestie muche askede concerninge my opinion of the new weede tobacco, and said 'it woud, by its use, infuse ill qualities on the braine, and that no lernede man ought to taste it, and wishede it forbidden.' (*Nugae Antiquae*, ed. Thomas Park, 1804, vol. I, pp. 367–9.)

Ranging from the grave to the trivial, touching on poetry, politics and religion, and moving into philosophy and the supernatural, spiced with wit and a tinge of indecency, such a conversation has a demanding, expectant air, and suggests a milieu with plenty of thought circulating through it.

It would be difficult to conceive of Charles in a similar situation. Correctness of manner and his more reserved character inhibited free exchange of opinion in a way which his education had done little to counteract. He was taught by David Murray, a competent but unmemorable tutor; then Dr George Hakewill, an Oxford divine whose main work would be *An Apologie or Declaration of the Power and Providence of God* (1627), was sent in to improve the Prince theologically. His education was by no means as invigorating as his father's. His dominant pleasure, a passion for the fine arts, fostered first by his elder brother Prince Henry and then by his mother, tended to restrict him amongst an exclusive circle of friends. Temperamentally too, Charles was somewhat retiring. Ill health in youth and a speech impediment inclined him to quieter ways than his father frequented. His reticence seems to have been exacerbated by his journey to Spain in 1623 to woo the Infanta; there he contracted an admiration for the haughty aristocratic conduct that prevailed at the Escorial, and he seems to have adopted a similar style when he ascended the throne.

The difference between the public presentation of James and Charles might perhaps be summed up by suggesting that James had attributes whereas Charles had roles. James as King was a static figure invested with a distinctive iconography: symbols of Justice, Piety, Wisdom, Peace, Plenty, Providence and Empire define his royal character, and these symbols were imposed on him by the artists and writers of the Court in accordance with James's own estimation of his qualities and achievements and in succession to the apparatus of royal symbolism that had accumulated during the reign of Elizabeth. Charles, however, was inclined to make a dramatic presentation of his kingship, to project himself in roles, either directly (as upon the Whitehall stage in masques where he appeared variously as a British Emperor, Heroic Virtue, or a heroic lover) or indirectly (by having artists—especially Van Dyck—depict him in dramatic circumstances, as St George or as a triumphant Roman Emperor). Charles's own love of the theatre and the fact that he enjoyed appearing as an actor in masque point up his personal fondness for dramatic attitudes. A certain romantic strain in his character also contributed to the effect. Charles's daring ride with Buckingham, incognito through France into Spain to carry off the Infanta first revealed the Prince's capacity for dramatic action. Spanish aloofness gave him a style for his reign, and the conscious self-possession that accompanied this style is nowhere better seen than on the occasion when he received the news of Buckingham's assassination. The King was at prayer in the Chapel Royal at the time, but never flinched at the news and continued praying, surrounded by his courtiers, until the service ended. Immediately afterward, in the privacy of his chamber, he broke down and wept, and remained in a swoon of grief for two days. In matters of religion he found ritualism an appropriate mode of mediating with the Almighty, and he introduced a highly elaborated ritual into the Chapel Royal and into the Garter services, the religious areas immediately under his own control. Late in his life the role of patiently suffering King came naturally to him, and his ultimate parts were as saint and martyr. Marvell accurately gauged the King's nature in his 'Horatian Ode', where he described his execution as the last act of a long theatrical career, played out with perfect control before a grim, appreciative audience of his people:

> That thence the *Royal Actor* born
> The *Tragic Scaffold* might adorn:
> While round the armed Bands
> Did clap their bloody hands.
> He nothing common did or mean
> Upon that memorable Scene.

Appendix: the principal Court masques, 1605–40

(The author is Ben Jonson, unless otherwise stated.)

1605	*The Masque of Blackness*	1620	*News from the New World*
1606	*Hymenaei*	1620	*Pan's Anniversary*
1608	*The Masque of Beauty*	1622	*The Masque of Augurs*
1608	*The Haddington Masque*	1623	*Time Vindicated*
1609	*The Masque of Queens*	1624	*Neptune's Triumph* (unperformed)
1610	*Prince Henry's Barriers*	1625	*The Fortunate Isles*
1610	*Tethys Festival* (Daniel)		
1611	*Oberon*	1631	*Love's Triumph through Callipolis*
1611	*Love Freed from Ignorance and Folly*	1631	*Chloridia*
1613	*The Lords' Masque* (Campion)	1632	*Albion's Triumph* (Townshend)
1613	*Middle Temple Masque* (Chapman)	1632	*Tempe Restored* (Townshend)
1613	*Gray's Inn Masque* (Beaumont)	1634	*The Triumph of Peace* (Shirley)
1615	*The Golden Age Restored*	1634	*Coelum Britannicum* (Carew)
1616	*Mercury Vindicated*	1635	*The Temple of Love* (Davenant)
1617	*The Vision of Delight*	1638	*Britannia Triumphans* (Davenant)
1618	*Pleasure Reconciled to Virtue*	1638	*Luminalia* (Davenant)
1618	*For the Honour of Wales*	1640	*Salmacida Spolia* (Davenant)

Select bibliography

Adams, J. Q., *Dramatic Records of Sir Henry Herbert*, New Haven, Conn. 1917.

Aikin, Lucy, *Memoirs of the Court of Charles the First*, London 1833.

Akrigg, G. P. V., *Jacobean Pageant*, London 1962.

Andrewes, Lancelot, *Sermons*, ed. G. M. Story, Oxford 1967.

Anglo, Sydney, *Spectacle, Pageantry and Early Tudor Policy*, Oxford 1969.

Baker, L. M. (ed.), *The Letters of Elizabeth, Queen of Bohemia*, London 1953.

Bas, Georges, *James Shirley: Dramaturge Caroléen*, Lille 1973.

Bentley, G. E., *The Jacobean and Caroline Stage*, Oxford 1941–56.

Bergeron, David M., *English Civic Pageantry 1558–1642*, London 1972.

Birch, Thomas, *The Court and Times of James the First*, London 1849.

———, *The Life of Henry, Prince of Wales*, London 1760.

Brome, Richard, *The Dramatic Works*, 3 vols., London 1873.

Cammell, C. R., *The Great Duke of Buckingham*, London 1939.

Campion, Thomas, *The Works of Thomas Campion*, ed. Walter R. Davis, New York 1970.

Carew, Thomas, *The Poems*, ed. Rhodes Dunlap, Oxford 1970.

Chambers, E. K., *The Elizabethan Stage*, Oxford 1923.

Charlton, John, *The Banqueting House, Whitehall*, London, H.M.S.O. 1964.

Clarendon, Edward Earl of, *History of the Rebellion*, Oxford 1705.

Cornwallis, Sir Charles, *An Account of the Baptism, Life, Death and Funeral of . . . Frederick Henry, Prince of Wales*, London 1751.

Davies, Horton, *Worship and Theology in England, 1603–90*, Princeton, N.J. 1975.

Dekker, Thomas, *Dramatic Works*, ed. F. Bowers, Cambridge, 1955.

Donne, John, *The Sermons of John Donne*, ed. E. M. Simpson and G. R. Potter, 10 vols., Berkeley, Cal. 1953–62.

Figgis, John N., *The Divine Right of Kings*, London 1896.

Fuller, Thomas, *The Church History of Britain*, 1655.

Gilbert, Allan H., *The Symbolic Personages in the Masques of Ben Jonson*, Durham, N.C. 1948.

Gordon, D. J., *The Renaissance Imagination*, ed. Stephen Orgel, Berkeley, Cal. and London 1975.

Harington, Sir John, *Nugae Antiquae*, ed. Thomas Park, London 1804.

Harris, John, Stephen Orgel and Roy Strong, *The King's Arcadia: Inigo Jones and the Stuart Court*, London, Arts Council 1973.

Harrison, Stephen, *Arches of Triumph*, 1604.

Haynes, D. E. L., *The Arundel Marbles*, Oxford, Ashmolean Museum 1975.

Herbert, George, *The Latin Poetry of George Herbert*, ed. and transl. by M. McCloskey and P. R. Murphy, Athens, Ohio 1965.

Hervey, Mary, *The Life, Correspondence and Collections of Thomas Howard, Earl of Arundel*, Cambridge 1921.

Huxley, Gervas, *Endymion Porter*, London 1959.

Jonson, Ben, *Ben Jonson*, ed. C. H. Herford, Percy and Evelyn Simpson, 11 vols., Oxford 1925–52.

Kaufmann, R. J., *Richard Brome, Caroline Playwright*, New York 1961.

Leech, Clifford, *John Ford and the Drama of his Time*, London 1957.

——, *Shakespeare's Tragedies and Other Studies in Seventeenth Century Drama*, London 1961.

Lefkowitz, M. (ed.), *Trois Masques à la Cour de Charles Ier d'Angleterre*, Paris 1970.

Lever, J. W., *Tragedy of State*, London 1971.

McClure, N. E. (ed.), *The Letters of John Chamberlain*, Philadelphia, Pa. 1939.

McIlwain, Charles Howard (ed.), *The Political Works of James I*, Cambridge, Mass. 1918.

Michaelis, Adolf, *Ancient Marbles in Great Britain*, Cambridge 1892.

Millar, Oliver (ed.), 'Abraham van der Dort's Catalogue of the Collections of Charles I', in *Publications of the Walpole Society* XXXVII, 1960.

——, *The Age of Charles I*, London 1972.

Nicols, John, *The Progresses of James I*, London 1828.

Nicoll, Allardyce, *Stuart Masques and the Renaissance Stage*, London 1937.

Oglander, Sir John, *A Royalist's Notebook: The Commonplace Book of Sir John Oglander*, ed. F. Bamford, London 1936.

Orgel, Stephen, *The Jonsonian Masque*, Cambridge, Mass. 1967.

——, *The Illusion of Power*, Berkeley, Cal. 1975.

Orgel, Stephen, and Roy Strong, *Inigo Jones: the Theatre of the Stuart Court*, Berkeley, Cal. 1973.

Palme, Per, *Triumph of Peace*, London 1957.

Parry, Graham, *Wenceslaus Hollar in England*, Oxford, Ashmolean Museum 1977.

Peacham, Henry, *Minerva Britanna*, 1612.

——, *The Compleat Gentleman*, 1634.

Perrin, W. G. (ed.), *The Autobiography of Phineas Pett*, Publications of the Navy Record Society, London 1918

Phillips, Claude, *The Picture Gallery of Charles I*, London 1896.

Pickel, Margaret B., *Charles I as Patron of Poetry and Drama*, London 1936.

Rye, W. B., *England as seen by Foreigners in the Days of Elizabeth and James the First*, London 1865.

Sainsbury, W. N., *Original Papers Illustrative of the Life of Sir Peter Paul Rubens*, London 1859.

Sharpe, K. A. (ed.), *Faction and Parliament: Essays in Early Stuart History*, Oxford 1978.

Solve, N. D., *Stuart Politics in Chapman's Tragedy of Chabot*, Ann Arbor, Mich. 1928.

Spencer, T. J. B., and S. W. Wells (eds.), *A Book of Masques*, Cambridge 1970.

Stone, Lawrence, *The Crisis of the Aristocracy 1558–1641*, Oxford 1965.

Strong, Roy, *The English Ikon: Elizabethan and Jacobean Portraiture*, London 1969.

——, *Festival Designs by Inigo Jones*, London, Victoria and Albert Museum 1969.

——, *Van Dyck: Charles I on Horseback*, London 1972.

——, *Splendour at Court: Renaissance Spectacle and Illusion*, London 1973.

————, *The Cult of Elizabeth*, London 1977.

————, *The Renaissance Garden in England*, London 1979.

Sullivan, M., *Court Masques of James I*, New York 1913.

Summerson, John, *Inigo Jones*, Harmondsworth 1966.

Thomas, Peter R., 'Charles I of England', in *The Courts of Europe*, ed. A. G. Dickens, London 1977.

Trevor-Roper, H. R., *Archbishop Laud*, London 1940.

————, *The Plunder of the Arts in the Seventeenth Century*, London 1970.

Waller, Edmund, *The Poems*, ed. G. Thorn Drury, London 1893.

Walpole, Horace, *Anecdotes of Painting in England*, 4 vols., London 1876.

Wedgwood, C. V., *The King's Peace, 1637–1641*, London 1955.

————, *Poetry and Politics under the Stuarts*, Cambridge 1960.

————, *Truth and Opinion*, London 1960.

————, *The Trial of Charles I*, London 1966.

Whinney, Margaret, *Sculpture in Britain 1530–1830*, Harmondsworth 1964.

Whinney, Margaret and Oliver Millar, *English Art, 1625–1714*, Oxford 1957.

Willet, Andrew, *Ecclesia Triumphans*, 1604.

Williams, Franklin B., *Index of Dedications and Commendatory Verses in English Books before 1641*, London, The Bibliographical Society 1962.

Williams, John, *Great Britain's Salomon*, 1625.

Williamson, J. W., *The Myth of the Conqueror: Prince Henry Stuart*, New York 1978.

Willson, David Harris, *King James VI & I*, New York 1967.

Wilson, E. C., *Prince Henry and English Literature*, Ithaca, N.Y. 1946.

Wind, Edgar, *Pagan Mysteries in the Renaissance*, London 1958.

Wittkower, Rudolf, *Architectural Principles in the Age of Humanism*, London 1971.

Wotton, Sir Henry, *Reliquiae Wottonianae*, 1672.

Yates, Frances A., *Astraea: the Imperial Theme in the Sixteenth Century*, London 1975.

————, *The Rosicrucian Enlightenment*, London 1972.

————, *Shakespeare's Last Plays: A New Approach*, London 1975.

Index

175-C. Thurne of every